LETTERS OF MOZART

LETTERS
OF
MOZART

Edited by
HANS MERSMANN

Translated by
M. M. BOZMAN

DORSET PRESS
New York

This edition published by Dorset Press,
a division of Marboro Books Corporation,
by arrangement with
J. M. Dent and Sons Ltd.

1986 Dorset Press.

ISBN 0-88029-087-0

Printed in the United States of America

M 9 8 7 6 5 4 3 2

PREFACE BY A. EAGLEFIELD HULL

No English edition of Mozart's Letters has appeared since Lady Wallace's translations in 1865. The present translation of Hans Mersmann's selection is therefore particularly welcome, inasmuch as he has done the work of selection and arrangement so well. The selection covers Mozart's whole life, from small boyhood to his early death. Most of the letters are written to his father, sister and wife. Interspersed as the selection is with letters from the father, it gives a great deal of the composer's life-story.

A short biographical outline will supply all that the reader needs further to complete the view. It is interesting to note that the first orderly biography of Mozart was written by Edward Holmes in English in 1845.

Mozart was born at Salzburg on 27 January, 1756. He died of typhoid fever at Vienna on 5 December, 1791, at the early age of thirty-five. In 1762 his father, Leopold Mozart (himself a cultured musician, Court-Composer and Vice-Kapellmeister to the Archbishop of Salzburg) took Wolfgang (aged six) and his sister "Nannerl" (aged ten and a half) on a concert tour to Munich and Vienna. In 1763 the two children were taken to Paris. In the following year (1764) they visited England, staying there for fifteen months. They were much fêted and were frequently invited to Court. In 1766 the children played in Paris; in 1768 they appeared before the Court at Vienna. In 1769 Wolfgang was appointed Konzertmeister to the Archbishop of Salzburg, with a miserable pittance as a salary.

His chief operas were produced in the following order:

Bastien und Bastienne (Vienna)	1768
La Finta Semplice (Salzburg)	1769
Mitridate, Re di Ponto (Milan, 26 December) . .	1770

Amongst his vocal music are several Masses, the great *Requiem*, and much other church music, besides 44 arias. His orchestral music consists of 41 symphonies, the best known of which are the C major ("Jupiter"), G minor ("Venus") and E flat; 31 *divertimenti*, and about 45 other orchestral pieces; 6 violin concertos, 2 flute concertos, 25 piano concertos, 4 horn concertos, a clarinet concerto, 11 quintets, 30 string quartets, 32 violin sonatas, and a large amount of piano music, including the 4 well-known Fantasias, and 17 solo-sonatas.

Michael Kelly,[1] an Irish operatic singer much favoured in Vienna in Mozart's time, describes the composer's personal appearance thus:

He was a remarkably small man, very thin and pale, with a profusion of hair, of which he was rather vain. Though born of beautiful parents, Mozart himself possessed beauty only as a child; in his later years he retained nothing of his early looks but the pleasing expression. His features were marked and had strong individuality of character. The outward man of the composer presented no index to his genius. His eyes, which were rather large and prominent, had more of a languid than a brilliant and animated character. The eyebrows were well arched and the eye-lashes long and handsome. . . . His head was apparently too large for his body; but the body itself, and the hands and the feet, were formed in

[1] Quoted in Edward Holmes's *Life of Mozart* (Everyman edition, pp. 193, 268).

exact proportion, of which he was rather vain. The easy, natural and elegant movement of his small hands on the piano rendered it interesting to overlook him when playing, while the power which he occasionally exhibited raised astonishment. His nose, which had been handsome, became so prominent a feature in the last years of his life, from the emaciation of his countenance, that a scribbler in the *Morgenblatt* of Vienna honoured him with the epithet "enormous-nosed."

With regard to Mozart's method of composing, there is a *bona fide* letter of his written to a certain baron who had made him a present of wine and interrogated him about his method of composing.[1]

When I am, as it were, completely myself, entirely alone, and of good cheer—say, travelling in a carriage, or walking after a good meal, or during the night when I cannot sleep; it is on such occasions that my ideas flow best and most abundantly. *Whence* and *how* they come, I know not; nor can I force them. Those ideas that please me I retain in memory, and am accustomed, as I have been told, to hum them to myself. If I continue in this way, it soon occurs to me how I may turn this or that morsel to account, so as to make a good dish of it, that is to say, agreeably to the rules of counterpoint, to the peculiarities of the various instruments, etc.

All this fires my soul, and, provided I am not disturbed, my subject enlarges itself, becomes methodised and defined, and the whole, though it be long, stands almost complete and finished in my mind, so that I can survey it, like a fine picture or a beautiful statue, at a glance. Nor do I hear in my imagination the parts *successively*, but I hear them, as it were, all at once (*gleich alles zusammen*). What a delight this is I cannot tell! All this inventing, this producing, takes place in a pleasing lively dream. Still the actual hearing of the *tout ensemble* is after all the best. What has been thus produced I do not easily forget, and this is perhaps the best gift I have my Divine Maker to thank for.

When I proceed to write down my ideas, I take out of the bag of my memory, if I may use that phrase, what has been previously collected into it in the way I have mentioned. For this reason the committing to paper is done quickly enough, for everything is, as

[1] It is found in Holmes's *Life of Mozart*, Everyman edition, p. 255 *et seq.*

I said before, already finished; and it rarely differs on paper from
what it was in my imagination. At this occupation I can therefore
suffer myself to be disturbed; for whatever may be going on around
me, I write, and even talk, but only of fowls and geese, or of Gretel
or Bärbel, or some such matters. But why my productions take
from my hand that particular form and style that makes them
Mozartish, and different from the works of other composers, is
probably owing to the same cause which renders my nose so large
or so aquiline, or, in short, makes it Mozart's, and different from
those of other people. For I really do not study or aim at any
originality.[1]

Mozart's letters are unstudied, non-literary, conversational,
and therefore vivid, vital and intimately personal; they were
not written with a view to publication. They contrast strongly
in almost every way with the letters of Richard Wagner, which
are often "essays." The letter of Mozart's regarding composition, which is quoted above, stands almost alone of its kind.

The spelling, punctuation and grammar are wildly erratic,
this being partly due to the half-formed state of the German
language as a literary medium, and partly due to Mozart's
South-German dialect. The letters are dotted with scraps of
foreign languages with which his travels made him more or
less familiar. The result is most entertaining, though difficult
to convey in a translation.

We gather from these letters Mozart's high-spirited, boyish
impression of his journeys through Europe as an "infant-
prodigy." We see his great love and reverence for his father
brought into conflict with, though never actually embittered
by, his manhood's natural instinct for independence. We
sympathise with his early struggles and adventures at the
various Courts in which he tried to get a foothold—his grief
for his mother's death—his first love affairs—his broader
flirtations with a female cousin (who would nowadays be
called "hot stuff")—his tragic wrestlings with poverty—his
hatred of Salzburg and particularly of his father's tyrannous

[1] Compare this with Beethoven's letters to the Archduke Rudolph—No. 355
(page 304) and others in the Dent edition of *Beethoven's Letters*.

and brutal patron, the archbishop who ordered a lackey to kick "that young whipper-snapper, Wolfgang," out of the house—his true love for Constance Weber, and his marriage —his growing sense of power as a composer—his increasing pecuniary difficulties up to his tragic death on the very threshold of an assured fortune. On the whole, the letters are practical and personal; only occasionally do we get revealing flashes of musical criticism.

The character which emerges is that of a most vital and joyous nature, warm-hearted and generous to a fault; a nature containing apparently none of that hard egotism and self-regardfulness sometimes associated with genius, though there is necessarily a powerful sense of, and faith in, his own genius and a natural desire to fulfil and express it. There is also a fine natural pride and an astonishing absence of a sense of social inferiority when amongst aristocrats and princes, all the more admirable because it is without that slight alloy of bumptiousness from which neither Beethoven nor Wagner were entirely free. This indeed seems to us very remarkable amongst all the formidable stiffness and artificiality of mid-eighteenth-century life in Europe. There is no vanity mingled with Mozart's pride, but instead we find a most engaging ebullition of youthful spirits—a love of brightness, gaiety and pleasure, combined with a radically "Puritan" standard of morals. He had an eye, too, for the *comédie humaine*, a wit of a somewhat primitive order, schoolboyish—not to say "street-urchinish"—and suggestive of Smollett rather than of Sterne. He was not a Romantic, but managed to combine realism and tenderness in personal relations. A tough courage bravely confronts poverty, disappointment and physical weakness, and an underlying, perhaps melancholy, philosophy is to be read rather *between* than *in* the lines of his letters, most of which, it must be remembered, were written to put a good face on things *for the sake of the recipients*—those near and dear to him.

A. E. H.

TRANSLATOR'S NOTE

THE happy-go-lucky spelling, grammar and punctuation which contribute something, at least, to the charming impression of spontaneity, informality and intimacy which Mozart's letters make upon the reader, cannot, of course, in the main, be conveyed in a translation. The translator has endeavoured, however, to "smooth out" as little as possible. Passages in languages foreign to Mozart—French, Italian, Latin and English—have been reproduced as Mozart wrote them; also his variable and haphazard spelling of the names of persons and places, for each of which the (or an) accepted spelling will be found in the index. Examples are *Cannabich*, spelled variously by him with one or two *n*'s; *Raaff*, spelled thus or *Raaf*; and *Strassburg* (Alsace), spelled thus, or *Strasburg*, or *Strasbourg*.

A few explanatory notes on matters of translation have been added in square brackets in the text, or as footnotes.

CONTENTS

LETTERS OF
WOLFGANG AMADEUS MOZART

EARLY JOURNEYS (1763-8) [1]

Leopold Mozart [2] *to L. Hagenauer, Salzburg*

WASSERBURG,[3] *11th June,* 1763.

The latest is that, upon going to the organ for our diversion, I explained the use of the pedal to Wolferl. He immediately began to try it, thrust the stool aside, and preluded, *stante pede* and treading the pedals, and that, indeed, as if he had practised for many months previously. Everyone was astonished and [indeed it] is a new grace of God, such as many receive only after much effort.

Leopold Mozart to L. Hagenauer

FRANKFORT, *20th August,* 1763.

Our concert was upon the 18th. It was good. Everybody was astonished. By the grace of God we are in health, God be praised, and are everywhere objects of admiration. As to our Wolfgangerl, he is extraordinarily gay, but naughty too. Little Nannerl no longer suffers by comparison with the boy, for she plays so that all the world talks of her and marvels at her proficiency.

Leopold Mozart to Frau Hagenauer

PARIS, *1st February,* 1764.

Four sonatas by *Mr. Wolfgang Mozart* are now being engraved! Do but picture to yourself the stir these sonatas will make in the

---

[1] A previous concert tour had been made in January 1762 to Munich, and another in September that year to Vienna, where the family had a great reception at the Imperial Court. On this occasion little Wolfgang proposed marriage to Marie Antoinette, afterwards the unfortunate Queen of France.

[2] Leopold Mozart (1719–89), father of the composer, was in the service of the Archbishop of Salzburg in a musical capacity. His two surviving children were Maria Anna ("Nannerl"), born in 1751, and Johann Chrysostom Wolfgang Amadeus ("Wolferl" or "Wolfgangerl"), born 27 January, 1756. Leopold Mozart was accompanied by both his children on these early tours, both being considered prodigies. L. Hagenauer was an intimate friend of Leopold Mozart.

[3] In Bavaria.

world when it is set forth on the title-page that this is the work of a child of seven years; and, when the incredulous are challenged to put the matter to the proof (as has happened already), he invites someone to write down a minuet, or such-like, and then forthwith (without touching the clavier) sets down the bass and, if desired, the second violin part besides! In due course you will hear how good these sonatas are; there is an andante among them of very singular *goût*. And I can assure you, my dearest Frau Hagenauer, that God daily works new miracles in this child. Upon our return home (if God will) he will be in a position to officiate at Court. Indeed he regularly accompanies at public concerts. When accompanying, he transposes the arias actually *à prima vista*; and everywhere he plays at sight such pieces as are put before him, whether Italian or French.

Leopold Mozart to L. Hagenauer

PARIS, *1st April,* 1764.

M. de Mechel, a copper-plate engraver, is working day and night to engrave our portraits, which Herr von Carmontel (an amateur) has painted very fine. Wolfgang plays the clavier, I stand behind his stool and play the violin, and Nannerl rests one arm upon the *clavecin* while she holds music in the other as though singing.[1]

Leopold Mozart to L. Hagenauer

LONDON,[2] *28th May,* 1764.

The King placed before him some pieces by Wagenseil, and also others by Bach,[3] Abel and Handel, and he played them all off, *à prima vista*. He played upon the King's organ in such a way that all esteem his organ performance far above his clavier playing. He then accompanied the Queen's singing of an aria and a flautist in a solo. Finally he took up the 'cello part of one of Handel's arias

[1] The children's dress on an earlier occasion is thus described by their father: "Wolferl's suit . . . is of lily colour, of the finest cloth, with double broad gold borders. . . . Nannerl's dress is the court costume of an Arch-Duchess. It is of white brocaded taffeta with all sorts of ornaments."

[2] The family lodged first in Cecil Court, St. Martin's Lane, during the father's convalescence at Dr. Randall's, in Fivefields, now Lower Ebury Street; and later at Mr. Williamson's, No. 51 Frith Street, Soho. (See G. H. Cunningham, *London.* Dent. 1927.)

[3] Johann Christian Bach, youngest son of the great John Sebastian, then music-master to the (English) queen.

(which chanced to lie before him), and upon the mere bass played the most beautiful melody, so that all were thrown into the extremest amazement. In a word, what he knew when we set out from Salzburg was a mere shadow compared with what he knows now. It is beyond all conception. He joins with us in presenting you his compliments from the clavier stool, where he sits at this moment playing through Kapellmeister Bach's trio, and not a day passes but he speaks at least thirty times of Salzburg and of his and our friends and patrons. His head is now forever full of an opera which he wishes to produce in Salzburg with none but young people. I have already frequently had to reckon up for him all the young people whom he may enlist for his orchestra.

Leopold Mozart to L. Hagenauer

VIENNA, 30*th January*, 1768.

But to tell the truth, the first idea of allowing little Wolfgang to write an opera came to me from the Emperor himself, who twice asked Wolfgang whether he would like to compose an opera and conduct it himself. He replied quite frankly, Yes, but indeed the Emperor could say no more, since opera is Affligio's [1] concern. The consequences of this enterprise (should God be pleased to aid us to accomplish it) would be so far-reaching but are also so plain to see that they need no elucidation. I must not, however, permit myself to regret any present expenditure, for the money will undoubtedly come back to us to-morrow, if not to-day.

Leopold Mozart to L. Hagenauer

VIENNA, 14*th September*, 1768.

Touching Wolfgangerl's opera,[2] I can but tell you briefly that the whole hell of music is in revolt to prevent the world from witnessing a child's cleverness. It is impossible for me to press for the performance of the opera, knowing that there is a conspiracy, should it come to the point, to produce it meanly and so spoil it. I had to await the arrival of the Emperor, else would the *bataille* have long since been joined. Believe me, I shall neglect nothing necessary to protect the honour of my child. I have long known of it. But I *guessed* it earlier yet. I actually spoke of the

[1] Affligio was the manager. There was much opposition to the Mozarts in Viennese musical circles at the time, the result of jealousy.

[2] *La Finta Semplice*. The opera was first performed in Salzburg in 1769.

matter to His Excellency Count von Zeyl, who, however, believed that all the *musici* had come under Wolfgangerl's spell, for he judged by appearances and knew naught of the hidden malice and spite of these cattle. Patience! Time will bring all to light and God permits· nothing to happen without purpose.

Leopold Mozart to L. Hagenauer

VIENNA, 14*th December*, 1768.

Wolfgang's *Mass*, performed on 7th December at Father Parhamer's in the presence of the Imperial Court, he himself taking the baton, has repaired the evil our enemies thought to do by obstruct-ing the opera, and has convinced both Court and public (who attended in astonishing numbers) of the malice of our opponents.

ITALIAN JOURNEYS WITH HIS FATHER (1769-73)

1. To his Mother

My very dearest Mama,

My heart is quite enraptured for pure joy, because I feel so merry on this journey, because it is so warm in our carriage, and because our coachman is a brave fellow who drives like the wind whenever the road at all permits it. My papa will have described the journey to my mama already, and the reason I write to mama is to show that I know my duty, and am with profoundest Respect her faithful son,

Wolfgang Mozart.

Carissima sorella mia
Siamo arivati a wirgel.

2. To his Sister

Indeed I rejoice with all my heart that you were so enraptured with this sledge-drive, and I wish you a thousand such occasions of delight, so that you may be very merry all your life. But one thing vexes me, and that is that you leave Herr von Mölk to sigh and suffer so interminably, and that you would not go sledging with him to give him an opportunity of overturning you! What a number of pocket-handkerchiefs he must have needed that same day—to weep into—on your account! He must, to be sure, have swallowed an ounce of tartar beforehand, and that will have purged away the horrible impurities from that belly of his! I have no news, save that Herr Gelehrt [1] the Leipzig poet is dead and since his death has written no more poetry.

---

[1] *Sic.* Gellert is the correct name.

Before beginning this letter I had just finished an aria from *Demetrio* which begins thus:

> *Misero tu non sei :*
> *Tu spieghi il tuo Dolore*
> *e se non dessti amore*
> *Ritrovi almen pietá.*
>
> *Misera ben so io*
> *che nel secreto laccio*
> *amo, non spero e traccio*
> *e l'idol mio nol sá.*

The opera at Mantua was beautiful—they played *Demetrio*. The *prima Dona* sings well but not loud, and if one did not see her acting but only singing, one would think she was not singing, for she cannot open her mouth but whimpers everything out. That, however, is no new thing for us to hear. *La seconda Dona* has a presence like a grenadier and also a powerful voice, and indeed she does not sing ill considering that this is her first appearance. *Il primo uomo*, *il musico*, sings well, but has an uneven voice. His name is Casselli. *Il secondo uomo* is getting old and does not please me. He is called — — *tenor* (*sic*). There is a man called Otini, who does not sing ill, though his voice is very hard like all Italian tenors, and he is our good friend. I do not know what the other's name may be— he is still young but he is nothing remarkable. *Primo ballerino*, good; *prima ballerina*, good; and they say she is no scarecrow, but indeed I have not seen her near at hand. The rest are just like all others. There is a *grotesco* who leaps well, but does not write as I do, that is, as the sows piss. The orchestra is not amiss. There is a good orchestra at Cremona, and the first violin is called Spangnoletto. The *prima Dona* is tolerable, but I think she is as old as the hills, sings less well than she acts and is the wife of a violinist at the opera called Masi. The opera is called *La clemenza di Tito*. The *seconda Dona* is no fright on the stage, young, but not remarkable. *Primo uomo*, *musico*, Cichognani—a fair voice and beautiful *cantabile*. The other two *castrati*, young and *passable*. The tenor is called *Non lo sò*. Has an attractive presence and is very like Le Roi of Vienna, who is come to Leman. *Ballerino primo*, good; *ballerina prima* good and a monstrous scarecrow. There was a girl dancer who did not dance ill, and, strange to relate of a *capo d'opera*, is not a fright either on the stage or off it. The rest are as usual. There was a *grotesco* there, too, who made a rude noise at each leap. I cannot tell you much about Milan. We have not yet been to the opera there; we heard that the opera was not going well. Aprile, the *primo uomo*, sings well and has a beautiful, even voice. We heard him in a church where a great festival was in progress. Madam Picinelli, of Paris, who sang at our concert, plays at the opera. Monsieur Bicch, who danced at Vienna, dances here in Milan. The opera is called *Di Done abbandonata*. This opera will soon come to an end and Sig. Piccini, who is writing the next opera, is here in Milan. Have heard that his opera is entitled *Cesare in eccito*. There are also *feste di ballo* here. As soon as the opera is over the *festa di ballo* begins. The Conte de Firmian's house-keeper is a Viennese woman and last Friday we dined there and next Sunday we are to dine there again. Farewell, and kiss Mama's hand a thousand times, *in vece mia*. I remain till death your faithful brother,

> Wolfgang de Mozart,
> Edler von Hochenthal,
> Freund des Zahlhausens.

26th January, 1770.

Leopold Mozart to his Wife

MILAN, *3rd February*, 1770.

I have nothing to tell you but that Wolfgang rejoices nightly in his good well-warmed mattress bed; that he can write no letters as he is composing two Latin *motetti* for two *castrati*, one fifteen and the other sixteen years old, who have begged him to do so and to whom he could refuse nothing because they are "comrades" and sing beautifully; that it greatly distresses me to see and hear such lads, but also to know that I cannot take them with me to Salzburg; and that I foresee that we shall remain in Milan longer than I fancied.

Leopold Mozart

His Excellence Count von Firmian was exceedingly moved by Wolfgangerl's talent, and distinguished us with his special favour and preference; and 'twould be too prolix to tell you in detail what proofs of his attainments our Wolfgang gave in the presence of the *Maestro* Sammartino and a large company of the most expert persons, astonishing them all. You know well enough what occurs on these occasions—you have seen it often enough.

3. *To his Mother and Sister*

Postscript to a letter from his father, 10th February, 1770.

"Speak of the Devil and he will appear." I am well, praise and thanks be to God, and can scarce await the moment of seeing your answer. I kiss Mama's hand, send my sister a smacking kiss and remain the undersigned——who then?—the undersigned *Jack-pudding*,

> Wolfgang in Germany, Amadeo in
> Italy, *De Mozartini.*

Leopold Mozart

We shall not, I am convinced, make much money in Italy. My sole satisfaction is that we are regarded with considerable interest and appreciation here, and that the Italians recognise Wolfgang's talents. For the rest, one must usually be content with admiration and applause in lieu of payment, though I must also tell you that we are everywhere received with every imaginable courtesy and are presented to the *haute noblesse* on all occasions.

4. *To his Sister*

Postscript to his father's letter of February 17th, 1770.

Here I am, you see! Oh, Mariandel, I am indeed rejoiced that you have been so exceedingly gay! Tell that baby Ursula, that I still think I sent *all* her songs back; but should I, absorbed in consideration of high and weighty matters, have brought them with me to Italy, I will not fail, if I find it is so, to enclose it in a letter. *Addio*, my children, farewell!

I kiss Mama's hand a thousand times, and imprint a hundred little kisses or smacks on that wondrous horse-face of thine! *Per fare il fine*, I am thine, etc.

5. *To his Sister*

Cara sorella mia,

I rejoice with all my heart that you have been so gay, but perhaps you may think that I have not been so, but indeed I have, and, I cannot count exactly, but I really believe we have been six or seven times to the opera and then to the *feste di ballo*, which come on after the opera, as in Vienna, only with this difference, that the dancing is better arranged in Vienna. We have also seen the *facchinata* and *chiccherata*, that is a *mascherata facchinata*, which is a fine sight because the people dress up as *facchini*, or domestic servants; and there was a *barca* full of people and many on foot, some four or six bands of trumpets and drums and also some bands of fiddles and other instruments. The *chiccherata* is a masquerade too; we saw it to-day. The Milanese mean by *chichera* what we call *petits maîtres*, or coxcombs and they all ride on horseback, which made a pretty sight. My happiness at hearing that Herr von Aman now goes on better is as great as was my sorrow at hearing that he had had an accident. What kind of a *masque* did Madam Rosa wear—and Herr von Mölk, and Herr von Schiedenhofen? Pray write and tell me, if you know, and you will be doing me a great favour. We have an invitation to-day from Count Firmian's major-domo to celebrate the last day of our stay and there we shall have something to prattle about you may be sure! *Addio*, farewell. Next post-day I will write you a Milanese letter. I am, etc.

Wolfgang Mozart.

Kiss Mama's hand for me 1000000000000 times. My compliments to all good friends and a thousand compliments to you from if-you-want-to-catch-him-you-have-him-already, and from Don Cacarella (particularly from behind).

P.S. *3rd March*, 1770.

Leopold Mozart   MILAN AND BOLOGNA, 13th and 24th March, 1770.

They are very anxious that Wolfgang should write the first opera for next Christmas.[1] The recitatives have to be sent to Milan by October, and by November 1st we must be in Milan so that Wolfgang may write the arias.

6. *To his Sister*

O Thou Industrious One!

Having been idle so long I thought there would be no harm in my setting to work again for a little while. Every post-day, when the German letters come in, my dinner tastes much nicer. Pray write and tell me who is singing in the oratorio. Tell me also what is the title of the oratorio. And write, too, how you liked the minuets by Haydn and whether they are better than the first. I am most heartily glad to hear that Herr von Aman is well again. Pray tell him he must take good care of himself and not over-exert himself. Tell him this, I beg you. And say too that I often think how we used to play at being workmen at Triebenbach and how he made the name "Schraltenbach." And tell him as well that I often recall him saying to me "Shall we divide ourselves up?" and how I always used to answer "How horrible!"

Simply to show you how slowly people dance, I shall presently send you a Minuet, which M. Pick danced at the theatre and which everybody danced afterwards at the *feste di ballo* at Milan. The minuet is, in itself, very fine. Of course it comes from Vienna and so is certainly by Teller or Starzer. It has many notes. Why? Because it is a theatrical minuet and moves slowly. But the Milanese or Italian minuets have many notes, and move slowly with many bars. For example, the first part contained 16, the second 20 and even 24 bars. At Parma we made the acquaintance of a singer whom we heard sing very beautifully in her own house. She is the celebrated Bastardella,[2] who has (1) a beautiful voice, (2) a rapid

---

[1] *Mitridate, re di Ponto.*

[2] Lucrezia Agujari (1743–83), a remarkable singer, who took London by storm in 1775. She could sing almost incredibly high notes with ease. She was known as *La Bastardella.*

execution and (3) can reach an incredibly high note. She sang the following notes and passages in my presence:

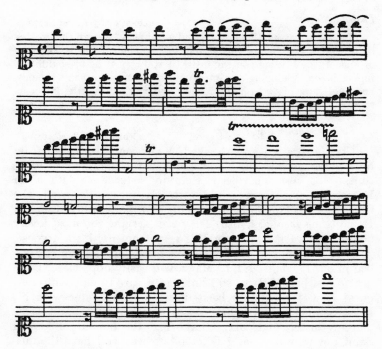

Leopold Mozart

BOLOGNA, 27th *March*, 1770.

What especially delights me is that we are uncommonly beloved here and that our Wolfgang is even more admired here than in other Italian towns; for this place is the seat, the residence, of numerous masters, artists and scholars. Moreover, he has been subjected to the severest tests here, with the result that his fame is increased throughout all Italy, for Padre Martino,[1] the idol of the Italians, having examined Wolfgang thoroughly, speaks of him with amazement. We visited Padre Martino twice, and on each

[1] Giambattista Martini, commonly called Padre Martini, a renowned composer and teacher.

occasion Wolfgang worked out a fugue, Padre Martino having written merely a few notes for *dux* or *guida* [theme].

Leopold Mozart   FLORENCE, 3rd *April*, 1770.

The affair passed off as usual, and admiration was all the greater in that His Excellency the Marchese Ligneville (who is Director of Music), the leading contrapuntist in Italy, put the most difficult fugues before Wolfgang and propounded the most difficult themes, and Wolfgang played off the former and worked out the latter as easy as shelling peas! That fine violinist Nardini also played.

7. *To his Mother and Sister*   ROME, 14th *April*, 1770.

God be praised and thanked, I am sound and well from top to toe, and miss my Mama and Nanerl a thousand (or 1000) times. N.B. My one wish is that my sister were with us in Rome, for this town would certainly please her well, the Church of St. Peter's being *regulair* and many other things in Rome being *regulaire*, also! They are carrying the most lovely flowers past, Papa tells me, this very moment. I am a goose, 'tis well known, and oh, I have one grief, for we have but one bed in our lodgings and, as Mama will easily appreciate, I can get no rest beside Papa, so I am glad we are to move into new ones! Now I have just been drawing Saint Peter with his keys, Saint Paul with his sword, together with Saint Luke and my sister, etc.; and I have had the honour of kissing Saint Peter's toe in Saint Peter's, but because I have the misfortune to be so little, someone had to lift up the undersigned old rascal,   Wolfgang Mozart!

Leopold Mozart
ROME, 21st *April*, 1770.

The farther we penetrate into Italy the more the wonder grows! Nor are Wolfgang's talents stationary, but increase daily, so that the greatest connoisseurs and masters are at a loss for words to express their admiration and publish their astonishment.

In Florence we met a young Englishman,[1] a pupil of the famous

[1] Thomas Linley, a gifted youth, who was accidentally drowned in his twenty-first year. Mozart never forgot him and always mentioned his name when in after-life he met English society in Vienna.

violinist Nardini. The lad, who plays very finely and is of Wolfgang's age and height, came to the house of the learned poetess
Signora Corilla, where we were admitted on M. Laugier's introduction. The two boys performed by turns throughout the evening
amidst continual embracing. The other day the little Englishman,
a most charming lad, had his violin brought to us and played all
the afternoon, Wolfgang accompanying him, also on the violin.
The following day we dined with M. Gavard, *administratore* of the
Grand Duke's exchequer, and the two children played by turns
the whole afternoon, not like boys but like men! Little Thomas
accompanied us home and wept the bitterest tears because we
were to leave the next day.

8. *To his Sister*

Postscript to his father's letter.
ROME, 21*st April*, 1770.

Cara sorella mia !

Pray will you look out the arithmetic tables, for you
wrote them out yourself, and I have lost them and so have
quite forgotten them. So I beg you will copy them for me
together with other examples in arithmetic and send them
to me here.

Manzuoli has contracted with the Milanese to sing in my
opera. On this account he sang me four or five arias in Florence,
besides several of mine which I had to compose in Milan
because they had heard no stage pieces of mine and wished
to see if I was able to write an opera. Manzuoli demands 1000
ducats. It is not known if Madame Gabrielli [1] will come for
certain. Some say Madame de' Amicis [2] will sing. We shall see
her in Naples. I want her and Manzuoli to appear. That would
make two good friends of ours. The libretto is not yet settled.
I have recommended one of Metastasio's [3] to Don Ferdinando
and Herr von Troyer.

I am working just now on the aria *Se ardire e speranza.* * * *

[1] Gabrielli, Catarina (1730–96), a brilliant *coloratura* singer.
[2] De Amicis, Lucia Anna, born *c.* 1740. A brilliant soprano. She made her
debut in London in 1763 under John Christian Bach.
[3] Metastasio (1698–1782), a celebrated Italian librettist. Mozart set four
of his libretti: *Il Rè Pastore* (1775), *Il Sogno di Scipione* (1772), *La Betulia
liberata* (1770–3), an oratorio, and *La Clemenza di Tito* (1791).

9. *To his Sister*

C. S. M.,

Vi prego di scrivermi presto e tutti i giorni di posta. Io vi ringrazio di avermi mandato questi books of arithmetic, *e vi prego, se mai volete avere mal di testa, di mandarmi ancora un poco questi* examples. *Perdonate mi che scrivo si malamente, ma la razione è perchè anche io ebbi un poco mal di testa.*[2] Haydn's 12th Minuet which you sent me pleases me very much; you have set the bass to it incomparably and without the smallest mistake. Pray make such essays more often.

Mama must not forget to have both muskets polished. Pray let me know how Mr. Canary does? Does he still sing? Does he still whistle? Do you know what has brought the canary to my mind? There is one in our front-room here which makes just such a noise as ours. *Apropos*, Herr Johannes will probably have received the letter of congratulation we wished to send him; but if he has not received it, I will tell him of its contents myself by word of mouth in Salzburg. We put on our new clothes yesterday; we were beautiful as angels! Remember me to Nandl and tell her she must pray for me diligently. An opera composed by Jomelli begins on the 30th. We have seen the king and queen at Mass in the royal chapel at Portici, and we have seen Vesuvius, too. Naples is beautiful, but as crowded as Vienna and Paris. Comparing the impudence of the towns-folk of London and Naples, I really do not know if Naples does not outdo London; for the populace here, the *lazzaroni*, have a chief of their own who gets 25 *ducati d'argento* every month from the king simply to keep the beggars in order.

Madame de Amicis is singing at the opera. We have been to visit her. Caffaro is the composer of the second opera, Ciccio

---

[1] At Naples they were entertained by the English ambassador, Sir William Hamilton, and his wife, the celebrated Lady Hamilton, who is described by Leopold Mozart as "an agreeable person " who "performs on the clavier with unusual skill."

[2] "Please write to me soon and every post-day. I thank you for having sent me the *arithmetic books* and beg you, if ever you wish me to have a headache, to send me a few more of these *examples*. Forgive me for writing so ill, but the reason is that I have a slight headache."

di Majo of the third, and the fourth is unknown as yet. Attend the Litanies at Mirabell[1] diligently, hear the *Regina cœli* or the *Salve Regina*, sleep sound and dream no ill dreams. My worst compliments to Herr von Schidenhofen—tralaliera—tralaliera—and tell him he must learn the Repeat Minuet on the clavier so that he *does* not forget it. He must *do* it soon, so that he may *do* me the pleasure of *doing* him an accompaniment sometime. And *do* remember me to all my other good friends, male and female, and *do* keep your health and *do* not die, so that you may *do* me another letter, and I may afterwards *do* one for you and so we may continue to *do* till we are *done* for, and *still* I will continue to *do* till there is no more to be *done*. Meanwhile I *do* remain,

W. M

10. *To his Sister*

C. S. M.

Vesuvius is smoking furiously to-day. *Potz Blitz und ka nent aini. Haid homa g'fresa beym* Herr Doll. *Dos is a deutscha Compositör und a brawa Mo.*[2] I shall now begin to write an account of my life. *Alle 9 ore qualche volta anche alle dieci mi sveglio, e poi andiamo, fuor di casa, e poi pranziamo da un trattore, e dopo pranzo scriviamo, e poi sortiamo, e indi ceniamo, ma che cosa? Al giorno di grasso, un mezzo pollo ovvero un piccolo boccone d'arrosto; al giorno di magro, un piccolo pesce; e di poi andiamo a dormire.*[3] *Est-ce que vous avez compris? Redma dafir soisburgarisch, don as is gschaida. Wir sand Gottlob gesund, da Voda und i.*[4] I hope you also are well, and likewise Mama. Naples and Rome are two sleepy cities. *A scheni Schrift!*

[1] A summer palace of the Archbishop of Salzburg.
[2] A piece of nonsense in dialect German. "Fed to-day with Herr Doll, a German composer and a good fellow."
[3] "I wake at nine o'clock, sometimes not till ten, and then we go out, and then we dine at an ordinary, and after dinner we write, and then we take a walk, and afterwards we sup. On a meat-day half a chicken, or a morsel of roast, on a fast-day a little fish; and then we go to sleep."
[4] "*You* may call this *low*, but it is very neatly done. We are well, praise be, Father and I." [Dialect.]

Net wor? [1] Write to me and don't be so lazy. *Altrimente avrete qualche bastonate di me!* [2] *Quel plaisir! Je te casserai la tête.* I look forward eagerly to the portrait,[3] *und i bi korios, wias da gleich sieht; wons ma gfoin, so los i mi und den Vodan a so macha.* Mädli, *las Da saga, wo bist dan gwesa, he?* [4] The opera here is by Jomelli; it is beautiful, but too discreet and old-fashioned for the theatre. Madame de Amicis sings incomparably and so does Aprile, who sang in Milan. The dances are wretchedly pompous. The theatre is handsome. The King is a rough Neapolitan in manners and always stands on a stool at the opera to appear a little taller than the Queen. The Queen is beautiful and courteous, for she has greeted me six times at least on the Molo (which is a public parade) in the friendliest manner.

P.S.—I kiss Mama's hand!

11. *To his Sister*

Postscript to his father's letter, Rome, 7th July, 1770.

C. S. M.

I am amazed indeed that you can compose so well. In a word, the song is beautiful. Try such things more often. Pray send me soon the other six minuets by Haydn. *Mlle, j'ai l'honneur d'être Votre très humble serviteur et frère Chevalier* [5] *de Mozart—Addio.*

12. *To his Mother*

Postscript to his father's letter, Bologna, 21st July, 1770.

My felicitations to Mama on her Name-day. I hope she may live many hundred years yet and ever in good health, a thing I ask of God continually, and pray for it daily and shall

---

[1] " Beautiful writing, isn't it ? " [Dialect.]

[2] " Otherwise you will get some whackings from me ! "

[3] The mother and daughter had been painted in miniature.

[4] " And I'm curious to see what it is like. If it pleases me I shall have myself and Father done in the same way. Where have you been, my girl, hey ? "

[5] *Chevalier.* At the age of fourteen Mozart was presented by the Pope with the Cross of the Order of the Golden Spur, the knights of which receive the title *Cavaliere.*

pray daily for you both. It is impossible for me to make any present, except a few Loretto bells and candles and caps and veils when I come back. Meantime I kiss Mama's hand 1000 times and am till death her faithful Son.

13. *To his Sister*

Postscript to his father's letter from Bologna, 4th August, 1770.

I am heartily sorry that Miss Martha is so ill, and I pray daily for her recovery; tell her from me that she must keep quiet and eat well-salted foods.

Apropos! Did you give my letter to Robinig? You tell me nothing of it. Pray tell him, when you see him, that he must not quite forget me. (I cannot write any better, for my pen is a music pen, not a letter pen.) My violin is now newly strung and I play every day. I only mention this because my Mama inquired once whether I still played the fiddle. Six times at least I have had the honour of going alone [1] to churches and splendid functions, and I have by now composed four Italian symphonies, besides arias (of which five or six at least are complete), and also a motet.

Does Herr Deibl come to see you often? Does he still honour you with his entertaining *discours*? And Herr Edler Karl von Vogt? Does he still permit himself the pleasure of listening to your intolerable voice? Herr von Schidenhofen must be diligent in helping you write minuets, or he shall have no sugar-sticks!

It would be my duty, if time permitted, to inflict a few lines on both Herr von Mölk and Herr Schidenhofen, but as it is impossible, I beg they will pardon my fault and let me postpone that honour to some future date.

Now I have done as you desired. I can scarcely believe that anything of mine will be chosen; for who would be so bold as to give, on his own authority, a piece composed by the son of the Capellmeister and whose Mother and Sister are among us? *Addio!* Farewell. My one amusement now consists in doing

[1] The father was confined to the inn after an accident on the road.

C

English dance steps and *caprioli*. Italy is a land of sleep! One is for ever sleepy! *Addio*, farewell!

Wolfgang Mozart.

4th *August*, 1770.

My compliments to all dear friends of the gentler sex! I kiss Mama's hand!

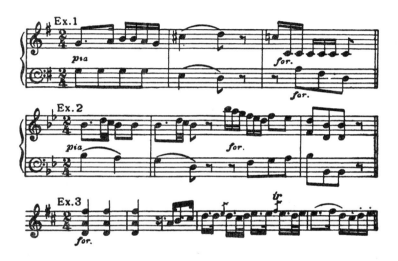

14. *To his Mother and Sister*

Postscript to a letter of his father's, Bologna, 21st August, 1770.

I too am still alive and in very good cheer. To-day the fancy took me to ride upon an ass; for it is the custom in Italy, and so I thought I must really try it. We have the honour of associating with a certain Dominican, who is held to be a holy man. I, indeed, do not altogether believe it, for at breakfast he often takes a cup of chocolate and directly afterwards a good glass of strong Spanish wine; and I have even had the honour of dining with this saint, who drank wine at table with a will and wound up with a whole glass full of strong wine, two good slices of melon, peaches, pears, five bowls of coffee, a whole plate full of cloves, and two full plates of milk with lemons. Well, I suppose he could do so if he tried hard, though I doubt it, for it would be far too much—and besides he takes many a dainty morsel in the afternoon

15. *To his Sister*

Postscript to a letter of his father's, Bologna, 22nd September, 1770.

I hope my Mama is well, and you likewise, and I wish in future you would answer my letters better, for indeed it is much easier to answer something than to think of something to say oneself. I like the six minuets of Haydn even better than the first twelve; we have had to play them to the Countess often, and we wished we could introduce the German *gusto* in minuets into Italy, because their minuets often last as long almost as a whole symphony. Forgive me for writing so ill— I could write better but am in haste. We should be glad of two little calendars for next year. *Addio*.

C. W. Mozart.

My hand-kiss to Mama

16. *To his Mother*

Postscript to a letter of his father's, Bologna, 29th September, 1770.

To make the letter a little longer, I will add a few words myself. I am grieved indeed at this prolonged illness of poor Miss Martha's which she is forced to endure with patience. I hope with God's help she will soon get well again, but if not, one must not grieve too much, for God's will is always best and God doubtless knows best whether it is better to be in this world or in the other. But she must take heart now that the rain is over and the fine weather is come. I kiss Mama's hands and bid her farewell. *Addio*.

Wolfgang Mozart.

Leopold Mozart

We remained in Bologna a few days longer because the *Accademia Philharmonica* unanimously elected Wolfgang into their Society and presented him with the patent of *Accademico Philharmonico*. All the necessary ceremonies and preliminary tests were, however, gone through. On the 9th of October, at four in the afternoon, he had to appear in the hall of the Academy. There the *Princeps Accademiæ* and the two *Censores* (all one-time kapellmeisters) gave him, in presence of all the members, an *antiphona* from an *antiphonarium*, which he was to set in four parts in an adjoining room, whither he was conducted by the *pedellus*, who locked the door on him. When he had completed this piece of work it was examined by the *Censores* and all the kapellmeisters and composers, who thereupon voted with black and white balls. All the balls being white, he was called in; his entrance was acclaimed by general clapping of hands and congratulations, the *princeps* of the accademy having previously informed him, in the name of the Society, of his election. He returned thanks and that closed the proceedings. Meanwhile Herr Prinsechi and I were locked into a room on the other side of the hall of the library of the Academy. Everyone was astounded at the rapidity with which he finished his task, as many have spent as much as three hours over an *antiphona* of three lines. You must know, however, that it is by no means easy, as a number of things are not permissible in this kind of composition, as he had been forewarned. He finished it in little over half an hour.

17. *To his Mother*

My dear Mama,

I can write but little, for much recitative writing has made my fingers very painful. I beg Mama to pray that my opera [1] may go well and that we may then be happily reunited. I kiss Mama's hand a thousand times, and I have much to tell my sister. But what? *That* God and I alone know, but, if it be God's will, I hope I shall soon be able to tell her by word of

[1] The opera referred to in this and subsequent letters is *Mitridate, re di Ponto*.

mouth. Meantime I kiss her a thousand times. My compliments to all our kind friends. We have lost our good Martha, yet we shall, by God's help, meet her again in bliss.

Leopold Mozart
MILAN, *15th December*, 1770.

Before the first rehearsal with the small orchestra, there were plenty of persons who made satirical remarks and cried down the music in advance as something immature and feeble—people who "prophesied," so to speak, affirming that it was impossible for a young boy, and a German into the bargain, to write an Italian opera; for although they recognised him as a great virtuoso, they could not believe he could have the requisite understanding of and insight into the *chiaro ed oscuro* of the stage. Since the night of the first small rehearsal, however, all these people have been struck dumb and left without a word to say. The copyist is full of glee—a good omen in Italy, since when the music is a success the copyist often makes more money through the distribution and sale of arias than the kapellmeister gets for the composition. The singers, male and female, are very well pleased and fully satisfied, the *prima donna* and *primo uomo* being particularly delighted with the duet. The *primo uomo* said "*Dass wenn dieses Duett nicht gefalle er sich noch einmal wolle beschnäzeln lassen!*" *Basta!* Now all depends on the caprice of the general public. In itself the affair is not of first importance to us, apart from a few barren honours. We have already ventured much in this strange world and God has always been our helper.

Leopold Mozart
MILAN, *29th December*, 1770.

God be praised, the first performance of the opera passed off on the 26th amidst universal applause. Two things occurred, unprecedented in Milan. In the first place (against all use and wont on a first *sera*, for it is not the custom to cry *fora* at a first production), one of the *prima donna's* arias was repeated; and in the second place, after almost every aria, with the possible exception of a few arias *delle ultime parti*, there was extraordinary hand-clapping and cries of "*Viva il Maestro, viva il Maestrino!*"

18. *To his Sister*

Postscript to his father's letter, Milan, 12th January, 1771.

Best-beloved Sister!

It is long since I wrote because I have been busy with the opera, but now that I have time I will be more mindful of my duty. The opera, thanks be to God, pleases the public so that the theatre is full every evening, and everyone is astonished at it and many say that they have seen no first opera so full as this one all the time that they have been in Milan. I and my Papa are well, God be praised and thanked, and I hope that I shall be able to tell Mama and you everything by word of mouth at Easter. *Addio!* I kiss Mama's hand. *Apropos.* Yesterday the copyist was with us and told us that he is now copying my opera for the court at Lisbon. Meanwhile, farewell my dear Mademoiselle Sister. I have the honour to be, and to remain, from now to eternity,

Your faithful brother.

19. *To his Sister*

Postscript to his father's letter, Milan, 24th August, 1771.

Best-beloved Sister!

The heat on our journey was very great, and the dust smothered us so audaciously that we should doubtless have been choked and suffocated if we had not taken care. It has not rained here for a whole month (say the Milanese), and though it began to drizzle a little to-day the sun is shining again now, and again it is very warm. That promise you made me (you know without my saying what that is—O thou dear one!) keep to it, I beg of you, and I shall indeed be indebted to you. Recently the princess *hatte das geschäftige Chatherl oder das — — schmeissen*[1]; otherwise I have no news. Do *you* write and tell me some. My compliments to all good friends. I kiss Mama's hand. I am puffing and blowing with heat—I am just going to burst! *Addio*, farewell,

Wolfgang.

[1] Obscure.

Above us is a violinist, beneath us is another, next us is a singing-master who gives lessons, and in the last room opposite us is an oboe-player. That is jolly for composing. It gives one plenty of ideas.

20. *To his Sister*

Postscript to his father's letter, Milan, 21st September, 1771.

I am well, God be praised and thanked. I cannot write much. Firstly, because I know not what to say; secondly, because my fingers ache with writing. Farewell. I kiss Mama's hand. I am always blowing my little whistle and no one answers me. Only two arias are wanting to the *Serenata*[1] and then I shall have finished. My compliments to all good friends. I have no longer any desire for Salzburg—I fear I might go mad too.

Wolfgang.

21. *To his Sister*

Postscript to his father's letter, Milan, 5th December, 1772.

I have still fourteen numbers to compose and shall then have finished. Really, one might count the terzet and duet as four numbers. I cannot possibly write much, for I have no news to tell you, and furthermore I do not know what I am writing because I think of nothing but my opera,[2] and am in danger of putting down an aria instead of words! I have to convey Herr and Frau Germani's compliments to Mama, to you and to Herr Adelgasser. I have learned a new game here in Milan called *Mercante in fiera* and we will play it as soon as I get home. Also I have learned a new language from Frau von Taste which is easy to speak, troublesome to write, useful, but a little—childish. However, it is good enough for Salzburg. *Addio*, farewell. My compliments to all good friends. Remember me to our beautiful Nandl, and to the canary bird, for these two and you are the most blameless creatures in our household. Fischietti, I suppose, is on the point of beginning an

[1] On this second short Italian journey Mozart successfully produced the stage serenade *Ascanio in Alba*.

[2] *Lucio Silla*. Mozart was beginning his third Italian tour.

opera buffa (in German, a "*närrische opera.*") *Addio.* I kiss Mama's hand.

22. *To his Sister*

Postscript to his father's letter, Milan, 18th December, 1772.

I hope you are well, my dear Sister. When you receive this letter, my dear Sister, it will be the very evening, my dear Sister, on which my opera is to be staged. Think of me, my dear Sister, and picture to yourself, my dear Sister, with all your might that you, my dear Sister, are seeing and hearing it too. Of course it is hard, as it is already eleven o'clock, else I should believe, and doubt not, that it is lighter by day than at Easter-time! To-morrow, my dear Sister, we dine out at Herr von Mayer's; and do you know why? Guess! Because he has invited us. There is a rehearsal to-morrow at the theatre. The impresario, however, Signor Castiglioni, has asked me to say nothing about it to anyone, else the public will pour in, and we do not want that. So, my child, I beg you will say nothing to nobody, otherwise too many folks will pour in, my child! *Approposito*, have you heard yet what has just happened here? Well, I will tell you all about it. We left Count Firmian's to-day to return home, and when we came to our street we opened our front-door, and what do you think happened? We went in. Farewell, my little heart. I kiss you, my little liver, and am as ever, my little stomach, thine unworthy

$$\left. \begin{array}{l} \textit{frater} \\ \text{brother} \end{array} \right\}$$ Wolfgang.

Pray, pray, my dear Sister, something is biting me—scratch me!

Leopold Mozart   Milan, 16*th* and 23*rd January*, 1773.

Wolfgang's opera has been performed seventeen times already and is to be performed some twenty odd times in all.

The theatre is astonishingly full every day. There have been twenty-six performances.[1]

---

[1] Nevertheless the Mozarts returned to Salzburg with their financial resources seriously impaired. Neither ever again visited Italy.

WITH HIS FATHER IN VIENNA (1773) AND MUNICH
(WINTER 1774-5)

23. *To Herr von Hefner* [1]

Enclosure in a letter to his sister, Vienna, 15th September, 1773.

To Herr von Hefner,

> *Ich hoff wir werden sie noch in Salzburg antreffen,*
>   *wohlfeiler freund*
> *Ich hoff sie werden gesund seyn, und nicht mir seyn*
>   *spinnfzund*
> *Sonst bin ich ihnen fliegenfeund,*
> *Oder gar wanzenfreund*
> *Also ich rathe ihnen bessere verse zu machen, sonst komm*
> *Ich meiner lebtag zu salzburg nicht mehr in Dom,*
> *Dan ich bin gar Capax zu gehen nach Constant-*
> *Inopel, die doch allen leuten ist bekannt*
> *Hernach sehen sie mich nicht mehr, und ich sie auch*
>   *nicht, aber*
> *Wen die Pferd hungrig sind, gieb man ihnen einen haber.*
>   *Leben sie wohl*
>   *Sonst werd ich toll*
>   *Ich bin zu Allezeit*
>   *Von nun an bist in Ewigkeit.*

[I hope we shall meet you in Salzburg, worthy friend.
I hope you will be in health, and will not be my "spider-
    enemy," [1]
Otherwise I shall be your "fly-enemy"
Or perhaps your "bug-friend."
Well, then, I counsel you, make better verse, else I'll come
Never more in my life into the Salzburger Dom,

---

[1] This gentleman held an appointment in the cathedral of Salzburg.
[2] "Spider-enemy"—a German metaphor for bitter hostility.

For I am quite *capax* of going to Con-
Stantinople, a town known to everyone.
After which you will see me no more, nor I you, but
When the steeds are hungry let them be given a bait;
    Live happy I pray,
    Else my wits will give way.
                      Both now and ever
                      I am forever——etc.]

Leopold Mozart
                          VIENNA, 12*th August*, 1773.

On the Feast of Saint Caietanus, the Fathers invited us to
dine and attend Divine Service, and since the organ was useless
to perform a concerto, Wolfgang borrowed a violin from Herr
Teiber and a concerto, and had the boldness to play the concerto
on the violin.

24. *To his Sister*
      Postscript to his father's letter, Munich, 16th December, 1774.

I have the toothache.

*johannes chrisostomus Wolfgangus Amadeus sigismundus
Mozartus Maria annæ Mozartæ matri et sorori, ac amicis
omnibus, præsertimque pulchris virginibus, ac freillibus, grati-
osisque freillibus*

                      S : P : D :

25. *To his Sister*
      Postscript to his father's letter, Munich, 30th December, 1774.

My compliments, pray, to Roxelana, and she is bidden
to take tea with the Sultan this evening. Give my very kindest
regards, I beg, to Miss Mizerl and tell her she must not doubt
my love and that she is ever before my mind's eye in her
enchanting négligée; I have seen many pretty girls here but
no such beauty as she. My sister must not forget to bring with
her the Variations on Ecart's [1] *minuette d'exaude* and my varia-

---

[1] Eckardt (1735–1809), a pianist and composer, renowned in his day.

tions on Fischer's [1] minuet. Yesterday I went to the comedy, according to the custom of the household. They did it very well. My compliments to all good friends, male and female. I hope you will—farewell—I shall soon see you, I hope, in Munich. I have to give you Frau von Durst's regards. Is it true that Hagenauer has become a professor of sculpture in Vienna? Herr von Mölk told Fathei Wasenau so in a letter, and Father Wasenau read me his letter. *Adieu.* I kiss Mama's hand and that is all for to-day. Keep really warm on the journey, I beg you, else you may spend your fortnight *sitting* indoors *sweating* over the fire, and who will *look after* you? I will not *overheat* myself. It's just beginning to thunder and *lighten.* [2]

> I am ever,
> Your Munich,
> Brother, 1774*th* 30 *Anno Decembre.* [3]

26. *To his Sister*

MUNICH, 11*th January,* '75.

We are all three well, thank God. I cannot possibly write much for I must go this minute to rehearsal. My chief rehearsal is to-morrow, and on Friday 13th my opera comes on.[4] Mama need have no care, all will go well. It grieves me very much that Mama should have cast suspicion on Count Seeau, for there is no doubt he is a friend and courtly gentleman and has more breeding than the majority of his like in Salzburg. Yesterday we went to the masked assembly. Herr von Mölk was so amazed and dumbfounded at hearing the *opera seria* that we were quite put out of countenance, for it was plain to all that he had never in his life seen aught beyond Salzburg and Innsbruck. *Addio.* I kiss Mama's hands.

> Wolfgang.

---

[1] Fischer (1733–1800), an oboist.
[2] The last five italicised words rhyme in German.
[3] An intentional jumble of names and figures.
[4] The comic opera *La Finta Giardiniera* which Mozart wrote for the Munich carnival.

27. *To his Sister*

My opera, thank God, was put on yesterday, being the thirteenth, and all went so well that I cannot possibly describe the uproar to Mama. In the first place, the whole theatre was packed so full that many people were forced to turn away. After each aria there was a terrible uproar with clapping and shouts of "*Viva Maestro.*" Her Highness the Electoress and the Dowager (who were *vis à vis* to me) also called "*bravo*" to me. The interval between the close of the opera and the beginning of the ballet was filled with clapping and shouts of "*bravo*" which no sooner died down than they broke out afresh, again and again. My papa and I afterwards went into a certain room through which the Elector and the whole Court have to pass and kissed the hands of their Highnesses the Elector and Electoress and other eminent persons, who were all very gracious. His Grace the Bishop of Chiemsee sent quite early this morning to congratulate me on the incomparable success of my opera. As to our return it will not be immediate and Mama must not even wish it, for Mama knows well how good it is to have a little breathing-space. We shall get home soon enough for [*an erasure here*]. But one just and valid excuse is that the opera is to be repeated next Friday and I must necessarily be present—otherwise nobody would recognise it again—for this is an odd place. I kiss Mama's hand a thousand times. My compliments to all good friends of both sexes. Remember me to M. Andretter and tell him I beg he will forgive me for not having answered him yet, but I had no time at all and I will now do so immediately. *Adieu!* A thousand kisses to *Bimberl.*[1]

[1] Bimberl (or Pimperl) was the dog, who plays a considerable rôle in the family correspondence.

A TOUR WITH HIS MOTHER THROUGH MUNICH AND AUGSBURG TO MANNHEIM (1777–8)[1]

28. *To his Father*

MUNICH, *29–30th September*, 1777.

It is true! We have many good friends but most, unfortunately, able to do little or nothing for us. I was with Count Seau at half-past ten o'clock yesterday and found him much graver and not so natural as on the first occasion. Still, it was but seeming, for to-day I waited on Prince Zeil, who said to me, using every civility, "I fear that we shall be unable to accomplish much here. I spoke privately with the Elector when dining with him at Nymphenburg and he replied that it was too soon as yet—that you ought to go to Italy and make a name—that he would deny you nothing, but that it was still too soon." So there it is! Most of these great gentlemen have such a terrible mania for Italy! Still, he advised me to go to the Elector and put my case before him as usual. To-day I privately spoke to Herr Wotschicka at table and he appointed 9 o'clock to-morrow, when he would certainly procure me an audience. We are·now good friends. He wished *absolument* to know the person, but I said to him, "Rest assured I am your friend and shall remain so. I for my part am fully convinced of your friendship. Let that suffice you." Well, to return to my story. The Bishop of Chiemsee also spoke quite privately with the Electoress. She shrugged her shoulders and said she would do what was possible, but that she had little hope. And now as to Count Seau. Count Seau asked Prince Zeil (after the latter had told him all): "Tell me, does not Mozart get enough from home to enable him to remain here with a

---

[1] Between 1775 and 1777 Mozart remained at Salzburg in the Archbishop's service, composing much and also performing. His salary was about £1 1s. per annum in English money! His father applied for leave to go on a tour to improve his straitened circumstances, but was refused.

little extra assistance? I should like to keep him." The Bishop
replied, "I do not know, but I am very doubtful of it. Still,
you might speak to him about it." This, then, was the reason
why he was so pensive the following day. I like being here;
and I am of opinion (like many kind friends) that, if I could
stay here a year or two, I could earn reputation and standing
by my work and consequently be in a position to be solicited
by, rather than to solicit, the Court. Since my arrival, Herr
Albert has had a project in mind which it seems to me it might
not be impossible to carry out. He would like to bring together
ten good friends, each willing to contribute the small sum
of one ducat a month, which would make ten ducats a month,
fifty gulden, six hundred florins a year. If in addition I were
to get only two hundred florins a year from Count Seau, that
would make eight hundred florins.—How does this idea please
Papa?—Is it not a friendly thought?—Ought it not to be
accepted if it is seriously proposed?—I am wholly content
with it. I should not be far from Salzburg and if you, my very
dearest Papa, were to take a fancy (as I wish with all my heart
you would) to leave Salzburg and live in Munich, things would
go very happily and smoothly. For seeing we had to live in
Salzburg on five-hundred-and-four florins, we could well live
in Munich on six hundred or eight hundred, could we not?—

I have 100,000 compliments to deliver from Countess La
Rose. She is indeed an amiable lady and our very good friend.
Herr von Dufresne told me recently that they two often
quarrelled with the *Praesidentin* on our behalf. Papa stands
in high favour with the Countess La Rosè. She says she has
seldom met so sensible a man!—and that you can see it in
his face!—I visit her every day. Her brother is not here.

To-day, the 30th, after talking with M. Wotschicka, I went
to Court at 9 o'clock. I found them all dressed for the hunt.
Baron Kern was gentleman-in-waiting. I should have gone
there yesterday evening, but that I could not offend Herr
Wotschicka, who had promised personally to get me speech
with the Elector. About 10 o'clock he led me into a narrow
little room through which his Electoral Highness had to pass

on his way to hear Mass before hunting. Count Seau passed by
and greeted me with a very friendly " Your servant, my dearest
Mozart!" When the Elector approached me, I said, "Will your
Highness permit me to lay myself and my services most
humbly at your feet?" "You want to leave Salzburg
altogether?" "Yes, altogether, your Highness." "Were you
dismissed?" "Oh! by no means, your Excellency, I merely
asked for leave of absence for a journey; it was refused, and
consequently I was forced to take this step. Notwithstanding,
I had long had in mind to go, for Salzburg is not the place
for me." "Indeed not. *Mon dieu*, what a lad! But your father
is still in Salzburg, is he not?" "Yes, your Highness. He is
your very humble, etc. I have already been to Italy three
times, have composed three operas, and at an examination by
the Academy of Bologna did my work in an hour when many
maestri have had to work and sweat over it for four or five
hours. This may bear witness that I am fit to serve in any
Court whatsoever. But my sole wish is to serve your Highness,
who is himself a great "——"Yes, yes, my dear child, but there
is no vacancy, I am sorry to say. If only there were a vacancy!"
"I do assure your Highness I should bring honour to Munich."
"Yes, but all that is no use, there is no vacancy," said he,
passing on, and I made respectful obeissance. Herr Wotschicka
advises me to let the Elector see me frequently. This afternoon
I went to see Count Salern. The Countess his daughter is now
lady-in-waiting. She joined in the hunt. I and Ravani were on
the road when the whole train came by. The Elector and
Electoress greeted me in very friendly fashion. Countess
Salern knew me at once. She waved to me a great many
times. Baron Rumling, whom I met previously in the ante-
room, was never so polite to me as on this occasion. I will tell
you what passed at the Salerns in my next letter—all very
kind, very courteous and sincere.

P.S.—*Ma très chère sœur*, I will soon write you a letter
all to yourself. Remember me to A. B. C. M. R. and other
letters of the alphabet. *Addio*. Pray take great care of your

health. I kiss Papa's hands 100,000 times and am and remain his

> Most obedient son,
> Wolfgang Amadé Mozart

A man built a house and wrote on it—

> *Das bauen ist ein grosse lust*
> *Dass so viell kost, hab ich nicht g'wust.*

[To build a house is joy, I trow,
How much 'twould cost, I did not know.]

During the night someone wrote underneath—

> *Und das es so viell kosten thut*
> *Hättst wissen soll'n, Du fozenhut.*

[But that 'twould take a deal of brass
You *should* have known, you silly ass.]

29. *To his Father*

MUNICH, *2nd October*, 1777.

Yesterday, being the 1st of October, I was again at Count Salern's house, and to-day, the 2nd, I dined there. I played quite enough on these three days; still, I did so very gladly. But do not let Papa suppose I was glad to be at the Salerns because of ——. No, for unfortunately she is in waiting and consequently never at home; but early to-morrow, at 10 o'clock, I am going to Court to visit her in company with Madame Hepp, formerly Mlle. Tosson. Then, on the following Saturday, the Court goes away and does not return till the 20th. To-morrow I am dining with Frau and Fräulein de Branca, in some sort a scholar of mine, for Siegl comes but seldom and Beeché,[1] who usually teaches her the flute, is away. For three whole days I played many things at Count Salern's "out of my head," and then, by heart, the two *casazioni* for the Countess, and the finale music, with the rondo to conclude. You cannot imagine how delighted Count Salern was; and he understands music,

---

[1] Beccke, a celebrated clavier-player of the day.

for he always says "*bravo*" when other cavaliers take a pinch of snuff, sneeze, clear their throats, or begin a conversation. I told him I only wished that the Elector were there to hear; he knows nothing about me, nor what I can do. A pity that these gentlemen simply believe what they are told and never investigate for themselves. I am willing to put the matter to the proof. Let him collect all the composers in Munich and send to Italy, France, Germany, England and Spain for others —I am confident I can compose with any of them. I told him of my Italian adventures and begged him to bring these matters to the fore if my name should be under discussion at any time, and he said, "I have very little influence, but what I can do I will, with all my heart." Furthermore, he believes that if I could manage to remain here for a time the matter would eventually settle itself. It would not be impossible for me to manage this alone, for I should get at least 300 florins from Count Seau and I need not worry about my board, as I should be constantly invited out; and when not, Albert would be delighted to have me to dinner. I eat little, drink water, and finish with a little wine and fruit. Provided my good friends saw no objection, I would make a contract with Count Seau to produce four German operas a year, some *buffé* and some *serie*. I should then get a benefit night on each for myself as is customary here, and that alone would bring me in at least 500 florins which, with my salary, would make 800 florins, though no doubt it would actually be more, for Reiner the actor and singer took 200 florins on his night, and I am a great favourite here. And how much more popular still I should become if I were to increase the German national stage in estimation in the sphere of music! I could certainly accomplish this, for on hearing the German musical drama I was at once filled with eagerness to write. The *prima donna's* name is Keiser. She is the daughter of a cook to a Count of these parts, a very pleasant girl and pretty on the stage, but I have not yet seen her near at hand. She was born here. When I heard her it was only her third appearance on the stage. She has a lovely voice, not strong but not weak either, very pure and with a good intonation. Valesi is her singing-master, and one can see from her singing that he understands singing as well as the teaching of it. On occasions, when she sustains a note for a couple of bars, I have very much admired her *crescendo* and *diminuendo*. Her trill is slow as yet and I am very glad of it, for it will be so much the purer and clearer when she quickens it. Besides, it is easier to do it fast. The people are very pleased with her—and I with them. Mama was in the parterre; she went at half-past four to secure a place. I did not go till half-past six as I can go into the boxes or anywhere, being well known. I was in the Branca box. I looked at Mlle. Keiser through my opera-glasses, and she drew many a tear from my eyes. I cried, "*Brava, bravissima!*" many times, for I never forgot that it was only her third appearance. The piece was called *The Fisher-Girl*, a very good translation with music by Picini.[1] They have no original pieces as yet, but they would like to give a German *opera seria* soon—and I think they would like me to compose it. Professor Huber, whom I mentioned, is among those who wish it. Now I must go to bed, otherwise I shall be fit for nothing. Ten o'clock to the second!

Baron Rumling recently paid me the compliment of saying to me, "The stage is my delight; good actors and actresses, good singers male and female, and to crown all so capital a composer as yourself!"—Of course that is mere talk—and it is easy to talk. But he never spoke to me like that before. I wish you a good night. To-morrow, if God wills, I shall have the honour of another pen-and-ink conversation, my very dearest Papa. 2nd October. No. 4 on the second story.

Leopold Mozart to his Son

6th October, 1777.

I feel sad at times because I cannot hear you playing the clavier and violin, and each time I come home a faint melancholy falls upon me, for as I draw near to our house I always half expect to hear the strains of your fiddle.

---

[1] Piccini, Nicolo (1728–1800), a very prolific operatic composer, much admired in his day. His rivalry with Gluck caused a social sensation in Paris in 1777.

30. *To his Father*

6th October, '77.

Mon très chèr Père!

Mama cannot write; in the first place she does not want to, and in the second place she has a headache! Consequently I must hold forth. I am on the point of going with the Professor to visit Mlle. Keiser. Yesterday there was an "ecclesiastical high time" or *altum tempus Eclesiasticum* at our house. There was dancing, but I danced only four minuets and was back in my room by eleven o'clock, for among the fifty females present there was only one who danced to time and she was Mlle. Käser, a sister of the secretary to Count Perusa who used to be in Salzburg. The Professor has been kind enough to miss his appointment with me; consequently I did not go to Mademoiselle Keiser, not knowing her house!

The day before yesterday, Saturday 4th, when the name-day of his Royal Highness the Archduke Albert was solemnised, we had a little concert. It began at half-past three and ended about eight o'clock. M. Dubreill, whom Papa will remember, was there. He is a pupil of Tartini.[1] In the morning he gave the youngest son, Carl, a violin lesson and I happened to come in while it was proceeding. I never believed much in him, but I perceived that he taught very assiduously, and when we fell into talk about the playing of the violin in concertos and in an orchestra he reasoned very well and was always of my persuasion. So I took back my earlier opinions and became convinced that I should find him an excellent companion and an accurate orchestral violinist. I therefore begged him to be so good as to join in our little concert in the afternoon. We began at once with the two quintets by Haydn. I am sorry to say I could scarcely listen to him! He was unable to play four bars without making a mistake. He could not manage the fingering and was not at all familiar with the rests. The best of the business was that he was very polite and praised the quintets, otherwise—well, I said nothing at all to him, but he himself kept on repeating, "I beg pardon, I am out again!

---

[1] Tartini, Giuseppe (1692–1770), composer and writer on musical theory.

The thing is tricky, but it is beautiful." *I* kept on saying, "Oh, it is of no consequence at all, we are just amongst ourselves." I then played the concerto in C in B flat and E flat and then my own trio. That was magnificently accompanied! In the adagio I had to play his part through six bars. Last but not least I played the last *casazione* out of my work in B flat. They all stared, I assure you! I played as if I were the greatest violinist in Europe. At three o'clock the following Sunday we visited a certain Herr von Hamm. I must write no more now, or I shall be unable to deliver the letter into Herr Kleinmayr's hands. The Bishop of Chiemsee has left for Strasburg to-day N.B. I enclose six duets *à clavicembalo e violino* by Schuster [1] for my sister. I have played them often here and they are not bad. If I stay here I shall compose six in the same *gusto*, for they are very popular here. I send them chiefly that you two may have something to amuse you. *Addio.* I kiss your hands 1000 times and beg you, my dear Nannerl, to wait a little longer in patience. I am your most obedient son,

Wolfgang Amadé Mozart.

Munich, *6th October*, 1777.

Leopold Mozart to his Son
1*5th October*, 1777.

You have stayed too long in Munich. You must give one or two concerts in Augsburg and make some money, be it much or little. Fair words, eulogies and *bravissimi* will pay neither postman nor landlord, and when there is nothing more to be made one must move on at once.

31. *To his Father*
AUGSBURG, 17–18*th October*, 1777.

To-day, the 17th, we dined with young Herr Gassner, the young and handsome widower of a young and beautiful wife. They had been married only two years. He is a most kind and courteous young man. We were entertained splendidly. A colleague of the Abbé Henri Bullinger, and Wishofer an ex-

[1] Schuster, Joseph (1748–1812), composer.

Jesuit, now kapellmeister at the cathedral here, were also at dinner. The latter knows Herr Schachtner well and was his choirmaster. His name is Father Gerbl. He asks me to convey his compliments to Herr Schachtner. After dinner Herr Gassner, a sister-in-law of his, Mama and I and our cousin went to see Herr Stein.[1] At four o'clock we were followed by the Herr Kapellmeister and by Herr Schmittbauer, organist at St. Ulrich's, an excellent suave old man. I played a sonata by Beeché at first sight, rather difficult, *miserable al solito*. The astonishment of the kapellmeister and organist was indescribable. Both here and in Munich I have frequently played all my six sonatas by heart. I played the 5th in G at a select peasants' parlour concert. The last, in D, goes excellently on Stein's pianoforte. He has, too, improved on the contrivance for exerting pressure by the knee. I can put it in action with the lightest touch, and when one slackens the knee-pressure a little there is no trace of an echo. Well, to-morrow perhaps I shall come to his organ—come to write about it, I mean. I shall save up his little daughter for the last! When I told Herr Stein that I should like to play his organ, since the organ was my passion, he was greatly surprised and said, "What! can such a man as you, such a great pianist, wish to play on an instrument devoid of *douceur*, of expression, of *piano* and *forte*, one which is always the same?"—"Oh, there is nothing in that. The organ is still, to my eyes and ears, the king of instruments."—"Well, just as you like——" and so we set off together. I could tell at once from his talk that he thought I should do little with the organ—that I should, *par exemple*, play it like the clavier. He told me he had taken Chobert,[2] at his own request, to the organ, and "I grew anxious," said he, "for Chobert told everybody and the church was fairly full; for I knew the fellow was all spirit, fire and speed, and that is unsuitable to the organ. However, as soon as he began I changed my mind." My sole reply was, "What do you think, Herr Stein, do you suppose I shall race about on the organ?"—"Oh, you—

---

[1] Stein was a renowned clavier-maker and organ-builder.
[2] The well-known Johann Schobert, pianoforte composer.

that is quite different." We reached the choir. I began to prelude; he smiled; then came a fugue. "I can well believe now," said he, "that you like playing the organ. When one plays like that——!" At first I found the pedal a little strange to me because it was not divided. It began with C, then D and E in series. In ours D and E are above, in his E♭ and F♯. However, I soon got used to it. I have also tried the old organ at St. Ulrich's. The stairs there are really terrible. I begged that someone else should play it to me while I descended to listen, for above you get no effect from the organ. I got nothing by it, however, for the young *regens chori* [choirmaster], a priest, skipped about on the organ in a manner completely unintelligible. When he tried for harmonies he produced nothing but discords, for it was out of tune. Afterwards we were invited into a reception-room, for my Mama, and cousin and Herr Stein were also there. A certain Father Emilian, a pompous ass, a feeble-minded would-be wit of his profession, was very familiar. He was constantly trying to make sport with my cousin, but she made sport of him. At length, when he had got a little drunk (which happened soon) he began to talk of music. He sang a canon and said I had never heard anything finer in my life. I said, "I am sorry I cannot sing with you for I am by nature incapable of intoning." "That is no matter," said he, and began. I made the third. But I set quite different words to it: "Padre Emilian, O you booby you, *leck Du mich im Arsch,*" *sotto voce* to my cousin! We spent another half-hour laughing, and he said to me: "If we only had longer together I should like to discuss the art of composition with you." "We should soon come to an end of the discussion," said I. *Schmecks kropfeter.*

To be continued in my next.

W. A. Mozart.

32. *To his Father*

Mon très cher Père

Yesterday, Wednesday the 22nd, my concert was held. Count Wolfeck was very zealous about it and brought several

canonesses with him. During my first few days here I went to
wait on him at his lodgings, but he was not there. A few days
ago, however, he returned, and hearing I was here, he did not
wait for me to come to him but himself came to my door as
I was in the very act of taking up hat and sword to pay him a
visit. Now I must describe the occurrences of the last few days
before I come to the concert. Last Saturday I was at St.
Ulrich's, as I wrote to you in my last. A few days previously
my cousin took me to visit the Abbot of Holy Cross, a
fine, honourable old man. On the Saturday before I went to
St. Ulrich's I again visited the monastery of Holy Cross with
my lady cousin because on the first occasion the Dean and
Procurator were not present, and my cousin told me that the
Procurator was a merry fellow.

"Indeed he *has* got it." Mama: "Oh no, I assure you; he
has written again and again that he has not got it yet." Wolfgang: "I hate argument. He certainly has it and that's an end
of the matter." Mama: "You are mistaken, Wolfgang."—"No,
I am not mistaken, I will show it you written down." Mama:
"Where, then?" Wolfgang: "There, read it." Mama is just
reading it now.——

Last Sunday I attended Divine Service at Holy Cross. At
10 o'clock, however, I went to see Herr Stein. That was on
the 19th, and we rehearsed a few symphonies for the concert.
Afterwards I dined with my cousins at Holy Cross, being
entertained with music at table. Badly as they fiddle, I would
rather have the abbey music than the Augsburg orchestra. I
performed a symphony and played Vanhall's concerto in B flat
on the violin with general approbation. The Dean is a good,
cheerful man, a cousin of Eberlin's. His name is Zeschinger
and he knows you well. In the evening, at supper-time, I
played the Strasburg violin concerto. It went like oil. All
praised the lovely pure tone. They then produced a small
clavichord on which I preluded and played a sonata and the
Fischer variations. All the others then whispered into the Dean's
ear that he ought to hear me play in organ style. I asked him
to give me a theme, but as he would not, one of the monks

gave me one. I worked upon it till mid-way (the fugue was in
G minor) I passed into the major, in playful style but in the
same *tempo*; then I returned to the theme, but reversed;
and at last I took it into my head to see if I could treat the
theme of the fugue in the same joking spirit. I did not have to
seek long, but came on what I wanted almost at once, and it
worked out as accurately as if a tailor had taken the measure-
ments. The Dean was quite beside himself with delight.
"Well," said he, "I could never have believed what I have
just heard. You're a wonderful fellow. True, the Abbot told me
he had never in his life heard anyone play the organ in so
compelling and solemn a style." (He had heard me a few days
previously when the Dean was not present.) At length someone
produced a fugued sonata for me to play. "Gentlemen," said
I, "this is too much; I must confess I shall not be able to play
this sonata so easily!" "I should think not, indeed," cried
the Dean zealously, for he was very much my partisan, "that
is too much. No one could do it!" "However," said I, "I will
just try it." All the time I could hear the Dean whispering
behind my back. "Oh, you arch-rascal!—Oh, you rogue! Oh,
you—you——" I played till eleven o'clock. I was bombarded
and besieged with subjects for fugues. Recently Stein brought
me a sonata by Beeché—I believe I have written about that
already. *Apropos* of Stein's little girl. Anyone able to see and
hear her play without laughing must be *stone* [1] like her father.
She sits opposite the treble notes, not in the middle forsooth,
for better occasion of throwing herself about and making
grimaces. She rolls her eyes and all kinds of nonsense. When
a passage occurs twice she plays it slower the second time,
when thrice, slower still. When she has a passage to execute
she lifts her arm high in the air, and if it needs emphasis she
uses the arm not the fingers, taking every care to do it heavily
and clumsily. Best of all, however, when it is necessary to
change the fingers in a passage which should run as smoothly
as oil, she does not worry her head at all, but at the critical
moment stops, lifts her hand, and begins again quite at her ease.

[1] A pun on the name Stein, which means stone.

Besides, that affords a better chance of surprising a false note and a very curious effect is produced! My sole object in writing this is that Papa may pick up ideas of clavier-playing and teaching which in due time he may be able to turn to account. Herr Stein is quite besotted about his daughter. She is eight and a half years old and plays everything by heart. Something might be made of her, she has talent, but on these lines she will come to naught. She will never acquire much speed because she is doing her best to become heavy-handed. She will never master the most necessary, the most difficult, the most important thing in music, namely the *tempo*, because she has been accustomed from infancy to disregard the beat. Herr Stein and I have discussed this point for two hours at a stretch and I have already gone far towards converting him. He asks my advice about everything now. He used to dote upon Beeché, but now he sees and hears that I play better than Beeché, that I do not grimace and yet play with so much expression that no one, by his own confession, has made such good use of his *piano-forte*. He sees, too, that I am always strictly in time. They all wonder at that. They cannot understand how I keep the left hand independent in the *tempo rubato* of an adagio, for with them the left hand always follows the right. Count Wolfeck and several more passionate adherents of Beeché recently said publicly at the concert that I put Beeché on the shelf. Count Wolfeck went about the room saying, "Never in my life heard anything like it!" To me he said, "I must tell you I never heard you play as you have done to-day. I shall tell your father so as soon as I arrive in Salzburg." What do you think came after the symphony? The concerto for three claviers. Herr Demmler played the first, I the second and Herr Stein the third. Then I played alone—the last sonata in D, for Dürnitz; then my concerto in B flat; then again alone in organ style a fugue in C minor, and then to conclude a magnificent sonata in C major with a closing rondo, my own invention. There was a prodigious tumult and hubbub. Herr Stein did nothing but make faces and grimaces of amazement. Herr Demler laughed and laughed. He is an odd fellow;

when anything really pleases him he can do nothing but laugh prodigiously. He even began to swear at me. *Addio.* I kiss Papa's hands and embrace my sister with all my heart.

I am your very obedient son,
Wolfgang Amadé Mozart.

24th October, 1777, augusta vindelicorum.

Leopold Mozart to his Son.

1st November, 1777.

I wish that you could get something to do in Mannheim. They constantly play German opera there. Perhaps you could get an order to compose one? Should this occur, you know without my telling you that I could never recommend you to do the frivolous type of work which is popular because easily understood. Great matters should be met in a great and exalted spirit.

33. *To his Father*

31st October, 1777.

Pray be patient with my deficiencies! To-day I was in Herr Danner's company at M. Canabich's [1] house. He was uncommonly polite. I played him something on his *pianoforte* (which is excellent) and we went to rehearsal together. I thought I should be unable to restrain my laughter when the people were introduced to me. A few who knew me *per renomé* were very civil, but others who knew nothing of me stared at me a great deal and no doubt found me ludicrous. They certainly think that because I am little and young there can be nothing great or venerable within me, but they shall soon see! To-morrow Herr Canabich himself is to take me to see Count Savioli, Intendant of Music. The best of it is that the Elector's name-day is impending. The oratorio in rehearsal is by Handel. I did not stay to hear it, however, for it was preceded by a rehearsal of a psalm, the *Magnificat*, by the vice-kapellmeister here, Vogler,[2] and the thing lasted an hour

[1] Christian Cannabich, 1731-98. Concert-master, director of chamber music and acting head of the Mannheim School founded by Johann Stamitz.
[2] The Abbé Vogler (1749–1812). His composition and playing were severely criticised by Mozart. See Letter No. 40.

at the least. Now I must close, for I have still to write to my
lady cousin. I kiss Papa's hand and embrace my dearest sister,
short and sharp.

* * * Johannes Chrisostomus * * Sigismundus
*Wolfgang Gottlieb Mozart.

* To-day is my name-day! * * this is my confirmation
name! * * * The 27th January is my birthday!

Our compliments to all our friends. Particularly to Count
Leopold Arco, Herr Bullinger, Mademoiselle Chatherl and the
whole tribe of them.

À Mad^{elle} Rosalie joli

Ich sag dir tausend danck mein liebste Sallerl,
Und trinke dir zur ehr ein ganzes schallerl,
Coffé und dann auch thee, und limonadi,
Und truncke ein, ein stangerl vom Pomadi
Und auch—auweh, auweh, es schlägt just Sex
Und wers nit glaubt der ist — — der ist — — ein fex.

[A thousand thanks to thee, my dearest Sallerl,
To toast thy right good health, I'd drink a barrel.
Coffee and tea to boot and lemonade
In which I sop a pellet of pomade.
Besides—but there chimes six, alack, alas!
And who believes me not—he is—he is—an ass!]

To be continued in my next.

34. *To his Father*

Yesterday forenoon at Herr Canabich's I composed the
rondo for the sonata for Mademoiselle his daughter, and afterwards they would not let me leave them. The Elector, the
lady, and the whole Court is very well pleased with me. On
both occasions when I played at the conceit the Elector and
his consort drew close to the clavier. Afterwards Canabich
procured me a word with his Highness. As I kissed the
Elector's hand he said, "I believe it is fifteen years since you

were here?"—"Yes, your Highness, it is fifteen years since I had that honour."—"You play incomparably." When I kissed the Princess's hand she said to me, "*Monsieur, je vous assure, on ne peut pas jouer mieux.*" Yesterday I was there with Canabich, as Mama has already written to you. I talked to the Elector as to a good friend. He is a very kind and gracious lord. He said to me, "I hear you wrote an opera at Munich." —"Yes, your Highness, I commend myself to your Highness's gracious favour. I wish nothing better than to be permitted to write an opera here. I beg that you will not entirely forget me. I can do something German, too, thank God."—"That may well be," said he. He has a son and three daughters, the eldest of whom, and the young Count, play the clavier. The Elector consulted me privately about his children. I answered quite sincerely but without prejudice to their master. Canabich agreed with my opinion. The Elector, in taking leave, thanked me very courteously. Directly after dinner to-day, about two o'clock, I accompanied Canabich to visit Wendling,[1] the flautist. All were prodigiously civil. The daughter (who was at one time the Elector's mistress) plays the clavier very prettily. Afterwards I played. I was in such good vein to-day that I cannot describe it to you. I played nothing but pieces out of my head and three violin duets which I had never seen before and whose author I had never heard of. They were all so delighted that I was compelled to kiss the ladies! I did not find it at all difficult in the daughter's case, for she is no scarecrow! Afterwards we visited the Elector's natural children. I played there with all my heart. I played thrice. The Elector himself kept on asking me to do so and sat near me motionless all the time. I let a certain professor give me a subject for a fugue and worked it out. Followed an outburst of congratulations.

My very dearest Papa!

I cannot write poetically, for I am no poet. I cannot artfully arrange my phrases so as to give light and shade. Neither

[1] Johann Baptist Wendling also belonged to the Mannheim circle. He was flautist to the orchestra and composer.

am I a painter; nor can I even express my thoughts by gesture and pantomime, for I am no dancer. But I can do so in sounds. I am a musician. To-morrow at Canabich's I shall *play* on the clavier my congratulations on your birthday and name-day! All I can do to-day is to wish you, *mon très cher Père*, with all my heart all those good things which I wish you every morning and evening—health, long life and cheerfulness! Moreover, I hope you are less displeased now that I have left Salzburg; for I have to confess that it was all my doing. They treated me ill; I did not deserve it. Naturally they took an interest—but too much! That you see was my chief and weightiest reason for leaving Salzburg so hurriedly. And so I hope my wish is fulfilled. Now I must close with congratulations—in music. I wish you may live as many years as one would need to leave nothing new in music to be composed! Now, fare you well. I beg you most submissively to go on loving me a little, and meantime to put up with these poor birthday wishes till my cramped and tiny brain-cupboard is fitted with new shelves in which I can store away the good sense which I hope I may yet acquire. I kiss Papa's hand 1000 times and remain till death,

Mon trés cher Pére,

Your most obedient son,

Wolfgang Amadé Mozart.

Mannhiem, 8th November, 1777.

35. *To his Father*

14–16th November, 1777.

I, *johannes Chrisostomus Amadeus Wolfgangus sigismundus* Mozart, confess my fault in that the day before yesterday, and yesterday (and on many previous occasions), I did not come home till 12 o'clock at night; and that from 10 o'clock until the hour aforenamed at Canabich's house, in the presence of, and in company with, Canabich, his wife and daughter, Herr Schazmeister, Ramm and Lang), I frequently—not gravely but quite frivolously—made verses; and those obscene ones, about dung, excrement and *arschlecken*, in thought and

word—but not in deed. But I should not have behaved so
impiously if the ring-leader, that is to say Lisel (Elisabetha
Canabich), had not urged me on and encouraged me to it so
lustily; and I must admit that I enjoyed it prodigiously. I
confess all these my sins and transgressions from the bottom
of my heart, and, in the hope of confessing them more often,
I am firmly resolved constantly to *improve on* the evil manner
of life which I have begun. Therefore I beg for holy dispensa-
tion, if it can be managed; and if not, it's all one to me, for
the game will go on all the same. *Lusus enim suum habet
ambitum,* says the sainted singer Meissner, cap. 9, page 24.
Furthermore, so says the holy Ascenditor, patron of the coffee-
bowl, of musty lemonade, of milk of almonds without almonds,
and more particularly of iced strawberries with lumps of ice
among them, for he himself was a great philosopher and artist
in such-like matters. As soon as possible I will have the
sonatas I wrote for Mlle. Canabich copied out on thin paper
and send them to my sister. Three days ago I began to teach
Mlle. Rose the sonatas. We finished the first allegro to-day. We
shall have most trouble with the andante, for it is full of expression and must be played accurately with *gusto, forte* and
piano just as it is written. But she is very apt and learns very
easily. The right hand is excellent, the left unfortunately has
been quite spoiled. I can tell you that I often feel very sorry
for her when I see her make so great an effort that she is quite
out of breath, and that not from stupidity but because long
habit, her whole previous training, has made it impossible for
her. I have told both her mother and herself that were I
formally her music-master I would lock up all her music, cover
the clavier with a handkerchief and make her play, at first
quite slowly, nothing but passages, shakes, *mordanten extra*
exercises with the right and left hands till the hand was fully
trained. After that I trust I could make a real pianist of her.
For it is a pity. She has so much talent, reads quite passably,
has much natural facility and much feeling. They both agreed
with me. Now, to the opera. A few words only. Holzbauer's [1]

[1] Holzbauer, Ignaz Jacob (1711–83), a voluminous composer.

music is very fine; the poetry is not worth such music. What amazes me most is that a man of his years should still have so much spirit, for you would not believe what fire there is in the music! Madame Elisabetha Wendling was *prima donna*—not the flautist's wife, but the violinist's. She is always out of health, and moreover the opera was not written for her, but for a certain Mlle. Danzi now in England, and therefore too high for her voice. Herr Raaf [1] has three of the four arias, and in one instance sang about four hundred and fifty bars in such a way that one noticed that the chief cause of his singing so ill is his voice. Were you to hear him begin an aria without bethinking yourself for the moment that it was Raaf, the once famous tenor, who was singing, you would be compelled to hearty laughter. There is no doubt about it, I have discovered it myself. If I did not know that this was Raaf I should double up for laughing, but as it is I merely get out my handkerchief and use it. Besides, as they tell me here, he could never act in his life; he should be heard but not seen. Moreover, he has not a good appearance. In the opera he had to die singing a long slow aria, and there he died, grinning! Towards the end of the aria his voice failed so much that it was unbearable. I sat near Wendling the flautist, in the orchestra. He had previously offered the criticism that it was unnatural to sing so long before dying and I said to him, "It seems a long time to wait." "But," continued I, "be patient. The end is near. I can hear it in his voice." "So can I," said he, and laughed. The second female singer, a certain Mlle. Strasser, sings very well and is an excellent actress. There is a permanent German national dramatic stage here, as in Munich. German operettas are given from time to time, but the singers, male and female, are wretched. Yesterday I dined with Baron and Baroness von Hagen. He is the Master of the Hunt. Three days ago I went to visit Herr Schmalz, a merchant, with an introductory letter from Herr Herzog, or rather from Nocker and Schidl. I expected to find a very civil, worthy man. I gave him

---

[1] Anton Raaff the tenor (1714-97) is repeatedly mentioned in the letters. Mozart wrote the part of Idomeneo for him.

the letter. He read it through, made me a little bow and—said nothing. At last I told him (after many apologies for not having waited on him long before) that the Elector had heard me play. "Indeed?"—*altum silentium!* I said nothing. He said nothing. Eventually I said, "I will not incommode you longer —I have the honour——" Here he broke in on me with, "If I can do you any service?"—"Then before I take my leave may I take the liberty of asking you——"—"You want money?" —"Yes, if you would——"—"Oh, I cannot do that. There is nothing in the letter about money. I cannot give you money. But anything else——"—"But indeed you can do *nothing* else for me. I have the honour to wish you good morning." Yesterday I wrote to Herr Herzog in Augsburg telling him the whole story. Now we must wait for an answer. Consequently Papa may still write to Mannheim. Please give my regards to all good friends of both sexes. I kiss Papa's hand 100,000 times, and embrace my sister with all my heart, and am your young brother and father—because in his last letter Papa wrote, "I am your old husband and son!" This letter has been finished to-day, the 16th, but who knows when this letter will be dispatched? "Have you finished it—the letter?"—"Yes, Mama, I have finished it—the letter."

36. *To his Father*

MANNHEIM, 29*th November*, 1777. *Evening.*

Mon trés cher Pére !

Yesterday morning I safely received your letter of the 24th, from which I perceive that you are unable to bear with equanimity good fortune—and evil, should these be our lot. Hitherto we four have been neither fortunate nor unfortunate, and I thank God for it. You reproach us undeservedly on many counts. We are incurring no unnecessary expense; as to what *is* necessary when travelling—you know it as well, or better, than we. It was on my sole responsibility that we stayed sc long in Munich; and had I been alone I should most certainly have remained in Munich. As to our fortnight's stay in Augsburg?—really I am almost driven to conclude that you did not get my letter from Augsburg. I wanted to give a concert in Augsburg—I was promised the opportunity. A week went by. I then resolved *absoulement* to leave, but they would not let me. They wished me to give a concert—I wished to be urged to do so. And it came off. I gave a concert. That accounts for the fortnight. As to our coming straight on to Mannheim— I explained that in my last letter. As to our being still here —well—can you suppose I would remain anywhere without reason? "But one might, surely, let one's father——" Good, then, you shall hear the reason, the whole course of events. God knows, nevertheless, that I did not wish to write about it because I could not (and cannot to-day) give a complete account and must consequently (as I well knew) have left you in a state of uncertainty and anxiety—a thing I have always endeavoured to avoid. But now that you attribute my course of action to negligence, thoughtlessness and idleness, I have only myself to thank for your good opinion of me, though I must deplore from my heart that you know me—your son—so little.

I am not careless, I am merely prepared for anything and can therefore await events in patience—and I can endure anything so long as my honour and that of the name of Mozart does not suffer. Well, what must be, must; only I would beg you not to give way prematurely either to joy or grief. Happen what will, all is well if one only keeps one's health; for happiness subsists—solely in the imagination. Last Tuesday week, the 18th, namely the Eve of St. Elizabeth, I called on Count Savioli in the morning and asked him whether it was possible that the Elector would keep me here for this winter; I was willing to give the royal children lessons. "I will suggest it to the Elector," said he, "and, in so far as it rests with me, it shall certainly be arranged." In the afternoon I was at Canabich's, and since it was on his advice that I had approached the Count, he at once asked me whether I had been to him. I told him all. "I should be very well pleased," said he, "if you were to stay for the winter, but I should be still better pleased if you to were remain permanently in the Elector's service." "Nothing would please me better," replied I, "than to remain in your neighbourhood; but I cannot see how this could be possible as a permanent arrangement. You have two kapellmeisters already and I do not see what post I could hold, for I should not care to be under Vogler!" "You would not be under him," said he, "for no musician here is under the kapellmeister, nor even under the Intendant. The Elector could well appoint you chamber-music composer. Wait a little and I will talk to the Count about it." There was a big concert on Thursday. On catching sight of me the Count apologised for not having mooted the subject as yet, owing to a series of gala days; when the holidays were over, however, namely on Monday, he would certainly speak. I let three days pass; then, hearing nothing, I went to him for news. "My dear M. Mozart," said he (that was on Friday—yesterday), "there was a hunt to-day and I could not possibly question the Elector in the midst of that. But by this time to-morrow I shall certainly be able to give you an answer." I begged him to be sure not to forget. Truth to tell, I left feeling somewhat provoked and accordingly decided to take the young Count my easiest six variations on Fischer's minuet (which I had already written out for the very purpose) and so make occasion to speak to the Elector myself. You cannot imagine how delighted the housekeeper was to see me. I was very civilly received, and when I produced the variations, telling her they were for the Count, she said, "Oh, that is splendid! But surely you have something for the Countess as well?" "Not yet," said I, "but if I remain here long enough to write something I will——" "Apropos," she broke in, "I am delighted that you are to remain here all the winter."—"I? I know nothing of it!"—"I am astonished," said she, "that is very odd! The Elector told me so recently himself. 'By the by,' said he, 'Mozart is staying here for the winter.'"—"Well, if he said that, it has been said by the person who has the best right to say it," replied I, "for naturally I cannot remain here except at the wish of the Elector." I then related the whole story to her. We agreed that I had better come on the morrow (that is to-day) at four o'clock bringing something with me for the Countess. She was to speak to the Elector before my arrival and I should then meet him myself. Now, I went there to-day, but he did not appear. But I shall go again to-morrow. I have composed a rondo for the Countess. Now, have I not reason enough to stay and await the issue? Ought I to leave now of all times, when the most important step has been taken?—now that I have the opportunity of speaking personally to the Elector? I really believe I shall probably spend the winter here. For the Elector likes me, thinks highly of me and recognises my capacity. I hope I shall be able to give you good news in a future letter. Again I beg you neither to rejoice nor grieve prematurely and to speak of this to no one save Herr Bullinger and my sister. I enclose for my sister the allegro and andante of the sonata I composed for Mlle. Canabich. The rondo will follow shortly. It would have made too big a packet to send all together. I fear you must put up with the original. It is easier for you to have it transcribed at six krone the sheet than for me at twenty-four krone. Is that not very dear?—*Addieu.* I kiss your hand 100,000 times, embrace my sister with all my heart, and remain your most obedient son,

Wolfgang Amadé Mozart.

You will probably have heard a fragment of the sonata, for it has been sung, played, fiddled or whistled at the Canabichs' at least three times a day—though I confess only *sotto voce!*

Leopold Mozart to his Son

4th December, 1777.

And so you think, perhaps, to coax me into a good humour by writing me a hundred droll letters? I am glad that you should be in good spirits; only instead of an alphabet of compliments I should have been more cheered by a rational account of the journey to Weilburg, its causes and circumstances, and your future plans; and you might have written me such an account last post-day but one, for the idea cannot have but just occurred to you, and moreover you could not have known that the Princess was there unless someone had advised you of it. In a word, when one entertains a project, it is not mere idle speculation to form two or three plans and make the corresponding necessary preparations, so that if one goes awry one can take up another without delay. To neglect to do this is to be either an imprudent or a frivolous person who, more especially in the modern world, will always fall behind in the race whatever his talents, and indeed is predestined for misfortune; for he will always be imposed upon by flatterers, by those who offer lip service and by the envious. Mark well, my son, if you find one man in a thousand who is your true friend, apart from self-interest, it is one of the greatest miracles in this world. Investigate all who call themselves or show themselves your friends, and you will discover their reasons for being so. If their interest is not directly personal, then it concerns some other friend of theirs who can be useful to them; or perhaps they befriend you in order to disconcert some third party through your advancement.

37. *To his lady Cousin* [1] *at Augsburg*

Ma très chère Cousine!

     * * * I *should have* safely received your letter of November 25th had you not written that you had had head-, neck- and arm-ache, but that now, for the present, just now, for the moment, you were rid of your pains and I have accordingly safely received your letter of November 26th. Yes, indeed, my very dear Mistress Cousin, so it is in this world; one has the purse and another the money. What do you hold with? With the ☞, do you not? [2] *Hey, presto, coppersmith!* It is gospel truth. He who believes it shall be saved and he who believes it not shall go to heaven—straight as a dart, not like my writing! And so you see I can write as I like, a smooth-flowing hand or a wild one, straight or crooked. A little while ago I

---

     [1] Maria Anna Mozart of Augsburg. On 18 October, 1777, Leopold Mozart writes of her: "I am vastly glad to find that Miss my Cousin is beautiful, sensible, amiable, talented and merry. I have no objection whatever but, on the contrary, desire the honour of making her acquaintance. Only it appears to me that she has too much acquaintance with clerics. If I am mistaken I will beg her pardon on my knees. So I only say, 'It seems to me'—and appearances are deceptive, especially at such a distance as from Augsburg to Salzburg, and more particularly now with so much fog that one can scarce see thirty paces ahead."
     [2] A common nursery "catch" in Germany.

was in a bad humour and so wrote beautifully, smoothly, solemnly; to-day I am at peace with myself so I write wildly, crookedly and merrily. Now the point is simply which you prefer? You must choose one or t'other, for I have nothing between; smooth or ragged, neat or crooked, grave or merry, the first three words or the last three. I await your decision in your next letter. My resolution is taken. When needs must I'll walk, but when circumstances permit—why, I'll run. I am very much obliged to you, my dear Fräulein Cousin, for the kind regards of Fräulein Freysinger which the dear Fräulein Juliana has been so good to convey. You tell me that you *could* say much more, but too much *is* too much;—I submit that it is too much for one letter, but little by little one may write reams. You see, in this matter of the sonata one must arm oneself with patience yet a little longer. If it had been for my little Cousin it would have been ready long ago—and who knows if Mlle. Freysinger still remembers it——? Notwithstanding I will finish it as soon as possible, write a letter to accompany it and beg my dear little Cousin to hand it over in the correct manner. *Apropos*—I wonder what you will think of my being still in Mannheim—right in? I have gone nowhere else, for I have not yet left it! But I believe now that Mannheim will shortly set out on its travels. However, Augsburg, writing from you, can continue to address letters to me at Mannheim till further notice. My Herr Cousin, my Frau Cousin and my Fräulein Cousin desire to be remembered to my Mama and to me. They were growing anxious lest we should be ill because they had not heard from us for so long. The day before yesterday they were at last rejoiced to receive our letter of November 26th and to-day, being December 3rd, they have the pleasure of answering me. And so I mean to keep my promise to you? Well, you are delighted. Only do not forget to compose Munich for the sonata, for what one has performed that one must promise. One must always be a word of one's man. But now let us be sensible!

I must tell you something at once. I did not dine at home to-day, but with a certain M. Wendling. Now you must know

that he always dines at half-past one, that he is married
and has a daughter who, however, is a permanent invalid.
His wife is singing in the coming opera and he plays the flute.
Now just picture to yourself how at half-past one we all sat
down to table (except the daughter, who remained in bed)
and—dined.

Compliments from us both to all good friends, male and
female. Those to your parents will be found on page 3, line 12.
Now I have no more news save that an old cow * * * * *
and now *adieu Anna Maria Schlosser* [Locksmith] *née*
Schlüsselmacher [Key-maker]. Live happily and love me.
Write to me *soon*, its near full *noon*. If your word you do not
keep, I will drown me in the *deep*. *Addieu, mon Dieu.* Thousand
kisses I *send thee*, and now I must *end me*

> *Mannheim*
> *ohne Schleim*
> *den* 3ten *Decembr.*
> *Heut ist nicht Quatembr.*
> *1777 zur nächtlichen Zeit*
> *von nun an bis in Ewigkeit*
> > *Amen.*

> *Ma très chère Cousine*
> *waren Sie nie zu Berlin ?*
> *Der aufrichtige wahre Vetter*
> *bei schönen und wilden Wetter*

> > *W. A. Mozqart.*
> > * * * *das ist hart.*

[(Rhymed nonsense :)

> Mannheim
> without slime
> Of December the 3rd day
> (To-day is not Quarter Day)
> Night-time, seventeen seventy-seven
> From this day till the Kingdom of Heaven
> > Amen.

Ma très chère cousine
You've not seen Berlin?
Your true and honest Cousin
In rain and eke in sunshine

W. A. Mozart
* * * that is hard!]

38. *To his Father*

MANNHEIM, 10*th December*, 1777.

Mon trés cher Pére!

Well, there is nothing to be hoped from the Elector now.
I was at the concert at Court the day before yesterday, hoping
to get an answer. Count Savioli definitely avoided me. I went
up to him, however. When he saw me he shrugged his
shoulders. "What," said I, "still no answer?" "I am very
sorry," said he, "but it is all in vain." "*Eh bien*," said I, "but
the Elector might have told me *that* sooner." "Yes," replied
he, "and he would not have made up his mind now if I had not
pressed him to do so and represented to him that you had been
kept waiting here a great while wasting your money at an
inn." "That is what annoys me most, also," rejoined I. "It is
not at all handsome. But, for the rest, I am very much obliged
to you, Herr Count (he is not addressed as 'Excellency') for
having acted so zealously on my behalf, and beg you will
thank the Elector in my name for this gracious, though somewhat tardy information, and assure him that he would certainly
never have regretted it had he engaged me." "Oh," said he,
"I am more convinced of that than you, perhaps, can believe."
Afterwards I told Herr Wendling of this decision. He flushed
deeply and said with great heat, "Then we must find a way.
You must stay here—at least for two months till we can go to
Paris together. To-morrow Canabich returns from the hunt;
then we can talk of it further." Thereupon I left the concert
and went straight to Madame Canabich. On the way I told
the whole story to the Chancellor, a most worthy man and a
good friend of mine. You cannot imagine how angry he was
about it. As we entered the room he opened the subject at

once, saying, "Well, here's a man who has experienced the usual handsome treatment at Court!" "What!" cried Madame, "has nothing come of it?"—I then told her all, and she began to relate all kinds of like instances which have occurred here. When Mademoiselle Rose, who had been occupied with the linen three rooms away, came in, she said to me, "We will work really hard at our lesson to-day." "Indeed, I think we should," rejoined I, "for there will not be many more of them." "What? How's that? But why?" and she turned to her mother, who told her all. "What?" said she "Is it certain? I cannot believe it!" "Yes, there is no doubt about it," said I. There-upon she played my sonata very gravely. I tell you I could not forbear weeping. In the end tears came to the eyes of the mother, the daughter and the Chancellor also, for she played the sonata perfectly and it is the favourite of the whole family. "The Herr Kapellmeister's departure (they all call me that here) makes us all weep," said the Chancellor. I must say that I have good friends here, for circumstances like these prove them. They are not friends in word only, but in deed.

Listen to the following. The other day, going as usual to dine with Wendling, he said to me, "Our Indian (that is a Dutch gentleman living here on his fortune, an amateur of all branches of learning and a great friend and admirer of mine) is a most excellent man. He will give you two hundred florins if you will write him three little short easy concertos and a couple of quartets for the flute. Through Canabich you can get at least two pupils who will pay well. You can write duets for clavier and violin and have them engraved by sub-scription. You can sit at our table both morning and evening and lodge with the Herr Chancellor, so all that will cost nothing. As for Madame your mother, until you have written home about all this, we will search out a cheap little lodging for a couple of months." After that Mama can go home and we go to Paris. Mama is satisfied with the arrangement and now all depends solely on your consent, of which I feel so certain that, if it were time to start, I would leave for Paris without awaiting your answer; for nothing else could be expected from a father so wise and so careful hitherto of his children's welfare. Herr Wendling, who sends you his compliments, is a bosom friend of our bosom friend, Grimm. He talked much with him about me when he was here—that is when he came here after leaving us at Salzburg. As soon as I get your answer to this letter I shall write to him, for, as I heard from a stranger dining here one day, he is now in Paris. I would like to ask you furthermore (we do not leave before March 6th) to procure me if possible a letter to the Queen of France, through Herr Messmer [1] of Vienna or through some other. But only if you can do so easily! For it is no great matter—but it is certainly better to have one. That is another piece of advice given me by Herr Wendling. I imagine that the matters of which I write to you strike you as strange because you are now living in a town where one is accustomed to having foolish enemies and simple weak friends, sycophantic because the bitter bread of Salzburg is indispensable to them and they live from hand to mouth. You see that the very reason why I have always written you letters full of childishness and jest with little sense in them is that I wished to await the issue here, to spare you anxiety and to shield my good friends, whom you blame as though they had privately conspired against me, when, as a fact, it is not so and they are innocent. *I* know who is the cause of it! But your letters have compelled me to tell you the whole story. I beg of you, however, by all I hold dear, do not grieve for the event. God willed it so. Bethink you of the all-too-certain truth that all a man's projects cannot be accomplished. We often think that this or that would be a good thing when it would be a very evil thing, and if it came to pass we should find it to be so by sad experience. Now I must go and compose. I shall have enough to write in these two months, three concertos, two quartets, four to six duets for the clavier, and then I have it in mind to do a big new Mass and to present it to the Elector. *Addieu.* Pray send me speedy answers on all

---

[1] Dr. Mesmer, a Viennese gentleman of musical tastes, "probably to be identified with the discoverer of animal magnetism" (Grove). It was at his house that Mozart's operetta, *Bastien and Bastienne*, was first performed.

points. I kiss your hands 100,000 times and embrace my sister with all my heart. I am your obedient son,

Wolfgang Amadé Mozart.

Baron Dürnitz was not in Munich when I was there. I will write to Prince Zeil next post-day to push matters forward in Munich. If you would write to him too, I should be very glad. But plain and to the point—no fawning, for I cannot abide it. One thing is certain—he can do it if he likes; all Munich told me that.

Leopold Mozart to his Son
11th December, 1777.

Nannerl plays your whole sonata very well and with full expression. Should you leave Mannheim, as I now suppose you will, I will have it copied and sent to you, a sheet in each letter, so that you have the sonata in your possession again for possible use in another place, without the detestable labour of writing it out again. But I will send it you only a sheet at a time, to avoid making the letters too bulky, and, moreover, should a letter go astray, it would be easier to re-copy a single sheet than the whole sonata, should that be lost. The sonata is exceptional. It has something of the mannered Mannheim taste about it, but not enough to disguise your own good style.

Leopold Mozart to his Son
18th December, 1777.

The one thing I will not have is that you should lodge with some anonymous Herr Councillor ——? while Mama lodges alone. As long as Mama is there you must remain at her side. You shall not and must not leave her alone among strangers while you and she are together. Let the room be as small as it may, there *must* be room for a bed for you.

39. *To his Father*
20th December, 1777.

I wish you, my very dearest Papa, a right happy New Year, and that your health, which I value so much, may improve to the welfare and the happiness of your wife and children, to

the delight of your true friends and to the chagrin and vexation
of your enemies! I beg you to love me as fatherly in the coming
year as you have ever done! I for my part will do my best
endeavour increasingly to deserve the love of so excellent a
father. I was heartily glad of your last letter, that of December
15th, for it told me that you were, thanks be to God, sound and
well. We, too, are both in very good health by God's grace. I
must succeed indeed, for I bestir myself diligently enough. I
am writing this at eleven o'clock at night, as I have no time
else. We cannot rise before eight for the light does not reach
our room (it being on the ground floor) before half-past eight.
Then I dress quickly and at ten o'clock sit down to compose
till twelve or half-past twelve. I then go to Wendling's, where
I write a little more until half-past one, when we sit down to
dinner which brings us to near three o'clock. Then I have to
go to the Mainzische Hof (an inn) to give a Dutch officer
lessons in *gallanterie* [1] and thorough-bass for which, if I am not
mistaken, I am to get four ducats for a course of twelve lessons.
At four I return home to give the daughter a lesson. We never
begin, however, before half-past four when lights are brought
in. At six o'clock I go to Canabich's to teach Mademoiselle
Rose and remain to sup. Then there is conversation—or at
times a little music, but I always draw a book from my pocket
and read—as I used to do in Salzburg. I have told you that
your last letter filled me with joy. That is true! But one thing
therein grieved me a little—your question as to whether I
had perhaps forgotten to make my confessions. I do not mean
that I have any objection to make—only let me beg you not
to think too ill of me! I like to be merry, but be assured that I
can be grave despite everyone. Since leaving Salzburg (and
even in Salzburg itself) I have found myself in company whose
words and acts I should be ashamed of were they mine, and
that among men, ten, twenty and even thirty years older than
myself!—I therefore beg you again most humbly to have a
better opinion of me. Please remember me to Herr Bullinger,
my best of friends, and convey him my warmest New Year's

---

[1] ? The ornamental or gallant style in music.—Ed.

wishes. My compliments to all good friends, male and female.
N.B. To Father Dominicus.

Meine liebste Sallerl, mein schazerl !

Meine liebste Nannerl mein schwesterl !

*Ich thue mich halt bedanken, für deinen glückwunsch
    Engel,*

Und hier hast ein von Mozart, von den grob-einzign bengel,

*Ich wünsch dir glück und freude, wens doch die sachen
    gibt,*

*Und hof Du wirst mich lieben, wie Dich der Woferl
    liebt ;*

Ich kan Die wahrlich sagen, dass er Dich thut verehren

Er luf Dir ja ins feuer, wens Dus thatst a begehren,

Ich meyn ich muss so schreiben, wie er zu reden pflegt !

Mir ist so frisch vor augen, die liebe die er hegt

Für seine joli sallerl, und seine schwester Nanzerl !

*Ach kommt geschwind her ihr lieben, wir machen
    geschwind ein tanzerl*

Es sollen leben alle, der Papa und d'Mama,

Die schwester und der bruder, huisassa hupsasa !

*Und auch d'metress von woferl, und auch der woferl
    selbst*

Und das so lange lange—so lang als er noch krelbst

So lang als er noch Prunzen, und wacker scheissen kan

So lang bleibt er und d'Sallerl, und's schwesterle voran.

*Ein saubers g'sindel—auweh ! ich mus geschwind nach
    schlaraffen,*

*Und das izt gleich um 12 uhr; dann dort thut man schon
    schlaffen.*

[My dear little Sally, my sweetheart!

   My dear little Nanny, my sister!

      For your good wishes, angels, I thank you from my
          heart,

      And here are some to you, from that clumsy ass Mozart.

   If in this world they're to be found I wish you joy and
          pleasure

And hope you'll still love Wolfgang, as he you, in fullest
     measure.
Love you indeed he does, for to do your least desire
I can with truth assure you he would run into the fire.
As he is wont to prattle I feel constrained to write
The love he ever cherished is so fresh before his sight
For his pretty sweetheart Sally and his little sister
     Nance.
Oh, do but come, my darlings, and we'll straightway have
     a dance.
     Long live we all, Papa, Mama,
     Sister and brother, hurrah, hurrah!
     Wolfgang's sweetheart and Wolfgang's self
     And never be put upon the shelf.
     While he can ——— and he can ———
     He, Sally and Sister shall dwell in bliss
A pretty rabble truly,—but alas! to bed I should be
     creeping
For the hour is striking midnight, when all honest folk are
     sleeping.]

                    Wolfgang Amadé Mozart.
                    Marie anna Mozart.

Extract from a Letter to his Father

                              27th December, 1777.
   I have now made the acquaintance of Herr Wieland.[1] But at
present I know him better than he knows me, for he has heard
nothing of mine as yet. I do not find him at all as I pictured him.
A somewhat childish voice; everlasting tippling; a kind of pedantic
insolence and yet from time to time a foolish condescension. I am
not surprised, however, that he should be satisfied with such a
bearing here (whether or no it is the same in Weimar and elsewhere),
for people in this town look at him as though he had descended from
heaven. People are prodigiously shy of him, do not open their
mouths, keep as still as mice, concentrate on every word he utters
—only it really is a pity they often have so long to wait for that
word, for he has some defect of speech so that he talks very slowly
and cannot say six words without coming to a halt. Otherwise he

   [1] Wieland, Christoph Martin (1733–1813), the poet and writer.

is, as we all know him to be, a man of excellent parts. His face is frankly ugly, thickly pock-marked and with a fairly long nose. In stature he must be approximately a little taller than Papa.

40. *To his Father*

MANNHEIM, 17th January, 1778.

On Wednesday next I am going for a few days to Kirchheim-Poland to visit the Princess of Orange; people speak so well of her here that I have at last resolved to go. A Dutch officer, a good friend of mine, got a terrible scolding from her for not bringing me with him when he went to pay her his New Year's compliments. I shall get eight louis d'or at the least; for since she is extraordinarily fond of singing I have had four arias copied for her, and as she has a really elegant orchestra and gives concerts daily I intend also to present her with a symphony. It will not cost me much to have the arias copied as this has been done for me by a certain Herr Weber,[1] who is to accompany me on my journey. He has a daughter just fifteen years of age who sings admirably, having a pure and lovely voice. She only needs to study action, when she might be *prima donna* on any stage. Her father is a good honest German who brings up his children well, and for that very reason the girl is persecuted with attentions here. He has six children, five girls and one son. He, his wife and children, have been obliged to live for fourteen years on an income of 200 florins; since he has always served well and has provided the Elector with a very talented singer he now gets—a whole four hundred florins! She sings my aria for De Amicis with those terribly difficult passages most excellently, and she is to sing it at Kirchheim-Poland.

Now for something else. Last Wednesday there was a big party at our house to which I was invited. There were fifteen guests and the young lady of the house was to play during the

[1] Fridolin Weber, singer, prompter and copyist at the Mannheim Court Theatre. Mozart was friendly with two of his daughters, Aloysia, who later married Lang, the actor, and Constance, Mozart's future wife.

evening the concerto I had taught her. About eleven in the
morning the Herr Councillor came to see me bringing Herr
Vogler. The latter desired *absolument* to make my better
acquaintance—he had plagued me so often already to come to
him, and had finally conquered his pride so far as to make me
the first visit. For the matter of that, people say he is very
much changed now because he is no longer such an object of
admiration; for at first they made an idol of him. Accordingly
I went upstairs with him at once; the other guests began to
arrive and we did nothing but chatter. After dinner, however,
he sent to his house for two claviers, tuned to one another,
and also for his tedious published sonatas. I was forced to
play them and he accompanied me on the other clavier. At
his urgent request I was then obliged to send for my own
sonatas. N.B. Before dinner he bungled through my concerto
(the one which the daughter of the house plays—Mme. Litzau's)
prima vista. The first movement went *prestissimo*, the andante
allegro and the rondo still more *prestissimo*. He played the
the bars for the most part not as it is written and from time
to time entirely changed both harmony and melody. At that
pace nothing else is possible; the eyes cannot see the music
nor the hands perform it. But what kind of sight-playing is
that?—Useless. The listeners (I mean those of them who are
worthy to be so named) can only claim to have *seen* music and
clavier playing. They hear, think and *feel* as little during the
performance as the player himself. You may easily conceive
how insupportable it was, for I could not well say to him
"Much too fast!" Moreover, it is much easier to play a thing
quickly than to play it slowly. In the former case certain notes
can be dropped out of the runs without being missed; but is
that desirable? In rapid playing the right and left hands can
be changed without anyone seeing or hearing it; but is *that*
desirable? And in what does the art of *prima vista* playing
consist? In this—in playing the piece in correct time, as it
should go, with appropriate expression and taste in every note,
phrase, etc., so that one would suppose the performer had composed it himself. His fingering, moreover, is wretched. His left

thumb is like that of the late Adlgasser,[1] and he executes all ascending runs in the right hand with the first finger and thumb.

Leopold Mozart to his Son

5th February, 1778.

You are but a young man, twenty-two years of age; accordingly you cannot have such settled gravity as would discourage any young fellow of whatever station in life—an adventurer, a roisterer—or any impostor, old or young—from seeking your friendship and acquaintance to draw you into his company and then by degrees into his toils. One steps into them so unnoticeably and then can find no return. I will not even speak to you of women, for there the greatest reserve and prudence are necessary, Nature herself being our enemy. He who does not exert his judgment to the utmost to keep the necessary reserve will exert it in vain afterwards to extricate himself from the labyrinth; a misery ended in most cases by death alone. You may perhaps already have learned a little by experience how blindly we may be led on at first by meaningless jests, flattery and play in a way for which reawakened reason blushes; but I do not mean to reproach you. I know that you love me, not merely as a father but as your truest and surest friend. I know that you understand and perceive that our happiness and unhappiness, nay, more, my long life or speedy death is, under God, so to speak in your hands. If I have read you aright I have nothing but joy to expect from you, and this must console me when robbed by your absence of the fatherly delight of seeing you, hearing you and folding you in my arms. Live as a good Catholic Christian. Love and fear God. Pray to Him with fervour, trust in Him with devotion; live so Christian a life that if I should see you no more the hour of my death may be free from apprehension. From my heart I give you my paternal blessing and am till death your faithful father and most sincere friend,

Leopold Mozart.

41. *To his Father*

Monsieur mon très cher Père!

I could not possibly wait as usual for Saturday, because it is already too long since I had the pleasure of talking with you

[1] Adelgasser, Anton Cajetan (1728–77), from 1751 cathedral organist in Salzburg. His church music was very much esteemed in his day.

by letter. First of all I must tell you how things went with me
and my good friends in Kirchheim-Poland. It was a real holiday
journey, neither more nor less. We set off from here at eight
o'clock on Friday morning after I had breakfasted with
Herr Weber. We had a fine covered chaise with four places. We
arrived in Kirchheim-Poland about four o'clock and proceeded
at once to the castle to leave our cards. Early next morning
Herr Concert-master Rothfischer came to see us. He had been
described to me in Mannheim as a most worthy man and I
found him so. In the evening, that is to say Saturday evening,
we went to Court, where Mademoiselle Weber sang the three
arias. I pass over her singing with one word—admirable! Indeed
I have recently described her merits to you; and yet I shall
not be able to close this letter without writing more of her,
for not till now have I really come to know her and consequently to perceive her true value. Afterwards we dined at
the officers' table. Next day we went some little way to Church,
for the Catholic church is not very near. That was Sunday.
At midday we again dined at Court, but as it was Sunday there
was no music in the evening. For the same reason they have
only three hundred musical evenings a year. We might nevertheless have supped at Court in the evening, but we did not
wish to do so, preferring to be privately together at home.
We would all have been unanimously and heartily glad to
dispense with meals at Court, for we never enjoyed ourselves
better than when we were alone, only we had to think a little
of economy—we had to spend enough as it was. The following
day, Monday, there was music again, as also on Tuesday and
Wednesday. Mademoiselle Weber sang in all thirteen times and
played the clavier twice, for she plays not at all ill. What
surprises me most is her good sight-reading. Only consider
that she played my difficult sonatas, slowly yet without a
single mistake, *prima vista*! On my honour I would rather hear
my sonatas played by her than by Vogler! I played a dozen
times in all, once by request on the organ in the Lutheran church,
and I waited on the Princess with four symphonies and got no
more than seven louis d'or in silver money, mark you, and my

poor dear Mlle. Weber only five! I really did not suppose it
could turn out so, and although I never hoped for much I
thought I should get at least eight for each work. *Basta!*
We have lost nothing by it, for I have 42 florins profit and
the inexpressible delight of acquaintance with a thoroughly
honourable good Catholic Christian family. I am very sorry
that I did not get to know them long ago. Now I come to an
important point to which I beg a speedy reply from you.

Mama and I, having discussed the matter together, are
agreed that the Wendlings' way of life does not please us
at all.

Wendling is a thoroughly honourable and good man, but
unfortunately he is without religion and so is his whole family.
It is enough to say that his daughter has been the Elector's
maîtresse. Ramm is a fine fellow but a libertine. I know myself
well enough to be sure that I have enough religion never at
any time to do what I could not do openly before all the
world; but the mere idea of travelling alone in the society of
people whose way of thinking is so different from my own
(and from that of all honourable people) frightens me. They
can do as they wish. I have no heart to travel with them—I
should not have a happy hour—I should not know of what
to talk. For, in a word, I do not fully trust them. Friends who
have no religion cannot last. I have already given them a
slight hint in advance of any intention. I have told them that
during my absence three letters have arrived of which I could
not tell them more, but that I am unlikely to be able to travel
to Paris with them. Perhaps I might follow them—perhaps go
elsewhere; they are not to rely on me. My idea is as follows.

I propose to stay here and finish at leisure my music for
De Jean, which will bring me in my two hundred florins. I
can stay here as long as I like, for neither food nor lodging
costs me anything. During this time Herr Weber will endeavour
to get engagements at concerts with me. Then we will travel
together. If I travel with him it will be just as if I were travelling with you. The very reason he is so dear to me is that,
apart from outward appearance, he is just like you and has just

your character and way of thinking. My mother, were she not, as you know, too lazy and comfortable to write, would tell you just the same! I must confess that I much enjoyed travelling with them. We were happy and merry; I heard a man talk as you do; I did not have to trouble about anything; I found my torn clothes mended; in a word I was waited on like a prince.

This unfortunate family is so dear to me that my dearest wish would be to make them happy; and perhaps I may actually be able to do so. My advice is that they should go to Italy. Therefore I want to ask you to write to our good friend Lugiati, the sooner the better, and find out how much, and what is the most, they give a *prima donna* in Verona—the more the better, one can always climb down—and perhaps one could also get Mme. Ascenza in Venice? As to her singing, I would lay my life that she will bring me renown. Even in so short a time she has greatly profited by my instruction, and how much greater will not the improvement be by then? I am not anxious about her acting, either. If our plan succeeds, we — M. Weber, his two daughters and I—will do ourselves the honour of spending a fortnight with my dear Papa and my dear sister *en route*. My sister will find a friend and comrade in Mademoiselle Weber, for her reputation for good breeding here is like that of my sister's in Salzburg, her father's like my father's, and the standing of the whole family like that of the family of Mozart. True, there are envious folk as there are with us, but when it comes to the point they are forced to speak the truth. Honesty triumphs in the end. I can tell you I shall be glad to come to Salzburg with them, if only that you may hear her sing. She sings my De Amicis arias, as well as the bravura aria, *Parto, m'affretto* and *Dalla sponda tenebrosa* superbly. I beg you will do your best to get us to Italy. You know my greatest inclination—to write operas.

I will gladly write an opera in Verona for fifty *zechini* merely that she may make her name, for if I do not write I fear she will be victimised. Before then I shall have made so much money on the other journeys we propose to undertake together that it will do me no harm. I think we shall go to

Switzerland and perhaps also to Holland. Only write to me soon on the point. If we stay long anywhere the other daughter, the elder, will be useful to us, for as she can cook we can set up our household. *Apropos*, you must not be too surprised that I have only forty-two florins left out of seventy-seven. That is merely the result of my joy in being again in the company of honourable and like-minded people. I spent it in paying a half-share of the expenses, but that is not usually so on our journeys when, as I have already told you, I pay only for myself. Afterwards we stayed five days at Worms, where Weber has a brother-in-law, namely the Dean of the monastery. N.B.—the fear of Herr Weber's sarcastic quill! We had a merry time there and dined and supped at the dean's table. One thing I can say, and that is that this little journey was fine practice for me on the clavier. The dean is a very excellent and sensible man. Well, it is time for me to make an end. Were I to write all I think I should have no paper left. Answer me soon I beg you, and do not forget my ambition to write operas. I am jealous of everybody who writes one. I could weep for vexation when I hear or see an aria! But Italian, not German; serious, not *buffé*. You should not have sent me Heufeld's letter; it gave me more mortification than pleasure. The fool thinks I shall write a comic opera—and that at once, on chance, a wretched speculation! Ah well! he is a real Viennese clown; or else he imagines people stand still at twelve years of age. Well, I have written all I have in my heart. My mother is content with my way of thinking. I cannot possibly travel with people—with a man—who lives a life of whom the veriest stripling could not but be ashamed; and the thought of helping a poor family without injury to oneself delights my very soul. I kiss your hand a thousand times and am till death,

Your most obedient son,

Wolfgang Amadé Mozart.

Mannheim, 4th February, 1778.

My regards to all good friends of both sexes; particularly to my best friend Herr Bullinger.

Leopold Mozart to his Son

SALZBURG, 12th February, 1778.

My dear Son!

I have read your letter of the 4th with amazement and horror! I am beginning to answer it to-day, the 11th, for I was unable to sleep the whole night through and am so wearied that I can only write slowly, word by word, and so gradually finish what I have to say by to-morrow. Recently, thank God, I have been in good health; but this letter, in which I only recognise my son by virtue of the failing which causes him to believe everyone at the first word spoken, to expose his kind heart to every glib flatterer, to let others sway him at will, and to be led by whimsies and ill-considered fanciful projects to sacrifice his own good name and interests, and even the interests and the assistance due to his aged and honourable parents, to the interests of strangers—this letter, I say, has crushed me all the more completely in that I had entertained reasonable hopes that certain experiences through which you have already passed, together with my own reminders, both spoken and written, could not have failed to convince you that, for the sake, not only of one's happiness but also of one's mere livelihood in this world, and in order to attain at length the desired goal in a world of men, in varying degrees good and bad, fortunate and unfortunate, it is essential for you to hedge your warm heart about with the strictest reserve, to undertake nothing without full consideration, and never to allow yourself to be carried away by enthusiastic notions and blind fancies. Pray, my dear son, read this letter and reflect upon it—take time for mature consideration as you read! Merciful God! those moments, so blessed for me, are passed when you, as child and boy, never went to your bed without standing upon the chair and singing me the *oragnia figatafa*,[1] kissing the end of my nose again and again afterwards, and telling me that you would put me in a glass case when I grew old and protect me from every breath so that you might always keep me with you and honour me! Listen to me, then, with patience! You are fully acquainted with our Salzburg distresses—you know my wretched income, why I kept my promise to let you leave us, and all my

---

[1] In Mozart's childhood "before he went to rest at night a little solemnity took place which could not on any occasion be omitted. He had composed a tune which was regularly sung by himself at this time, standing in a chair, while his father standing near him sang the second. The words were merely, ' *oragna figata fa marina gemina fa* '" (Edward Holmes).

various troubles. The objects of your journey were two—either to find a good permanent post, or, if you should be unsuccessful in this, to betake yourself to some great city where large earnings are possible. Both plans were designed to support your parents and to help forward your dear sister, but above all to build up your own name and fame in the world. The latter has already been in part accomplished during your childhood and boyhood, and it now depends on yourself alone to raise yourself by degrees to a position of consequence, the greatest ever yet obtained by a musician. You owe that to the extraordinary talents bestowed on you by a most beneficent Providence; and now it depends solely on your judgment and way of life whether you die a common musician utterly forgotten by the world, or a famous kapellmeister, of whom posterity will read,—whether you leave this world, having been captured by some petticoat, bedded on straw and penned in with an attic-full of starving children, or whether, after a Christian life, you leave it full of contentment, honour and renown, all your family well provided, your name respected by all. You travelled to Munich—with what purpose you know—but nothing could be made of it. Well-meaning friends wished to keep you there—you wished to remain. It occurred to someone to form a committee— but I need not recapitulate in detail. At the moment you thought the matter practicable—and I thought it not so. Look up the letter in which I replied to you. You have a sense of honour. Would it have conduced to your honour, had the scheme come to pass, to be dependent on the monthly charity of ten persons? At that time you were prodigiously taken up with the little singer [1] at the theatre and your dearest wish was to forward the cause of the German stage; now you declare you would not even write a comic opera! You were no sooner outside the gates of Munich than (as I prophesied) all your friendly committee of *subscribers* had forgotten you—and what would it have been like in Munich by now? One can always see the providence of God after the event. In Augsburg, too, you had your little romance, amusing yourself with my brother's daughter, who now must needs send you her portrait! I wrote you the rest in my first letters to Mannheim. In Wallerstein you amused all the company prodigiously, took up your fiddle, pranced about and played, so that people cried you up to absent friends as a merry, high-spirited, hare-brained fellow, giving Herr

---

[1] Mlle. Keiser, the Munich singer mentioned in Letter No. 29.

Becke occasion to disparage your merits, although now your compositions and your sister's playing (for she always says, "I am only my
brother's pupil") have set you before the two gentlemen in another
light, so that they now have the highest esteem for your art and
are more inclined to exclaim against Herr Becke's bad composition.
In Mannheim you did well to get into the good graces of Herr
Canabich. It would have done you no good, though, if he had
not been seeking a double advantage for himself thereby. I have
already written to you about the rest. Mademoiselle, Herr Canabich's
daughter, was next loaded with praises, her temperament portrayed
in the *adagio* of a sonata, in short she was for the time reigning
favourite. Then you made the acquaintance of Herr Wendling.
Now *he* was the most honourable of friends—and what happened
next I need not repeat. Suddenly you strike up a new acquaintance,
with Herr Weber; the past is past and forgotten; now *this* family
is the most honourable, the most Christian of families, and the
daughter is assigned the leading rôle in the tragedy to be played
out between your own family and hers! In the transports into which
your kind and too open heart has thrown you, you think all your
ill-considered fancies as reasonable and practicable as if they were
bound to be accomplished in the course of nature. You propose
to take her to Italy as prima donna. Tell me, do you know of any
prima donna who has appeared as prima donna in an Italian theatre
without having appeared many times previously in Germany? In
how many operas has not Signora Bernasconi[1] of Vienna acted,
and those operas of the greatest renown and under the very severe
criticism and direction of Gluck and Calzabigi[2]? In how many
operas did Mlle. Deiber sing in Vienna, under Hasse's[3] direction
and taught by that one-time singer and very famous actress Signora
Tesi,[4] whom you saw at Prince Hildburgshausen's, and whose negress
you kissed as a child? How many times did Mlle. Schindler appear

[1] Bernasconi, Antonia, a celebrated operatic singer, the first Aspasia in
Mozart's *Mitridate* in Milan.

[2] Calzabigi, Raniero (1714–95), wrote libretti for Gluck.

[3] Hasse, Johann (1699–1783), one of the most prolific composers of the
eighteenth century, and much admired for his dramatic music. In 1771 both
he and Mozart were invited to compose in celebration of the marriage of the
Archduke Ferdinand at Milan. Mozart composed a serenata, Hasse an opera.
The old and the young musicians met with great cordiality. Mozart's father
writes: "The *serenata* pleases wonderfully. . . . In short, I am sorry; for
Wolfgang's serenata has so knocked Hasse's opera on the head that it is
indescribable!"

[4] Tesi, Vittoria (1700–75), a famous singer, a teacher of de Amicis.

at the theatre of Vienna, after making her début in a private production at Baron Fries's country seat under the direction of Hasse and Signora Tesi and Metastasio? Did any of these persons venture to throw themselves at the head of the Italian public? And how much patronage, what powerful recommendations, they needed before they were able to attain their ends! Princes and counts recommended them, renowned composers and poets stood sponsors for their ability. And now you want me to write to Luggiati! You propose to write an opera for fifty ducats, because you know the Veronese have no money and never commission a new opera! I am to remember Mlle. Ascensa, when Michelagata has not even replied to my two previous letters! I read that this Miss Weber sings like a Gabrielli; that she has a splendid voice for the Italian stage, etc.; that she has the build of a *prima donna*, so that you can vouch for her capacity to act! It is ludicrous! There is more than that in acting. Old Hasse's childish, albeit most kindly meant, good-hearted efforts on behalf of Miss Devis banished her from the Italian theatres for ever, she having been hissed off the stage the first night and her part given to de' Amicis. Even a practised male actor, let alone a female, may well tremble at a first appearance in a foreign land. And do you think even that is all? By no means! *Ci vuole il possesso del teatro*, particularly in the case of a female, as regards costume, *frisure*, ornaments, etc. But you know all this yourself will you but consider. I know that serious reflection on all these points will convince you that, kindly as your plan is meant, it needs time and much preparation and must be approached in a very different fashion if, eventually, it is to be carried out. What *impresario* would not laugh were one to recommend him a sixteen- or seventeen-year-old girl who had never yet appeared on the stage! As for your proposal (I can scarcely write when I think of it)—your proposal to travel about with Herr Weber *and*, be it noted, *his two daughters*—it has almost deprived me of my senses! My dearest son! How can you have allowed yourself to be bewitched by such a monstrous idea even for an hour! Your letter is simply written like a romance—and you can really make up your mind to drag about the world with strangers?—to set aside all thought of your renown—your aged parents—your dear sister?—to expose me to the mockery and laughter of the Prince and the whole town which loves you? Yes, to expose me to mockery and yourself to scorn, for I have always had to say, in reply to repeated questions,

that you were to go to Paris. And now, after all, you intend to
wander about at random with strangers! Nay, you *can* no longer
dream of doing so after a little reflection! But that I may convince
you of your rash precipitancy, let me tell you that the time is
coming when no man of sense could countenance such a scheme.
Circumstances are now such that it is impossible to guess where
war will *not* break out, for everywhere the regiments are either
already on the march or under marching orders. Switzerland?—
Holland?—why there it is dead all summer; and in winter, in
Berne and Zurich, one can make just enough not to perish of
hunger, but no more—and nowhere else. As for Holland, they have
other things to think of now than music, and in any case half one's
takings are eaten up by Herr Hummel and concert expenses. Moreover, what of your renown? Those are places for the lesser lights,
for half-composers, for scribblers, for charlatans, Zappa, Ricci,
and the like. Name me one great composer who would deign to
take so abject a step! Off with you to Paris—and that soon! Find
your place among great folk—*aut Cæsar aut nihil*. The mere thought
of seeing Paris ought to have preserved you from all passing fancies!
From Paris the name and fame of a man of great talent resounds
through all the world. There the nobility treat men of genius with
the greatest condescension, the greatest esteem and courtesy;
there you may see a manner of life which contrasts most astonishingly with the coarseness of our German cavaliers and their ladies,
and there you may perfect yourself in the French tongue. As to
Wendling's company, etc., you have no need of it whatever. You
have known them a long time—and if your Mama did not perceive
it, were you *both* blind? Nay, I know how it must have been. You
were set upon it and she dared not oppose you. It angers me that
you should both have lacked the trustfulness and frankness to
inform me circumstantially and straightforwardly of all. You
treated me similarly in that matter of the Elector, and in the end
all came out notwithstanding. You "wish to spare me anxiety,"
and in the end you overturn a whole barrel-full of anxieties at
once upon my devoted head, so that it almost kills me! You know,
you have a thousand proofs of it, that the good God has given me
sound understanding, that my brains are still in their right place
and that in tangled circumstances I have often found a way out
and foreseen and conjectured much. What withholds you, then,
from asking my advice and always rendering me obedience? My

son, you should regard me rather as your most faithful friend than as a severe father. Consider if I have not ever treated you kindly, served you as a servant his lord, even provided you with all possible entertainment, and assisted you in all honourable and decorous pleasures, even at great inconvenience to myself?

42. *To his Father*

7th February, 1778.

Herr von Schidenhofen ought to have let me know long ago through you that he intended soon to marry. I would have composed him a new minuet for the occasion. From my heart I wish him happiness. But indeed it is merely another of those marriages for money—no more. *I* should not care to marry so; I want to make my wife happy, not to make my fortune by her. Therefore I will let the matter wait and enjoy my golden freedom until I am in a position to support a wife and children. Of course Herr von Schidenhofen was obliged to choose a rich wife; that is the penalty of his nobility. Noblemen must never marry for fancy or for love, but solely for *interest* and all manner of side issues. It would not at all become such an exalted personage to go on loving his wife once she has done her duty and presented him with a bouncing heir. We common folk, though, not only ought to take a wife whom we love and who loves us, but may, can and will do so, because not being noble but, on the contrary, lowly, base and poor, we do not need a rich wife; for our wealth simply dies with us, being stored in our brains—and these no man can take from us, unless they chop off our heads, in which case—we want nothing more! We safely received your letter of February 2nd. I have already written you a letter telling you my principal reason for not travelling to Paris with these people. My second reason follows from mature reflection on what I should have to do when I got there. I could scarcely manage without taking pupils, and that is work for which I was not born. I have had a practical example of this here. I could have had two pupils; I visited each three times; then

I found one of them out and consequently never went there again! I will gladly give lessons to oblige, particularly when I see that my pupil has talent, delights in music and is eager to learn. But to have to go to a certain house at a certain hour—or to have to wait at home for a pupil—that I cannot do however much I could make by it. The thing is impossible to me. I leave that to people who can do nothing but play the clavier. I am a composer and born to be a kapellmeister. I dare not and cannot bury in teaching the talent which the good God has so richly bestowed on me—(I may say it without pride, for I feel it now more than ever)—and yet that would happen if I had many pupils, for it is a very troublous profession. I would rather, so to speak, neglect the clavier than composition, for the clavier is merely an accessory with me, albeit, thank God, a very powerful accessory. Well then, my *third* reason is my uncertainty as to whether our friend Grimm is in Paris. When he is in Paris I can still follow at any moment by the mail-coach, for a splendid mail-coach runs from here to Paris by way of Strasburg. We always travelled thus and they too are going that way. Herr Wendling is inconsolable now that he hears I am not going with him, but I think self-interest has more to do with this than friendship. I have told him, besides the reasons I wrote of to you in my last letter (namely that three letters had come for me during my absence, etc.), my further difficulties about taking pupils, and have begged him to look out for some safe opening for me, in which case, if my other affairs should render it possible, I should be glad to follow him to Paris—particularly if it were an opera! My head is full of operatic projects now, French rather than German, but Italian rather than either. All the Wendlings think my music would be extraordinarily well-received in Paris. Certainly I have no fears at all on that head, for, as you know, I can assimilate and imitate every sort and style of composition very fairly. I have set a French air for Mlle. Gustl (the daughter) to some verses she gave me and which she sings incomparably. I have the honour to present you with it herewith. It is sung daily at Wendling's; they all dote on it. Below is a satire which comes from Munich. I do not know if it is known to you or not, but at any rate here it is:

Die Guten Ostereicher.

> *um unser gräntzen zu decken*
> *ganz redlich und Pflichten getreu*
> *schikt Joseph dem Friedrich* [1] *zum schrecken*
> *uns seine soldaten herbey*
> *da sind sie die nachbarn vom osten*
> *voll freundschaft bezoh schon ein thor*
> *hüpsch ordentlich wachen und Posten*
> *und Joseph verlangt nichts davor.*
> *Er gibt uns nur schutz; und wir raumen*
> *ihm alles vom herzen gern ein.*
> *wem sollte was böses wohl traumen*
> *wie könnten wir ruhiger seyn?*
> *gesezt nun sie sollten lang bleiben*
> *gesezt auch es wäre betrug;*
> *Die frevler von uns abzutreiben*
> *sind wir noch stets muthig genug.*
> *wir haben zwar wenig soldaten*
> *das wär ein zu kostbare waar,*
> *doch haben wir tänzer, kastraten*
> *und Pfaffen in zahloser schaar*
> *geschweige der Erz-bruderschaften*
> *leviten-schwänz, jäger und hund*
> *ach Joseph! wenn diese sich straften*
> *sie stürzten dich wahrlich zu grund.*
> *wir haben auch viel generalen*
> *vielleicht auch noch mehr als wie Du,*
> *Du müstest die Zeche bezahlen,*
> *Drum lass uns ja lieber in ruh.*
> *Wir hoffens und bleiben hier still;*
> *Die Preussen lass uns nicht herein!*
> *das ist unser baierischer will*
> *du sollst unser schutz-Engel seyn.*

[1] Frederick the Great.

Josephs resolution folgt im Copert.
Josephs recreation
im erhabenen Ton
Barone ! sind ruhig ! ich komme zu schützen
und das geschützte zu besitzen.

[*The Kind Austrians*

Our frontiers to guard from our foemen
In accordance with treaty and right,
Joseph sends us his spearmen and bowmen
King Frederic of Prussia to fight.
Behold them, these neighbours from eastwards
For pure friendship defending our lands,
Spick and span all, from vanguard to rearguard,
And Joseph asks naught at our hands!
Our hearths and our homes he's protecting,
Our hearts and our gates we unbar.
Who so base as of treason suspect him,
Or with doubts our placidity mar?
Suppose they should stay here forever,
Suppose we are really betrayed?
Why, we'll drive back the scoundrel and never
Shall they boast that they found us afraid!
True our army is small, and for arms, sirs,
Why, they're more than our purse will afford,
But we have castrati and dancers
And of parsons a numberless horde,
Not to speak of that brotherly band, Jew
Money-lenders—and huntsman, and hound.
Ah, Joseph! if *these* fell upon you
You would surely be cast to the ground!
Our *Staff* is more numerous and riper
Than your own, though our *army* be less,
I assure you 'tis you'll pay the piper
Unless you will leave us in peace!
We hope it; meanwhile we do nothing,
And you'll keep back the foe at our plea—
We appoint you our Guardian Angel!
That is our Bavarian decree!

Joseph's reply follows:

Joseph laughs aloud: "Gentlemen, be at your ease! I come to protect—and to possess what I protect!"[1]]

In my last letter I forgot to mention Mademoiselle Weber's chiefest merit, which is her superb *cantabile* singing. Pray do not forget about Italy. I commend this unfortunate but excellent little Miss Weber to your interest with all my heart —*caldamente*, as the Italians say. I have given her three of Mme. de' Amicis' arias, Mme. Duchek's[2] *scena* (I am about to write to her) and four arias from *Il Re Pastore*. I have also promised to have some arias sent her from home. I hope you will do me the favour of sending me the same; but *gratis*, I beg you, and you will really be doing a good work! The list of arias is on the French song which her father wrote, and the paper is also a present from him. Now I must close. I kiss your hands a thousand times and embrace my sister with all my heart. Our compliments to all good friends, especially to Herr Bullinger. *Addio.* I am your most obedient son,

W. Mzt.

Thank you for the four-handed sonatas and Fischer's variations.

43. *To his Father*

Monsieur, mon trés cher Père!

MANNHEIM, *19th February*, 1778.

I hope you received my last two letters safely. In the last I discussed my Mother's homeward journey, but I see from your letter of the 12th that this was quite unnecessary. Not for a moment did I ever suppose that you would do anything but disapprove the journey with the Webers, for I myself never entertained the idea, *in our present circumstances*, be it understood. But I had given my word of honour to write

---

[1] See note, page 87.

[2] Dussek (or Duschek), Josephine, a very celebrated singer in her day (b. 1756), wife of Franz Dussek, a Bohemian, one of the best pianists of the time and a warm friend and admirer of Mozart.

to you as I did. Herr Weber does not know how we stand. Indeed I tell no one; and greatly desiring to be in a position of independence, with prosperity for us all, I forgot, in the intoxication of the moment, the present impractibility of the matter—and consequently also forgot to inform you of what I have now done. My last two letters will have informed you sufficiently of the reason why I did not go to Paris. If my mother herself had not opened the subject I should certainly have travelled with the Wendlings, but observing that she did not like the prospect, I began to dislike it myself, for as soon as I feel myself mistrusted I cease to trust myself. The days when I used to stand upon a chair and sing you the *oragna fiagata fà*[1] and wind up by kissing the end of your nose are past indeed, but do I therefore honour, love and obey you the less?—I will say no more. As to your reproaches on the subject of the little singer in Munich,[2] I must confess myself an ass to have written you so palpable a lie. Indeed she does not yet know what singing is. True, she sang excellently for a person who had been studying only three months and had, besides, a very pleasing, pure voice. The reason why I praised her so may well have been that I heard nothing from morn to night but "There is not a better singer in all Europe. If you have not heard her you have heard nothing." I did not venture to contradict, partly because I wanted to make friends, partly because I had come straight from Salzburg where the impulse to contradict is broken in a man. Once I was alone, however, I could not help laughing at it all! Why, then, did I not laugh in my letter to you? I cannot understand why I did not!

I am deeply wounded by your very biting comments upon my merry converse with your brother's daughter. Since things are not as you represent them to be I have nothing to reply. I am at a loss what to say about Wallerstein; I was very reserved and grave at Beecke's, was serious even at the officers' table where I dined, and spoke not a word to anyone. We will pass over all that, for surely you wrote in heat!

[1] See note, page 69.   [2] See note, page 70.

What you say about Mademoiselle Weber is all very true. Even as I wrote I knew as well as you do that she is still too young, that she needs to learn acting and appear many times on the boards. Only, with some people, one has to proceed— by degrees. These good folk are weary of being here, just as— well, *you* know whom and where! Consequently they will believe any scheme is practicable. I promised them I would write to my father, but meantime, while the letter was on its way to Salzburg, I kept on saying, "After all, you must be patient a little longer. You are still rather too young," etc. And they will take anything from me for they rely on me very much. On my advice her father has now spoken with Madame Toscani (*comedienne*) and has asked her to instruct his daughter in acting. Everything you write about Mlle. Weber is true except one thing, namely that she "sings like a Gabrielli"; for I should be far from pleased if she did sing like that! Whoever has heard Gabrielli sing says, and will say, that she was no more than a virtuoso in runs and roulades; these she executed in a manner so remarkable that she aroused admiration, which did not, however, survive a fourth time of hearing. She could not please ultimately for one soon grows weary of runs; and she was unfortunate in being unable to *sing*. She could never sustain an entire note properly, she had no *messa di voce*, she did not understand *sostenuto*; in a word, she sang with technique but without understanding. This lady, however, sings from the heart and prefers to sing *cantabile*. I have brought her on through the great arias to runs, for if she gets to Italy she will have to sing bravura arias. She will certainly not forget the *cantabile* for that is her natural bent. Raff himself (certainly no flatterer) said, when asked his frank opinion, "She sang not like a student, but like a professoress." Well, now you know all. I commend her to your interest with all my heart; and pray do not forget the arias, cadenzas, etc. Farewell. I kiss your hands 100,000 times and am your most obedient son,

Wolfgang Amadé Mozart.

I cannot write, I am so hungry!

My mother will notify you of our great store of wealth.

I embrace my sister with all my heart; she is not to weep for every good-for-nothing, else I will never, never return! My compliments to all good friends, particularly to Herr Bullinger.

Leopold Mozart to his Son

23rd February, 1778.

What is the use, then, of all my precise thinking, all my care, and consideration, my paternal efforts in pursuance of a most urgent and weighty enterprise if you (when faced with an apparently grave obstacle which Mama might really have perceived long ago) fail to give your father your full confidence, and only change your mind when, caught between two fires, you can neither advance nor retreat? Just when I believe that things are on a better footing and taking their proper course, I am suddenly confronted with some foolish unforeseen whim of yours, or else it appears that matters were not after all as you represented them to me!—And so I have guessed aright again?—You have got only 96 florins, instead of 200?—and why?—because you completed only two concerti and only three quartets. How many *were* you to have composed for him, then, since he would only pay you half?— Why did you lie to me, writing that you had only to compose three small, light concertos and a couple of quartets? And why did you not listen to me when I wrote expressly telling you to satisfy this gentleman as speedily as you were able? Why did I tell you to do so? So that you might make sure of getting your money, for I know men better than you do. Have I not guessed all? It appears that I see more and judge better at a distance than you do with these people under your very nose! You must be ready to believe me when I mistrust people, and to act as prudently as I direct; indeed you must have learned the justice of this, for you have bought experience latterly at a somewhat heavy cost to us all. True, you have arranged with Herr Wendling that the sum in question is to be paid later and that you will send the work on. Yes—and if Herr Wendling in Paris can advantageously dispose of what you have yet to deliver to friends at Flautraver, he will try to get something out of it. One party has to pay; the other sucks advantage from it.

Furthermore you wrote to me of a few pupils, and in particular of the Dutch officer, who would pay you three, or as you were

inclined to believe, four ducats for twelve lessons. And now it comes
out that you might have had these pupils but that you gave them
up simply because you had failed to find them within doors on one
or two occasions! You would rather give lessons gratuitously—no
doubt you would!—and you would rather, I suppose, leave your
poor old father in need! The effort is too great for you, a young
man, however good the pay, and it is more seemly, no doubt, that
your fifty-eight-year-old father should run hither and thither for
a wretched fee so that he may win the needful subsistence for
himself and his daughter in the sweat of his brow and, instead of
paying off his debts, support you with what remains over, so that
you, in the meantime, can amuse yourself giving a girl lessons
for nothing! Pray bethink yourself, my son, and give your common
sense a hearing!

My dear Wolfgang, all your letters convince me that you are
ready to accept, without proper consideration or reflection, the
first heated fancy which comes into your head, or is put into it
by others. For instance, you write, "I am a composer, I must
not bury my talent," etc. Who, then, says that you ought to do
so? But you really *would* do so by gipsy wanderings. If you are
to make a name as a composer it must be either in Paris, Vienna,
or Italy. You are now nearest Paris. The only remaining question
is: "Where have I the best hope of distinguishing myself?—In
Italy, where, in Naples alone, there are at least three hundred
maestri and where, throughout the land, these *maestri* have work in
hand at theatres which pay well, for two years ahead?—or in Paris,
where perhaps two or three write for the theatres, and where other
composers may be counted on one's fingers?" The clavier must
bring you first acquaintances and win you the favour of the great.
After that you can have something engraved by subscription,
which is rather more profitable than composing six quartets for
some Italian cavalier and getting a few ducats—perhaps a purse
of three—for your work.

44. *To his Father*

Monsieur, mon trés cher Père!

I have been confined to the house for two days and have
been swallowing *antispasmotisch*, black powder and elderberry
tea to induce sweating, because I have had catarrh, cold in

the head, headache, sore-throat, eye-ache and ear-ache. But now, thank God, I am better and to-morrow I hope to go out again because it is Sunday. I have safely received your letter of the 16th together with the two open letters of introduction for Paris. I am glad that you like my French aria. Pray pardon me if I write you but a short letter this time. Indeed I cannot write much; I fear I might get headache again; and besides I am not at all in the vein for it—one cannot write all one thinks—at least I cannot. It is better to say it than to write it. My last letter will have told you just how things stand. Pray believe anything of me—what you will—only nothing evil. There are people who believe it is impossible to love a poor girl without forming evil designs upon her; and that pretty word *maiträsse*, wh—e in our tongue, is far too pretty for me!—I am no Brunetti,[1] no Misliwetceck![2] I am a Mozart, a young, right-minded Mozart, so I hope you will forgive me for occasional excess of ardour — because I must talk like that—although I would rather say it than *write* it, as of course I am obliged to do. I have much to say on this subject, but I cannot write it down. I find it impossible. Among my many faults this one is included—namely an obstinate belief that the friends who know me—know me! Consequently few words are needed. But if they know me *not*, oh, how could I ever find words enough! It is bad enough that one needs words at all— and letters in addition! This is not written against you, my dear Papa. No, indeed! You know me too well and besides are too excellent a man lightly to injure a man's reputation! I mean only those people—they know I mean them—those people who believe *this* of me!

I have made up my mind to remain within doors to-day, although it is Sunday, because it snows so hard. To-morrow I must go out because our domestic nymph, Mademoiselle Pierron, my very-much-to-be-revered pupil, is to reel off Litzau's

[1] A solo violinist in the Archbishop's household, for whom Mozart wrote several sonatas for violin and piano.

[2] A composer surnamed *Il Boemo* by the Italians, who wrote some thirty operas before his death in Rome in his forty-fourth year. He was patronised by Gabrielli, who liked to sing in his operas.

fine concerto at the French concert, which is held every Monday. I, too, prostitution though it be, must strum something, and I shall see whether I cannot hammer it out *prima vista*; for I am a born clog-dancer, good for nothing but to thump the clavier a little! Now I pray your leave to stop, for I am not at all disposed for letter-writing to-day, rather for composition. Once more I beg you not to forget to do as I asked you in foregoing letters with reference to the cadenzas and the *aria cantabile*, etc. I am already obliged to you for having had the arias I asked for copied so speedily. That proves that you *have* confidence in me, and believe me when I recommend anything to you! Fare you well. I kiss your hands a thousand times and embrace my sister with all my heart. I remain your most obedient son,

Wolfgang Amadé Mozart.

MANNHEIM, *22nd February*, 1778.

Compliments to all good friends of both sexes, particularly to my dearest friend Herr Bullinger.

45. *To his Father*

28th February, 1778.

Monsieur, mon trés cher Pére!

We have safely received your letter of the 23rd. I hope I may get the arias next Friday or Saturday, although you make no further reference to them in your last, and I consequently do not know whether you dispatched them by the diligence on the 22nd. I hope it was so; for I should like to play and sing them through to Mlle. Weber while I am still here. Yesterday I was at Raff's and took him an aria which I wrote for him during the last few days. The words are *Se al labro mio non credi, bella nemica mia*, etc. I do not think they are Metastasio's. He was altogether delighted with the aria. One must go to work in a particular fashion with a man of that type. I chose those words with especial care because I knew he already had an aria to them; consequently he will sing them more easily and with greater pleasure. I said to him he must tell me frankly if it did not suit him or did not please him, as I was willing to alter the aria to his taste or to make another. "Heaven forbid!" said he, "the aria must remain as it is, for it is very fine. Only may I beg you to shorten it a very little for me, as my voice has less staying power now." "I will gladly do so as much as you wish," I replied, "for one can always cut down, though addition is not so easy." When he had sung the other part through he took off his spectacles, stared at me and said, "Beautiful, beautiful! That is a lovely *seconda parte*." And he sang it thrice. When I left he thanked me very civilly, and I for my part assured him that I would arrange the aria so that he should have real pleasure in singing it; for I love to have an aria as exactly fitted to its singer as a well-cut suit of clothes. As an exercise I have also composed the aria *Non sò d'onde viene*, etc., so beautifully done by Bach,[1] for the reason that I know Bach's composition so well and like it so much that it is continually in my ears, and I wished to try if, in spite of this, I could make an aria entirely unlike Bach's! And, indeed, it is not at all like, not in the least. At first I intended this aria for Raff, but almost at once I saw that it was too high for Raff, while I liked it too well to alter it. Moreover, the instrumental accompaniment seemed better for a soprano, so I decided to make the aria for Mademoiselle Weber. I laid it aside and took up the words *Se al labro*, etc., for Raff. But it was in vain. I could not possibly write, for the first aria kept running in my head. Accordingly I wrote it down and set to work to adapt it perfectly for Mlle. Weber. There is an *andante sostenuto* (preceded by a short recitative), in the midst of the second part, *Nel sero à destarmi*, and then *sostenuto* again. When it was finished I said to Mlle. Weber: "Learn the aria yourself; sing it according to your own taste; then let me hear it and I will tell you frankly what I like and what I do not like." Two days later I went there and she sang it to me, accompanying herself. I could not but confess that she sang it in every particular exactly as I would have wished and as I intended to teach it to her! Well, it is the best aria she has now, and she will

---

[1] Johann Christian, as throughout these letters. Cf. note, page 2.

certainly win applause with it wherever she appears. Yesterday at Mme. Wendling's I sketched out the aria I promised her, with a short recitative. The words were her own choice from *Didone*: *Ah non lasciarmi nò*. She and her daughter simply dote on this aria. I have promised the daughter some more French *ariettes* and have begun one to-day. When it is ready I will write it out small with the earlier ones, and send them on. I have still two of the six clavier sonatas to do, but there is no haste as I cannot have them engraved here. It is impossible to raise a subscription here; it would be beggarly, and the engraver will not engrave them at his own costs and wishes to go halves with me in the sale. So I prefer to have them engraved in Paris, where the engravers are glad to get something new and pay well; besides one can make something there by subscription. I would have had the sonatas copied one by one long since and sent them to you but that I thought I would rather send them to you engraved. Most of all I look forward to the *concert spirituel* in Paris, as I shall probably have to compose something for it. The orchestra is said to be large and very fine, and my favourite type of composition, the chorus, can be well performed there. I am indeed glad that the French prize it highly. Their only objection to Piccini's new opera *Roland* is that the choruses are too weak and thin, and that the music on the whole is a little monotonous; otherwise the work has been a success. To be sure they are used to Gluck's choruses in Paris. Rely upon me. I shall strain every nerve to bring honour to the name of Mozart and I have no fears for the event. My previous letters will have told you how things are now and what my intentions were. I beg you will not often entertain the idea of my forgetting you!—for I cannot bear it. My chief purpose was, is, and will ever be, to endeavour to bring about our speedy reunion—our happy reunion! But that means patience. You know, even better than I, how often things go awry—but they will go well yet. Only—patience! Let us hope in God, He will not forsake us. I shall not be found wanting. Can you really doubt me?—Does it not dearly concern me to work my best so that I may the sooner have the joy of clasping my best, my dearest father to my heart? There, you see!

Should war break out in Bavaria[1] follow me at once, I beg you! I put my trust in three friends, all three mighty, invincible; namely in God, in your brain and in my brain! True our brains are not alike, but each in its kind is good, serviceable and useful; and I hope that with time my brain may gradually approach yours in those departments in which it is now inferior. Well, fare you well, and may you be happy and care-free. Bethink you that you have a son who has never, knowingly, forgotten his filial duty to you, who will endeavour to grow increasingly worthy of so good a father and who remains unalterably your most obedient,

Wolfgang Mozart.

I embrace my sister with all my heart!

My compliments to all good friends, particularly to Herr Bullinger.

If by any chance you have not already dispatched the arias I beg you to do so as soon as possible, and you will make me really happy. Ah, if only the Elector of Bavaria had not died! I would have composed and produced a Mass which would have made a great stir here. I was all ready to do so when the devil softly wafts that accursed doctor hither!

46. *To his Cousin*

Mademoiselle, mon très chère Cousine!

You may perhaps believe, or opine, that I am dead!—that I am defunct!—or insane!—but no, I beg you will think no such thing, for to think is one thing and to do another! How could I write so beautifully if I were dead? Tell me now, would it be possible? I will not offer a word of apology for my long silence, for you would never believe me; though what is true *is* true! I have had so much to do that I have had

---

[1] The War of the Bavarian Succession, which broke out early in 1778, following on the death, in December 1777, of the Elector Maximilian Joseph. The Austrians occupied Bavaria. See the lampoon in Letter No. 42.

time to *think* of my little cousin but not to *write* to her, consequently I have had to leave it undone. Now, however, I do myself the honour of inquiring how you are and how you do? Have you good *digestion*? Have you, perhaps, *congestion*? Can you tolerate me, do you *think*? Do you write with pencil or *ink*? Do you ever think of me, so far *away*? And are you not sometimes inclined to *felo de se*? You may have been *angry*, with me, poor *zany*, but if you will not *recognise me* I'll make a noise, will *scandalise ye*! There, you are laughing —*victoria*! Our *arsch* shall be emblems of peace between us. (I thought she would not be able to resist me much longer!) I go to Paris in a fortnight. If you wish to answer this *letter*, from Augsburg you had *better*, write soon, or I'll not get it— — — *Dreck!!* . . . Well, to turn to other matters, I suppose you have been very merry this Shrove Tuesday, for it is more amusing in Augsburg on such occasions than here. I wish I were there to go gallivanting with you. My mother and I both present our compliments to your father and mother and to my cousin, your brother, and hope they are all well. So much the better—the better so! *Apropos*, how is the French getting on? May I soon write you a letter all in French? From Paris, for instance? Tell me, have you done the *spuni cuni* yet? I expect so. Well, now, before I close, for I must finish soon because I am in a hurry, having nothing at all to do, and no more room, as you see, and my paper is almost out and I am tired, and my fingers ache from writing and, finally, if I had more room I should not know what to write, except this story which I have a mind to tell you. You must know, then, that all this occurred not long ago. It happened in the country near us and made quite a stir, for one would have thought it impossible, and (between ourselves) people do not even yet know what the end of it all will be. To cut a long story short, it occurred some four hours' journey from here. I cannot remember the place, but it was a village or something of the kind. Well, whether it was Tribsterill, where the sewage runs into the lake, or Burmesquik, where they make the crooked *arschlöcher*, it is all one. In a word, it was a place. There there lived a herdsman, or shepherd, already well advanced in years but robust and strong to all appearance, who was a man of means, a well-to-do man who kept a good table. But to be sure there is one thing I must tell you before I continue my story—he had a very ugly tone of voice so that one dreaded to hear him speak. Well, to go straight to the point, you must know that this herd, or shepherd, possessed a dog whom he called *Bellot*, a monstrous fine great dog, white, with black spots. Well, one day, he set out with his sheep, of which he had eleven thousand, holding a stick in his hand with a beautiful rose-coloured band on it, for he never went out without his stick. It was a habit of his. To proceed with my story. When he had walked an hour or more he grew tired and sat down by a river. There he fell asleep and dreamed that he had lost his sheep. He awoke in terror, but to his great joy saw all his sheep about him. At last he arose and went on, but not for long, for when scarcely half an hour had passed he reached a bridge, very long, but well walled on both sides to prevent folk falling into the water. There he regarded his flock and, as he had to pass over the bridge, he began to drive his eleven thousand sheep over. Now if you will but have the goodness to wait till the eleven thousand sheep have crossed over I will tell you the whole story to the end; I told you in advance that the issue is as yet unknown! I hope, however, that they will all have crossed before I write to you again, and if not it doesn't matter to me, for as far as I am concerned they might have stayed where they were! In the meantime you must be content to wait. I have written you all I know of the matter and it was better to stop than to invent a false ending. Then you would not have believed any of my story; as it is believe— half of it! I must cease upon the *spot*, even though I like it *not*; He who begins must make an *end*, or he'll soon find he has no *friend*; My compliments to every*one*, who likes me not he shall get *none*; from now until the Judgment *Day*—or till I've learned some sense, you'll *say*; and that will take so many *years*, that even I am filled with *fears*! — — — —

Adieu little coz. I am, I was, I should be, I have been, I had been, I should have been, oh, if I only were, oh, that I were, would God I were; I could be, I shall be, if I were to be, oh, that I might be, I would have been, oh, had I been, oh, that I had been, would God I had been—what? A dried cod! *Adieu ma chère Cousine*, whither away? I am your faithful cousin,

Wolfgang Amadé Mozart.

Mannheim, 28*th February*, 1778.

47. *To his Father and Sister*

Monsieur, mon trés cher Pére !

We have had no letter from you to-day, but we hope the only reason for it is that the bad weather has made the diligence unpunctual, or that you have not written at all. I safely received your last of February 26th. I am very much obliged to you for all the trouble you have taken about the arias. They are exact in every detail. After God comes my Papa— that was ever the motto, the axiom of my childhood and I cling to it still! True, you are right when you say "learning is power." For the rest, apart from your trouble and many exertions, you should regret nothing, for Mademoiselle Weber is indeed deserving. I can only wish that you could hear her sing my latest aria of which I wrote to you recently. I can only say that it was made for her. A man like yourself, who understands what *portamento* singing is, would certainly find complete satisfaction in her performance. If I am fortunate in Paris and our circumstances improve, as they will do, I hope, by God's help, and we are all in better spirits, I will write to you of my thoughts in more detail and beg you for a very great favour. But I must tell you that I was greatly shocked and that the tears came to my eyes when I read in your last letter that you had to go so ill-clad. My very dearest Papa, that is through no fault of mine—you know that! We save all we can here. Food and lodging, light and firing have cost us nothing here, which is just as one would wish. As to clothing, you know that one cannot go ill-clad in strange places. One must always keep up a certain appearance. I have now set all my hopes on Paris, for the German princes are all niggards. I shall strain every nerve to have the satisfaction of being able soon to release you from your present troublous circumstances. Now to our journey. A week to-day, being the 14th, we leave here. We are unfortunate as regards the sale of the carriage and have found no buyer to date. We shall have to be content if we get four louis d'or for it. People here advise us, if we cannot dispose of the carriage, to hire a hackney coachman and drive in it as far as Strasburg, for it should be easier to sell it there. However, as it is cheaper to travel post I shall leave the carriage here in charge of honest people. You must know that since this is not a commercial town no carriers go to Paris and everything is sent by the post. I am told that the fare from here to Strasburg is half a louis-d'or for each passenger, so I think it should not cost us more than fifteen gulden in all. Meantime farewell. Let us hope in God and He will surely not forsake us. I shall write you one, or even two, more letters before we leave here. I wish I were in Paris now, for I dislike the thought of the journey thither. Herr Wendling writes that he found the journey vastly tedious. Now I must close in order to leave a little room for Mama. I kiss your hands a thousand times and am your most obedient son,

Wolfgang Mozart.

Mannheim, *7th March*, 1778.

PARIS (1778–9)

48. To his Father

PARIS, *le 24 di mars,* 1778.

Mon trés cher Pére !

Yesterday, Monday 23rd, at 4 o'clock after noon, we arrived, thank God, safe and sound, having been nine and a half days upon the journey. We believed we should hardly survive it. Never in my life have I endured such tedium! You may imagine what it was like to leave Mannheim and with it so many good friends, and then to be compelled to exist for nearly ten days not only without those good friends, but without anyone, without one single soul with whom to associate or converse! Well, now, thank God, we have reached our destination. I hope that with God's help all will go well. To-day we are to take a *fiacre* and seek out Grimm and Wendling. Early to-morrow, however, I am to wait on the Palatine ambassador, Herr von Sückingen, a great student and passionate amateur of music, to whom I have two letters from Herr von Gemmingen [1] and M. Canabich. Before I left Mannheim I had the quartet, which I composed of evenings at the inn at Lodi, the quintet, and the Fischer variations, copied out for Herr von Gemmingen. Thereupon he wrote me a very civil note, expressed his pleasure in the memorial I was thus leaving him, and sent me a letter to his good friend Herr von Sückingen with the words, "I am convinced that you will recommend the letter more powerfully than it can do you!" To cover the expenses of copying he sent me three louis d'or. He assured me of his friendship and begged for mine. I must say that all the gentlemen who knew me, privy councillors, other persons of standing, and all the Court musicians, were

---

[1] Von Gemmingen, subsequently author of the libretto of *Semiramis*, a duo-drama composed by Mozart, now lost (Edward Holmes).

very unwilling and sorry to see me go. There is no doubt of that. We left on Saturday the 14th, and on the preceding Thursday there was a concert at Canabich's where my concerto for three claviers was played. Mlle. Rosl Canabich played the first, Mlle. Weber the second and Mlle. Pierron (our maid-servant) the third. We had rehearsed thrice and it went very well. Mademoiselle Weber sang two of my arias, the *Aer tranquillo* from *Rè pastore* and the new one, *Non so d'onde viene*. My dear Mlle. Weber did herself and me incomparable honour with this last, for everybody said they had never been so deeply moved by any aria before; indeed, she sang it just as it should be sung. The moment the aria was over Canabich cried at the top of his voice, "*Bravo, bravissimo maestro! Veramente scrittor da maestro!*" It was the first time I had heard it with orchestral accompaniment and I wished you were able to hear it too, produced and sung as *she* sang it, with such exactitude in taste, *piano* and *forte!* Who knows, perhaps you may yet hear it—I hope so. The orchestra are perpetually praising the aria and talking about it. I have many good friends in Mannheim (people of position and means) who are very anxious to keep me there. Well, my place is where people will pay me well. It may yet come off—I hope so, for I am like that—always hopeful. Canabich is an honest, excellent fellow and my very good friend, but he has one failing which is that, though no longer young, he is a little volatile and absent-minded. If one is not perpetually at him he forgets everything, but when a good friend is spoken of he roars like a bull, espousing his cause, and that has its effect, for he has *credit.* For the rest, however, I cannot say much on the score of civility and gratitude, for I cannot deny that the Webers, despite their poverty and although I have done less for them, have shown themselves more grateful; for Madame and Monsieur Canabich have not said a word to me, let alone offered me the least keepsake, even the merest *bagatelle* to show kindness of feeling; but nothing at all— not so much as thanks, when I have spent so much time and trouble on their daughter that she could certainly appear anywhere now! For a fourteen-year-old girl and a *dilettante* she plays quite well; and that is due to me, as all Mannheim knows. She now has *gusto*, trill, *tempo* and better fingering, none of which she had formerly. I fear she will soon be spoiled again, or spoil herself, for if she has not an intelligent master about her it will all be in vain; she is too much a child, too fickle to practise seriously and to any purpose by herself. Out of the kindness of her heart Mlle. Weber has knitted two pairs of socks and bestowed them on me in remembrance and as a small acknowledgment. Herr Weber has done all the copying I needed for nothing, supplied me with music paper, and finally presented me with Molière's Comedies (knowing that I had never read them) with this inscription: *"Ricevi, Amico, le opere del molière in segno di gratitudine, e qualche volta ricordati di me."* Once, when alone with Mama, he said: "Our best friend, our benefactor is now going away. Your son has done much for my daughter, has interested himself on her behalf, and she cannot be sufficiently grateful to him." The day before I left they wished me to sup with them once more, but I could not do so as I was obliged to remain at home. But I could not forbear to give them an hour or two before supper, when they never ceased to thank me and to wish that they were in a position to prove their gratitude. When I left they all wept. Pardon me, but tears fill my eyes when I remember it! Herr Weber descended the stairs with me and remained standing at the door till I turned the corner, when he cried a final *Adieu!* The expenses of our journey, for food and drink, lodging and gratuities exceeded four louis d'or, for the farther we penetrated into France the dearer things became. I have just received your letter of the 16th. Do not be anxious, I shall certainly do well. Only, I beg you, show a happy spirit in your letters; and if war comes too near you, come and join us! My compliments to all good friends of both sexes. I kiss your hands a thousand times and embrace my sister with all my heart.

I am your most obedient son,

Wolfgang Amadé Mozart.

Leopold Mozart to his Son

20th April, 1778.

My dear Wolfgang,

I rejoice from my heart that you already have work, only I am sorry that you have been obliged to hurry over the composition of the choruses, a work which to do you honour needs time. I wish and hope that success may be yours. In the opera you will of course be guided by the French taste. If one can but win applause and get well paid, the deuce take the rest!

You know me, and you know I value honour and fame above everything. You won them in childhood and you must continue to do so now. That always has been and is my object. The coming years are now in your own hands, to be used for your benefit and for that of us all.

49. *To his Father*

PARIS, *le* 1 *may*, 1778.

Mon trés cher Pére !

We have safely received your letter of April 12th. I waited for it and that is the reason why it is so long since I wrote. Pray do not be offended if from time to time I leave you without a letter for a space, for postal charges here are very heavy, and if one has nothing very necessary to communicate it certainly is not worth while to expend twenty-four sous, and indeed often more. I had intended to postpone writing until I had news and could tell you more about our circumstances, but I now feel compelled to give you an account of certain small matters, which still hang in the balance. The little violinist Zygmontofsky is here with that worthless father of his. I may have told you of it already—but I merely mention it in passing, because I have just remembered that I met him at a house of which I wish to tell you, namely that of Madame la Duchesse de Chabot. I went there with a letter of introduction from M. Grimm.[1] The principal purport of this letter was to recommend me to the Duchesse de Bourbon

---

[1] Grimm, Friedrich Melchior (1723–1807). A renowned *littérateur* in Paris, 1750–89, and an enthusiastic amateur of music. He left Paris in the Revolution and obtained office under Catherine II. of Russia. See Letters Nos. 54, 55, 56.

(who was at a convent there), to reintroduce me to her and recall me to her mind. A week went by without any news whatsoever. However, she had told me to call after the lapse of a week, so I kept my word and presented myself. On my arrival I was made to wait half an hour in a great ice-cold unwarmed room, unprovided with any fire-place. At length the Duchesse de Chabot came in, greeted me with the greatest civility, begged me to make the best of the clavier since it was the only one in order, and asked me to try it. "I am very willing to play," said I, "but momentarily it is impossible for my hands are numb with cold," and I begged she would at least have me conducted to a room with a fire. "*Oh, oui Monsieur, vous avez raison,*" was all the answer I received, and thereupon she sat down and began to sketch, continuing for a whole hour in company with a party of gentlemen who sat in a circle round a big table. There I had the honour of waiting fully an hour. The windows and doors stood open, and not only my hands, but my whole body and my feet were chilled. My head also began to ache. *Altum silentium* prevailed, and I did not know what to do for cold, headache and tedium. I kept on thinking, "If it were not for M. Grimm I would leave this instant." At last, to be brief, I played on the wretched, miserable *pianoforte*. Most vexing of all, however, Madame and her gentlemen never ceased their sketching for a moment, but remained intent upon it, so that I had to play to the chairs, table and walls. Under these vile conditions, I lost patience. I began to play the Fischer variations, played them half through and stood up. At once I received a host of compliments. I, however, said what was quite true, namely that I could not do myself justice with that clavier and should be very glad to choose another day when a better clavier would be available. But she would not consent to let me go; I must wait another half-hour till her husband came. He sat beside me and listened with close attention and I—I forgot cold and headache and in spite of all played the wretched clavier as —as I do play when I am in the vein! Give me the best clavier in Europe with an audience who understand nothing, desire to understand nothing and do not feel with me in what I play, and I would have no joy in it! I have told Herr Grimm the whole story. You write that I ought to be assiduous in paying visits to form new acquaintances and revive the old ones. But this is not possible. The distances are too great for walking— or else the roads too dirty, for the filth of Paris is indescribable. As to driving—one has the honour of expending four to five *livres* a day—and all in vain; people return your compliments and there's an end. They bespeak me for such and such a day, I play, and they say, "*O c'est un prodige, c'est inconcevable, c'est étonnant!*" and so—*adieu!* At first I wasted money enough in this way—and often entirely in vain, for I found the people from home. If one were not here one could not believe how hopeless it is! Altogether Paris is greatly changed. The French are not as polite as fifteen years ago. Their manners now border on coarseness and they are terribly discourteous. Now I must give you a description of a *concert spirituel*. I may tell you briefly in passing that my work on the choruses was, so to speak, in vain. Holzbauer's *Miserere* is long in any case; consequently they gave two instead of four of my choruses, leaving out the best. That, however, mattered little, for few knew that any work of mine was included in the programme, and many had never heard of me. However, there was great applause at rehearsal and I myself (for I set no store by Parisian praise) am very well satisfied with my work. Now with respect to the *sinfonie concertante* there is another imbroglio. In this case, however, I believe there is something going on behind the scenes, for I have enemies here also. Where, indeed, have I not had them? But that may be regarded as a good sign! I was obliged to compose the symphony with the greatest expedition, but I put out all my powers and the four *concertanti* were and are entirely in love with it. Le Gros [1] had it for four days for copying, but I always found it lying in the same place. At length, on the last day but one, I could not find it, but on searching under the pile of music discovered it—hidden away. I did not do anything at once, but said to

[1] Director of the *Concert spirituel*.

Le Gros: "*Apropos*, have you sent the *sinfonie concertante*
to be copied yet?"—"No, I had forgotten it." Since I naturally
could not *order* him to have it copied and prepared I said
no more. The two days went by upon which it should have been
performed at the concert. Then Ramm and Punto came to
me in a great heat and asked me why my *sinfonie concertante*
had not been given. "That I do not know," said I. "It is
the first I have heard of it. I know nothing about it." Ramm
fell into a raging passion and abused Le Gros in French, there
in the music-room, saying it was most unhandsome of him,
etc. What vexes me most in the whole affair is that Le Gros
said no word to me about it—kept me in the dark. If he had
only excused himself on the ground of lack of time or the like
—but nothing!—I believe, however, that Cambini,[1] an Italian
maestro here, is at the bottom of it, for I, in all innocence,
offended him at our first meeting at Le Gros' house. He has
written some quartets, one of which I heard at Mannheim,
and they are very pretty. I praised them to him and played
the opening of one; but Ritter, Ramm and Punto who were
present forced me to continue, saying I could invent where
I did not know. I did so and Cambini was beside himself.
He could not help saying, "*Questa è una gran testa!*" but I am
convinced he did not like it! If this were a place where people
had ears to hear, hearts to feel and some measure of understanding of and taste for music, I could laugh heartily over
all these things, but (as regards music) I am living among mere
brute beasts. How can it be otherwise? It is the same with
all their dealings, passions and affections—there is, I am sure,
no place in the world like Paris. Do not think I exaggerate
when I speak thus of the condition of music here—ask anyone
(not a born Frenchman), and if he knows anything at all of
the matter he will say the same. Well, I am here. I must
support it for your sake, but I shall thank Almighty God if
I escape with taste unvitiated. I pray God daily to give me
grace to endure here steadfastly, to do honour to the whole

[1] Cambini, Giovanni (1746–1825), an Italian operatic composer who met
with some success in Paris but died in poverty.

German nation, putting His glory first, and to grant me to gain fame and money so that I may be able to help you out of your present embarrassed circumstances and effect our speedy reunion, when we may all live together in joy and prosperity. For the rest, may His will be done on earth as it is in heaven. But I pray you, dearest Papa, to do your best in the meantime to make it possible for me to revisit Italy [1] soon, where I may be recalled to life after this experience! Do me this favour, I beg you. But now pray be of good cheer—I shall hew my way through as best I can. If I can but come through it a whole man! *Addieu.* I kiss your hand a thousand times and embrace my sister with all my heart.

                              I am your most obedient son,
                                        Wolfgang Amadé Mozart.

Leopold Mozart to his Son
                                            11th May, 1778.
My Dear Wolfgang!

    I will now answer you on all your points. Indeed I know by experience that one may take a hundred walks in Paris for nothing, as I told you beforehand in a previous letter. I am also aware that the French pay in compliments. You will undoubtedly find enemies in every place—that is inevitable for every man of outstanding talent. All those who are at present in repute in Paris and have found a niche there are determined not to be driven out; they cannot but be apprehensive of the lowering of that consequence with which their interest is bound up! Not Gambini only, but Stamitz,[2] Piccini and others will certainly grow jealous. Is Piccini still in Paris? And will not Gretry [3] grow jealous? — Wendling tells you that music has altered, but I do not put much faith in that. Instrumental music—yes, that was improving even then, but vocal music will not improve so quickly. But you must on no account let yourself be discouraged or put out of countenance by the envious. It is the same everywhere. Only remember Italy— your first opera, your third opera, D'Ettore, etc., Mme. de' Amicis' intrigues, etc.—but one must make a way through it all for oneself by force!

---

[1] See note, page 24.
[2] Anton Stamitz, son of the founder of the Mannheim School.
[3] Grétry, André (1742–1813), a successful and prolific composer.

You tell me you are to write an opera; take my advice, then, and remember that your whole reputation hangs on your first piece. Listen before you write and study the national taste. Hear and witness their operas. I know you and I know that you can imitate anything. Do not write in haste—no man of sense does so. Go over the words in advance with Herr Baron Grimm and with Noverre.[1] Compose sketches, and get the same kind of men to hear them. Everyone does the same. Voltaire reads his poems to his friends, listens to their verdict and alters accordingly. Your object is to get fame and money, and once we have money we can return to Italy. If you write anything for publication, make it popular and easy for amateurs. Do not write in a hurry! Strike out what does not satisfy you. Do nothing for nothing, and see that you get paid for all.

50. *To his Father*

14th May, 1778.

I have already so much to do that I wonder what will happen in winter! I believe I told you in my last letter that the Duc de Guines, whose daughter is my pupil in composition, plays the flute incomparably, and she plays the harp *magnifique*. She has much talent and genius and in particular an incomparable memory so that she can play all her pieces, actually some two hundred, by heart. She, however, has grave doubts as to whether she has any talent for composition—especially on the score of ideas. But her father (who, between ourselves, dotes on her somewhat overmuch) says she certainly has ideas—it is all mere bashfulness and lack of self-confidence. Well, we shall see. If she develops no ideas (for at present she really has *none*) it is useless, for God knows *I* can give her none! Her father's intention is not to make a great "composeress" out of her. "She is not," says he, "to compose operas, arias, concertos, symphonies, but simply great sonatas for her instrument and for mine." To-day I gave her her fourth lesson, and as regards the rules of composition and harmony I am fairly satisfied with her. She set quite a good bass to the first

[1] Noverre, Jean Georges (1727–1810), a dancer and ballet-master in Paris, London, etc. He contributed greatly to the development of his art.

minuet when I put it before her. She managed it, but she soon
found it tedious. I cannot help her, however. I cannot get
any farther. It would be too soon to say so if there really were
genius there, but unhappily there is none—everything has to
be done artificially. She has no ideas at all—nothing comes.
I have tested her in every possible way. Among other things
it occurred to me to write a quite simple minuet and see if
she could not make variations on it. It was all in vain. "Well,"
thought I, "she does not know how to begin," so I set to work
upon the first bar and told her she must go on, keeping to that
idea. Eventually she did not do so badly with it. When that
was over I said she should make something of her own, only
the first part, the melody. She thought for a quarter of an hour
and produced nothing. Then I wrote four bars of a minuet
and said, "See what an ass I am! I have begun a minuet and
cannot even finish the first part. Pray be so kind as to do it
for me." She did not think she could, but at last, with a prodigious effort, she produced something. I was glad indeed to
see something for once! I told her then to finish the minuet
—that is to say only the top part. As homework, all I asked
her to do, however, was to alter my four bars and make something of her own—to find a new opening—the harmony being
the same and only the melody different. Well, to-morrow I
shall see. I shall soon, I believe, get the libretto for my *opera
en deux acts* and shall have first of all to show it to the director,
Monsieur de Huime, for his approval. There is not a doubt of
that, however, for it comes from Noverre and De Huime has
Noverre to thank for his post. Noverre is also about to design
a new ballet and I am to compose the music for it. Rudolph
(the French horn-player) is in the royal service here and is a
good friend of mine. He has a thorough grasp of the principles
of composition and writes beautifully. This man has tendered
the post of organist at Versailles for my acceptance. The
position carries with it 2000 livres a year and the condition
that I spend six months each year at Versailles, the other six
in Paris or where I will. I do not think I shall accept, but I
have yet to hear my friends' advice on the subject. Two

thousand livres is after all no such great sum. True, it would be so in German money, but not here. It amounts, indeed, to 83 louis d'or 8 livres a year, in our money 915 florins and 45 krone—a large sum—but here only 333 thalers, 2 livres, which is little. It is terrible how quickly a thaler is spent here. I cannot really wonder that they think little of a louis d'or here for it does not go far. Well, *adieu!* Fare you well. I kiss your hands a thousand times, embrace my sister with all my heart, and am your most obedient son,

Wolfgang Amadé Mozart.

My compliments to all good friends, especially to Herr Bullinger.

28th May, 1778.

Leopold Mozart to his Son

You write that you have that very day been giving Monsieur le Duc's daughter her fourth lesson, and that you want her to do original work already!—Do you imagine everyone has your genius? —It will come soon enough! She has a good memory. *Eh bien!* Let her steal, or, more politely, appropriate—there is nothing to be done till courage comes. Your "variations" method is a good one and you should persevere with it!—

As to the opera you are to write, I called your attention to certain points in my last letter. I repeat that you should give thorough consideration to your subject-matter, read the verse through with Baron Grimm, come to an understanding with Noverre as to emotional expression, and follow the national taste in song, which your modulation and setting will then render superior to, and distinguished from, the work of others.

—And so Rudolph has offered you the post of organist at Versailles?—Does it really rest with him?—You say he is willing to get it for you! You must not throw *that* away so lightly. You must reflect that you earn your 83 louis d'or in six months—that the rest of the year is free for other activities—that it is probably a life appointment, sick or well—that you could leave it at any moment —that you would be at Court and consequently daily in the sight of the King and Queen and thereby in reach of fortune—that you might receive the post of one or other kapellmeister should either retire—that in time you might occupy the very profitable position of clavier master to one of the royal children—that you would be in no way hindered from writing for the theatre and *concert spirituel*, etc., or from having music engraved and dedicated to your acquaintances among the great, since many ministers of state stay in Versailles at least for the summer—that Versailles is a small town in itself, or at least has a number of eminent residents, among them, no doubt, pupils of either sex. Finally remember that it is your surest way of securing the Queen's protection and making yourself beloved. Read this letter to Baron von Grimm and listen to his opinion.

51. *To his Father*

29th May, 1778.

I am tolerably well, thank God, but my life often seems to be without rhyme or reason   I am neither hot nor cold—and take little joy in anything. My chief support and encouragement is the thought that you, my dearest Papa, and my sister are well, that I am an honest German, and that if I may not always speak I may at least *think* as I will! That is all, however. Yesterday I went for the second time to visit the Count von Sückingen, the Palatine ambassador (having already dined there once with Herr von Wendling and Raff), a charming man—I do not remember if I have already told you so—a passionate lover and true connoisseur of music. I spent eight hours quite alone with him. We were at the clavier morning, afternoon and evening till ten o'clock, playing, praising, admiring, analysing and criticising all kinds of music. He possesses nearly thirty operatic scores.

Well, I must not forget to tell you that I have had the honour of seeing your *Violinschule*[1] in a French translation. I believe the translation was made eight years ago at least. I happened to be at the music-seller's to buy a book of sonatas by Chobert for one of my scholars when I saw it, and I mean to go again and get a better look at it in order to be able to

[1] Leopold Mozart's *Versuch einer gründlichen Violinschule (An Attempt towards a Fundamental Course of Violin Study)* went into many editions during the eighteenth century. It is the earliest comprehensive method of violin-playing, and is of value even to-day.

send you a fuller account. And now, farewell. I kiss your hands a thousand times and embrace my sister with all my heart. *Mes compliments à tous mes amis, particulièrement à M. Bullinger.*

W. A. Mozart.

29th June, 1778.

Leopold Mozart to his Son

My dear Son can easily imagine that it is a species of martyrdom to me to know that he has composed much during all this time, while I, unhappily, can hear nothing of that which was once my chiefest delight!

52. *To his Father*

Paris, *ce* 3 *de juillet,* 1778.

Monsieur, mon très cher Père !

I have very sad and distressing news to give you, which is, indeed, the reason why I have been unable to answer your letter of the 11th earlier.—My dear Mother is very ill.[1] She had herself bled as she was used to do—it was indeed very necessary—and afterwards she felt better. Yet a few days later she complained of simultaneous chills and fever, accompanied by diarrhœa and headache. At first we employed merely our household remedies, *antispasmotisch* powder—and we should have used the black powder, but we had none and could get none here, where it is not known even under the name of *pulvis epilepticus.* As she grew steadily worse—found speech difficult, and lost her hearing so that one had to shout to make her hear —Baron Grimm sent us his physician. She is very weak, still has fever and is delirious. They give me hope—but I have not much. I have been day and night long between hope and fear —but I have surrendered myself wholly to the will of God— and I hope you and my dear sister will do the like. How else can we manage to be calm?—calmer, I should say, for more is not possible. I am resigned, come what may—for I know that God, who ordains all for the best, however strange it may

[1] Actually she had died the previous night.

appear to our eyes, will have it so. I believe (and none shall take the belief from me) that no physician, nor any other man, no accident, no chance, can either give life or take it, but God alone, though for the most part—not always—He works only through these instruments. We see people about us fall sick, sink and die—when their hour has come all means are useless—they rather hasten death than delay it. Did we not see it in the case of our dear departed friend Hefner? I do not therefore say that my Mother will and must die, that all hope is lost—she may recover health and vigour if God will. Having prayed with all my strength to my God for the health and life of my dear Mother I console myself with such re-flections because they hearten, soothe and comfort me—and you may easily imagine how greatly I need comfort! Now something else—let us leave these mournful thoughts! Let us hope, but not too much; let us trust in God and comfort our-selves with the thought that all is well if it be God's will, since He best knows what is requisite and necessary to our temporal and to our eternal happiness!

I had to compose a symphony to open the *concert spirituel.* It was performed with applause on Corpus Christi day, and I hear, moreover, that it has been noticed in the *Couriere de L'Europe*—so that you can see it has been exceptionally well received. I was exceedingly anxious at rehearsal, for never in my life have I heard a worse performance. You can have no conception of how they bungled and scrambled through it the first time and the second. Really I was quite frightened and would have liked to rehearse it once more, but there was so much else to rehearse that there was no time left. Accordingly I went to bed, fear in my heart, discontent and anger in my mind. I had decided not to go to the concert at all next day; but it was a fine evening, and I finally resolved to go with the proviso that if things went as ill as at the rehearsal I would certainly make my way into the orchestra, snatch Herr Lahouse's (the first violin's) instrument from his hand and conduct myself! I prayed God it might go well, dedicating all to His greater honour and glory, and *ecce !*—the symphony

began! Raff stood near me, and in the midst of the first allegro
came a passage I had known would please. The audience was
quite carried away—there was a great outburst of applause.
But, since I knew when I wrote it that it would make a sensation,
I had brought it in again in the last—and then it came again,
da capo! The andante also found favour, but particularly the
last allegro because, having noticed that all last allegri here
opened, like the first, with all instruments together and usually
in unison, *I* began with two violins only, *piano* for eight bars
only, then *forte*, so that at the *piano* (as I had expected) the
audience said "Sh!" and when they heard the *forte* began at
once to clap their hands. I was so happy that I went straight
to the Palais Royale after the symphony, ate an ice, said the
rosary I had vowed—and went home—for I always am and
always will be happiest there, or else with some good honest
German, who, if a bachelor, lives alone like a good Christian
or, if married, loves his wife and brings up his children well!
Now I have a piece of news for you which you may have
heard already, namely that that godless arch-rascal, Voltaire,
has died like a dog, like a beast. You have probably been long
since aware that I do not like being here. I have reasons in
plenty for this, but all are useless, simply because—I *am* here!
It is through no fault of mine and it shall not be, for I will
strain every nerve to do what I can.—Well, God will guide all
aright! I have a project in my head for which I daily pray God's
aid. If it is His Divine Will it will succeed—if not, I am also
content—I have at least done my part. If all goes as it should
and turns out as I wish, you will have to do *your* part to complete
the whole. I trust in your kindness to do so. Only do not indulge
in vain speculations on this matter. I would like to beg you
beforehand to grant me this, so that I need not expose my
idea before the time is ripe.[1]

It is very difficult at present to find suitable poems for
opera. The old ones, though they are the best, are not adapted
to the modern style, while the new are all useless, for poetry,
which was the one thing upon which the French could pride

[1] His hoped-for marriage with Aloysia Weber.

themselves, deteriorates daily—and yet poetry is the one thing that *must* be good here as they do not understand music! There are now two operas which I might compose, one in two acts, the other in three. That in two is *Alexandre et Roxeane*, but the poet who is writing it is still in the country; that in three is a translation of *Demofont* (by Metastasio), is interlarded with choruses and dances and is altogether adapted to the French stage. I have not yet been able to get a glimpse of this, either.

Write and tell me if you have Schrötter's[1] concertos in Salzburg?—and Hüllmandel's[2] sonatas? I would like to buy them and send them to you. Both works are very fine.

As to Versailles, I never thought of it. I listened to the advice of Baron Grimm and other good friends on the subject and they all thought as I did. The salary is small and one would have to pine for six months of the year in a place where nothing else is to be earned and where one's talent would be buried; for anyone in the royal service is forgotten in Paris. And then —organist! I should like a good appointment, but it must be a kapellmeister's with an ample salary. Well, fare you well. Take care of your health and trust in God—it is there you must look for comfort! My dear Mother is in the hands of the Almighty. If He will grant her to be with us, as I pray He may, we will thank Him for His grace, but if it be His will to take her to Himself, all our fears, all our cares and despair will be useless —let us rather submit ourselves steadfastly to the Divine Will, fully convinced it will be for our good, for He does all things well! Then farewell, dearest Papa, and for my sake care for your health. I kiss your hands a thousand times, embrace my sister with all my heart and am your most obedient son,

Wolfgang Amadé Mozart.

Leopold Mozart to his Son

13th July, 1778.

I congratulate you on your good fortune with your symphony at the *concert spirituel*. Your decision to break into the orchestra

---

[1] Schröter, Christoph (1699–1782), organist and composer; *or* Schröter, Johann (1750–88), pianist and composer.

[2] Hüllmandel, Nikolaus (1751–1823), distinguished clavier-player, and composer of some of the best music of his time for that instrument.

if things had gone ill was, of course, merely an overheated fancy. Heaven forfend! You must crush back this and all similar wild notions. You cannot have considered that such a step would have cost you your life, and no man of sense would risk that for a symphony!

53. To the Abbé Bullinger, Salzburg

PARIS, ce 3 juillet, 1778.

My best of Friends!
(For your eye alone).

Mourn with me, my friend!—This has been the saddest day of my life.—I am writing at two o'clock at night—I have to tell you that my mother, my dear mother is no more! God has called her to Himself—He willed to take her, I saw that clearly—and so I have surrendered myself to God's will. He gave her to me and it was in His power to take her from me. Picture to yourself the anxiety, the cares and fears I have had to endure for the last fortnight! She was quite unconscious at the time of her death—she went out like a light. Three days before she had confessed, received the Sacrament and extreme unction. Since then she was constantly delirious till to-day, when she was seized with convulsions at twenty-one minutes past five and immediately lost all feeling and perception. I pressed her hand and spoke to her, but she saw me not, heard me not, nor seemed sensible of anything. She lay thus five hours, that is, till twenty-one minutes past ten at night, when she expired. No one was present but I, M. Haina, a good friend of ours, and the nurse. To-day it is not possible for me to describe to you the whole course of the illness, but I believe that she was to die—that it was the will of God. Let me now beg you to do me one friendly service, to prepare my poor father very gently for this sad news! I have written to him by this same post, but only to say that she is gravely ill, and I now await his answer by which I shall be guided. God support and strengthen him! O my friend! not only am I now, but I have long been resigned! By the especial grace of God I have supported all with steadfastness and resignation. When the illness

became dangerous I prayed to God for two things only — a
happy death-hour for my mother, and then, for myself, strength
and courage; and God graciously heard my prayer and gave
me those two blessings in richest measure. I beg you then,
dearest friend, support my father! Inspire him with courage
so that when he knows the worst he may not take it too hardly!
I commend my sister to you also with all my heart. Go to
them both at once, I beseech you—do not say anything to them
yet of the death, but simply prepare them for it. Do what you
will—use every means—only ease my mind so that I need not
be apprehensive of a second blow. Preserve my dear father and
sister for me and pray send me a speedy answer.

—Adieu. I am,

Your most obedient and thankful servant,

Wolfgang Amadé Mozart.

Rue du gros chevet
vis à vis calle du croissant
à l'hôtel des quatre fils aimont.

54. *To his Father*

PARIS, *ce 9 juillet* 1778.

Monsieur, mon trés cher Pére

I hope that you are now prepared to hear some very
melancholy and distressing news with fortitude; indeed my
last letter, of the 3rd, will have led you to expect no good news.
On the evening of that same day, at twenty-one minutes past
ten o'clock, my mother fell happily asleep in God. Indeed,
when I wrote she was already experiencing heavenly joys—
all was then over—I wrote to you during the night; and I
trust that you and my sister will pardon me this slight but
very necessary deception, for when, after all my sorrow and
grief, I thought of what *yours* would be, I could not find it in
my heart to surprise you so suddenly with this terrible news!
Now, however, I hope that you have both prepared yourselves
to hear the worst and, that after giving way to natural and
all-too-well-justified grief and tears, you will be resolved to

submit to the will of God and to adore His inscrutable, un-
fathomable and all-wise providence. You will easily conceive
what I have had to go through—what courage and fortitude
I have needed to endure resignedly as things grew gradually
and steadily worse. And yet the good God gave me His grace.
I suffered grief enough—wept abundance of tears—but what
did it avail? I was forced to resign myself. Do you do the same,
my dear father, my dear sister! Weep—weep your hearts out
—but then take comfort—reflect that God Almighty will
have it so—and could or would we resist His will? Rather will
we pray and give thanks that she was so happy in her death—
for she was so. In those melancholy moments I took comfort
in three things—firstly, in whole-hearted, trustful submission
to God's will; secondly, in the sight of her very easy and
beautiful death, whereby I could picture to myself how she
had become happy in a moment of time (how much happier
she now is than we, so that I could have wished in that moment
to journey with her!) and—arising out of that desire as my third
comfort—in the thought that she is not lost to us for ever,
that we shall see her again and be more happily, more bliss-
fully together than ever in this world! It is only the time that
is unknown to us and that gives me no fears—when God wills
then will I also. May the divine, the most holy, Will be fulfilled!
Then let us say a devout Paternoster for her soul—and let us
turn to other matters, for all things have their appropriate time.
I am writing this in the house of Madame d'Epinai and Monsieur
Grimm, where I am now lodging. I have a pretty little room
with a very pleasant prospect, and as far as circumstances
allow I am happy. It will greatly assist such happiness as I
may have to hear that my dear father and my dear sister
have submitted wholly to the will of God, with resignation
and with fortitude—and have put their whole confidence in
Him in the firm assurance that He orders all things for the
best. O dearest and best father, take care of yourself! Dearest
sister, take care of yourself!—you have not yet tasted the fruits
of your brother's love towards you, for he has not yet been
in a position to provide them! My dearest pair! Take care

of your health—remember that you have a son, a brother, who will strain every nerve to make *you* happy, well knowing that you, some day, will not refuse his desire, his happiness— which is certainly not discreditable to him—and will do all in your power to see *him* happy. Oh, then we shall live at peace, honoured, blessed (as far as is possible in this world), and finally, when God wills, shall be reunited in that abode for which we are destined, for which we were created![1]

55. *To his Father*

PARIS, *ce* 31 *juillet*, 1778.

Monsieur mon trés cher Pére !

I hope you have safely received my last two letters, of the 11th and 18th (I believe). Meanwhile I have received yours of the 13th and 20th. The first drew tears of anguish from my eyes—because I was reminded of the sad death of my dear, sainted mother, and all the circumstances were brought back to me so vividly. Indeed, I shall never forget it all my life—for you know that I had never seen anyone die (though I could have wished to do so) and then my first experience must needs be the death of my mother! That moment was my chiefest dread, and I prayed to God with tears to give me strength. I was heard—it was given me. Sad as your letter made me, I was yet beside myself with joy when I saw that you had taken it all as it should be taken— and that I need consequently have no fears for my dearest father and sister. The moment I had read your letter through I fell upon my knees and thanked my dear God with all my heart for this grace. Now I am quite at ease, for I know that I have nothing to fear for the two persons who are dearest to me in this world. If evil were to happen to them it would be the greatest sorrow to me—I should be utterly crushed by it. Therefore I beg you both to preserve the health which is so precious to me, and accord to one who flatters himself that he is now your dearest in this world, the happiness,

---

[1] The whole of this and the succeeding letter have not been published here for considerations of space.

the joy, the bliss of soon folding you in his arms! Your last letter drew tears of joy from me, for after reading it I am for evermore perfectly assured of your true fatherly love and care. I shall strive with all my might ever to deserve that paternal love. I kiss your hand in tender gratitude to you for sending the powder—and am convinced you will be glad to know that I have had no occasion to use it. During my sainted mother's illness I came near needing it—but now, thank God, I am quite sound and well. Only from time to time I have melancholy fits, the quickest cure for which, I find, is letters, written or received; they cheer me up again. But I assure you that these attacks are not without reason. Would you like to know how much I had to pay for your last containing the powder? Forty-five sous! You would like some account of the illness and all its circumstances? You shall have it; only I beg you will permit me to be somewhat brief since it is all over now and can, alas! never be altered —and I must reserve room to write of matters touching our present situation. First of all, I feel I must tell you that my sainted mother *was to die*—no doctor in the world could have saved her this time, for it was clearly the will of God; her time had come—God willed to take her to Himself. You think she postponed the bleeding too long. It may be so; she did postpone it somewhat; but I am rather inclined to the opinion of the people here who advised her against bleeding and tried instead to persuade her to take a clyster. She would not, however, and I did not venture to say aught, because I know nothing of the matter and consequently should have been to blame if it had not suited her. If the case had been my own I should have consented at once, for it is very much in vogue here—when a man has inflammation he takes a clyster—and the cause of my mother's illness was nothing but internal inflammation, at least it was so diagnosed. I cannot tell you accurately how much blood she was let, for here it is measured not by the ounce but by the plate; they took not quite two platefuls. The chirurgeon said it was very necessary —but that day was so terribly hot that he dared not bleed

her any more. For a few days she improved, but then diarrhœa
set in. No one thought much of it as it is common here for
foreigners to find the strong water laxative. That is true
enough, too. I had it myself when I first came, but since I have
given up drinking plain water and always drink a little wine
mixed with it, I have been free of the trouble. Since, however,
I cannot do without plain water to drink, I purify it with ice
and drink it *en glace* — two glassfuls every day before I go
to bed. Well, to continue. On the 19th she complained of
headache, and that was the first day she remained all day in
bed; she was up for the last time on the 18th. On the 20th
she complained of chilliness and then of fever. I gave her an
antispasmotisch powder. All this time I wanted to send for
a physician, but she would never consent. When I pressed her
strongly she said she had no confidence in a French *medicum*,
and so I looked about for a German. Naturally I could not go out,
and so I waited anxiously for M. Haina, who was accustomed to
visit us unfailingly each day—only of course on this occasion he
stayed away two days! At last he came, but as the physician
was prevented from coming the following day we could do
nothing. He came at length on the 24th. The day before that
I would have given much to have him, for she suddenly lost
her hearing and I was in great anxiety. The physician (a
German of seventy years and more) gave her rhubarb powder
mixed with wine. I cannot understand that, for they usually
say wine is heating, but when I said as much everyone cried,
"Oh, by no means! What are you saying? Wine does not heat,
it merely strengthens. Water heats." And meantime the poor
invalid was pining for fresh water. How gladly would I have
given it to her! Dearest father, you cannot imagine what
I endured. There was no help for it, I had to leave her, in God's
name, in the hands of the doctors. All I could do with a good
conscience was to pray continually to God to order all things
for the best for her. I went about as if bereft of my senses.
I had time enough for composition, but I could not have
written a note. On the 25th the physician did not come. On
the 26th he visited her again. Imagine yourself in my place

when he said to me quite unexpectedly, "I fear she will not last out the night. Should she be taken with pains in the night and have to leave her bed she might die in a moment —so see that she has opportunity to make her confession." I ran out then, to the end of the *Chaussee d'Antin* beyond the *barriere* to seek out Heina, for I knew he was at music with a certain Count. He told me he would bring a German priest next day. On my way home I stopped for a moment in passing to call on Grimm and Madame d'Epinay. They were quite distressed that I had not spoken to them earlier, for they would have sent their own doctor at once. I had not done so because my mother did not want a Frenchman, but now I was driven to extremities—and they said they would send their physician that same evening. On my return, I told my mother that I had met Herr Heina with a German priest, who had heard much of me and was eager to hear me play and that they were to come to-morrow to pay me a visit. She was quite agreeable, and thinking she seemed better (although I am no doctor) I said no more to her then.—I see now that I cannot possibly tell it in brief—I want to write of it all in detail, and I believe you too would prefer that I should. So since there are matters of more present urgency to write of, I will continue my story in my next letter. In the meantime my last letter will have told you where I am lodging and that all my affairs and those of my sainted mother are in good order. When I come to this point you will see how we managed. Heina and I did everything. Clothes, linen, trinkets, indeed all her little possessions, shall be sent at the first suitable opportunity and with every precaution to Salzburg. I am arranging all that with Herr Geschwendtner. Now to business —but first I must beg you again (in respect of that matter of which I wrote to you in my last, begging permission to keep my own counsel till the time is ripe)—do not be in the least anxious. I cannot tell you about it yet, for indeed it is not yet time and I should thereby do more harm than good. For your ease of mind, let me say it concerns myself alone. It will not affect your circumstances either for better or

worse and I shall not think about it at all until I see you in
an improved position. But when we are happily reunited and
can live somewhere together, when that happy time comes—
God grant it may be soon!—then the moment will have come
and then it will rest wholly with you. So have no anxiety
about it, and rest assured that in all matters where I know
your peace and happiness are involved I will ever repose my
confidence in you—in my dearest father, my truest friend!
And I will tell you all circumstantially; if I have not always
done so hitherto it has not been entirely my fault. Monsieur
Grimm recently said to me: "What am I to write to your
father? What course of action have you decided on? Will
you stay here, or go to Mannheim?" I really could not refrain
from laughing. "What could I do in Mannheim now?" said
I. "If only I had never come to Paris—but, being here, I must
do all I can to make my way." "Yes," said he, "but I hardly
think you will be able to make your future here." "But why
so?" I asked. "I see a lot of wretched blockheads here who
are able to make their way, and why should not I, with my
talent? I told you that I liked Mannheim—that I would be
glad of an appointment there—but an honourable and reputable
one. I must be sure how I stand before I take any step."
"I am afraid," said he, "that you have not been active enough
here—you do not go about enough." "Well," I replied, "that
is just my greatest difficulty here." Recently, of course, my
mother's long illness has prevented me from going anywhere.
Two of my pupils are in the country and the third (the daughter
of the Duc de Guines) is betrothed and will no longer continue
her studies (no great loss to my reputation!). Moreover, I shall
lose no money by her, for the Duke pays no more than anyone
else here. Only conceive that the Duc de Guines, where I went
daily for two hours, let me give twenty-four lessons (when
it is customary to pay after the twelfth) and went away
into the country and returned after ten days without letting
me know a word of it, so that if I had not had the wit to make
inquiries myself I should not have known yet that the family
were here! Finally the housekeeper pulled out a purse and said,

" Pardon me if I only pay you for twelve lessons to-day as I have not money enough by me." There's *noblesse* for you! And she paid me down three louis-d'or, adding, " I hope this will content you, but if not you must tell me so." M. le Duc, then, has not a spark of honour about him and must have thought, "He's but a young fellow, a stupid German into the bargain (for all Frenchmen speak so of the Germans) and so will be quite content." But the "stupid German" was not at all content and I will not let the matter rest. He wanted, you see, to pay me for one hour instead of for two—added to which he has had a concerto of mine for flute and harp four months and has not yet paid me for it ! I shall accordingly wait till the wedding is over and then I shall go to the house-keeper and demand my money. What vexes me most of all here is that these " stupid Frenchmen " seem to think that I am still seven years old because that was my age when they first saw me ! This is perfectly true. Madame d'Epinay said as much to me in all seriousness—they treat me here as a beginner—with the exception of the musical experts, who think otherwise. But it is the majority that counts. After my conversation with Grimm I went the following day to Count Sückingen. He was quite of my opinion—namely that I should have patience, wait till the arrival of Raff, who will work for me to the very best of his ability, and then, if that is no use, go to Mayence, where Count Sückingen has himself promised to find me a place. Consequently my intention at present is to do my best to get along by means of pupils and make what money I can. I am doing so, indeed, in the fond hope of a speedy change of circumstances, for I cannot conceal from you, rather must I confess, that I shall be glad to be delivered from it ; for lesson-giving is no joke here, one is bound to wear oneself out considerably over it. If one takes few pupils one makes little money. You must not think this is laziness. No ! But it goes utterly against my genius, my habit of life. You know that I am so to speak wrapped up in music—that it is with me all day—that I love to speculate, to study, to reflect. Well, I am prevented from all this by my way of life here.

I shall have a few free hours, it is true, but these few hours will be needed more for rest than for work. I have already written of opera in a former letter. I cannot help it—I must write either a grand opera or none. If I write a little one I shall get little for it (for everything is taxed here). Then, should it be so unlucky as not to hit the taste of these "stupid Frenchmen" all would be over. I should get no more commissions to compose—I should have made little—and my name would have suffered. If I write a grand opera, however, I shall be better paid, I shall be doing the work I rejoice in—and I shall have more hope of success, for one has a better chance of making one's name with a big work. I assure you I shall have no fears whatever if I get the commission to write an opera. True, it is the devil's own language, and I see the full extent of the difficulties with which all composers have had to contend, but, notwithstanding, I feel able to overcome these difficulties as well as another. *O contraire*, when, I fancy, as I often do, that my opera is in train, I feel my whole body on fire and I tremble from head to foot with eagerness to teach the French once for all to know, to value and to fear the Germans! Why do they never entrust a Frenchman with a grand opera? Why must it always be a foreigner? The most odious part of the business for me would be the singers. Well, I am ready. I will begin no quarrel, but if I am challenged I shall know how to defend myself. But I should prefer to avoid a duel, for I do not care to fight with dwarfs. God grant some change may come soon! In the meantime I shall not fall short in zeal and industry. I set my hope on the winter, when they all return from the country. Meanwhile, fare you well and love me ever. My very heart laughs when I think of the happy day when I shall have the joy of seeing you again and embracing you with all my heart. *Adieu.* I kiss your hands a thousand times and embrace my sister brotherly. I am your most

obedient son,

Wolfgang Amadé Mozart.

The day before yesterday my dear friend Weber wrote

telling me among other things that, following on the arrival of the Elector the other day, it was given out that he was to take up his residence in Munich. This piece of news was like a thunderbolt to all Mannheim and completely quenched the joy of the inhabitants which had been expressed the preceding day by a general illumination. All the Court musicians were notified of it, with the addition that each was at liberty to follow the Court to Munich or to remain at Mannheim at the same salary. Within a fortnight the decision of each must be delivered signed and sealed to the Intendant. Weber, who, as you know, is in the most wretched circumstances, has written as follows: "In view of the confusion of my affairs I am not in a position, greatly as I should desire it, to follow his Highness to Munich." Before this occurred there had been a great concert at Court, on the occasion of which poor Mlle. Weber had been made to feel the strength of her enemies. She did not sing at it! They do not know who was at the bottom of it. However, afterwards there was a concert at Herr von Gemmingen's, and Count Seeau was present. She sang two of my arias, and had the good fortune to please in spite of these Italian scoundrels who have been spreading a report that her singing has deteriorated. When the arias were over, Canabich said to her: "Mademoiselle, I could wish that you may continue to 'deteriorate' in this fashion! To-morrow I shall write to Herr Mozart and commend your singing to him." Well, the kernel of the matter is that the Court would have moved to Munich by now if war had not already broken out, and that Count Seeau, being determined to have Mlle. Weber, would have made the greatest effort to get her taken too, so that there might have been hope of seeing the whole family in better circumstances. Now no more is said about the Munich journey, and this poor family may be kept long in suspense while their debts grow heavier day by day. If only I could help them! Dearest father, I commend them to you with all my heart! If she could but enjoy an income of 1000 florins for a few years!

Leopold Mozart to his Son

Since your pupils are now away, compose something again. Even if you get little for it in money it must, surely to God, make your name known! Let it be something short, easy and popular. Talk it over with an engraver and learn what he would prefer to have—perhaps easy quartets for two *violini, viola e basso*. You think, perhaps, you will lower yourself by such work? Not at all! Did Bach ever publish anything but such-like trifles in London? A trifle may be very great if it is natural, fluent, written easily and efficiently composed. It is harder to make it thus than to produce all those artificial and for the most part incomprehensible harmonic progressions and difficult melodies. Did Bach lower himself by such work? No, indeed! Good phrasing and construction— *il filo*—this is what distinguishes the master from the dullard even in a trifle. Were I in your place I would prepare something of that kind now, at the same time endeavouring by all possible means to get the writing of an opera. You must make an effort to strike a bargain with some engraver or other. Do you not need money to live? And what other means have you of making it when your pupils are out of town? Something *must* be done!

Leopold Mozart to his Son

Your dear mother saw it all, but she wished to spare me all annoyance and wrote at the end of the letter, "My dear Husband, you will perceive from this letter that when Wolfgang makes new acquaintances he is at once ready to dedicate life and goods for them. It is true she sings incomparably, but indeed it does not do to set one's own interests aside. I never approved the friendship with Wendling and Rahm, but I dared not offer any objections for he would never believe me. As soon, however, as he came to know the Webers he changed his mind at once. In a word, he prefers the society of others to mine. If I raise any objection when this or that displeases me he does not like it. Frankly, I do not think the journey with Wendling would be advisable, and I would rather accompany him to Paris myself. Perhaps you may get an answer from Herr von Grimm." This, my dear Son, is the sole postscript which your dear sainted mother, trusting in you, wrote without your knowledge during the whole period of your absence. And although she might have written more clearly and called things by their right names, she loved both you and me too dearly to speak more plainly.

I cannot forgive you for having neglected to go to Mayence during all your long stay in Mannheim. Examine the matter impartially and you will have to acknowledge that you very seldom followed my advice and precepts. A journey to Mayence would have been of more use to you than that fatal journey of yours to Kirchheim-Poland, for Mayence is after all a capital, where there were some prospects and where many of our acquaintance among the *noblesse* and others have friends. You see, then, that at present all your speculation must be directed solely to making your way effectively in Paris. As to all the rest about Mannheim, Mayence or Salzburg, we must wait and see, and not engage our thoughts with mere idle dreams which do nothing but render us incapable of dealing with the present necessary business.

You are forever writing about the embarrassed circumstances of these Webers, but tell me how, being in your right mind, you are for a moment able to entertain the idea that *you* could be the person capable of making these people's fortune? You are coming to know by degrees (or so I hope) how much money even a single man needs to keep himself with decency. One may of course make an effort to assist Mlle. Weber as far as is possible, and even achieve all you wish for with time, but are our powers sufficient to help even one child out of a family of six? Who can do this? I? You?— who have not even been able to help ourselves! How can you help others before you have helped yourself? You write: "Dearest father! I commend her to you with all my heart. If she only had an income of 1000 florins for a few years!" My dearest Son! Could I help fearing for your reason when I read this? Heavens above! I am to get her 1000 florins for a few years! If I could do it I would help you first, and then myself and your dear sister, who is already twenty-seven years of age and is without support, while I grow old! And where, pray, are the Courts, where is a single Court, which pays a singer 1000 florins? In Munich they get five, six or at most seven hundred, and do you imagine that a young person, unknown and considered a beginner, will get 1000 florins forthwith? Think about it day and night, and imagine it half done or easy to bring about, but you will never find it so; more particularly since, as you are constantly hearing and seeing, one must make a name for oneself, attain a certain notoriety, so to speak, before achieving one's fortune in this world. You may ponder the whole day through and dream of a thousand imaginary possibilities, and not only will this miracle not happen, but unless you turn your present circumstances to profit you will pass your life in ineffectiveness, unknown and poor, ruin yourself and me, and be incapable of *helping* anyone! You must write to Canabich and Raff and ask them to propose you as a composer for the German opera to the Elector and to Seau. Count Sückingen must write likewise to Baron Gemmingen and others. You should also write a French letter to the same effect to the Imperial ambassador, Baron Lerbach. Baron Grimm could deliver it for you. Briefly, you should write to everyone who might have any influence with the Elector, for German opera will always be played in Munich in future. On St. Charles's Day, November 4th, the opera by Wieland and Schweizer is to be performed and will probably be continued through the carnival. I shall also approach Count Seau from here. If you were to get only 600 florins it would be something. One has one's name to make. When did Gluck, when did Piccini, when did all the others first come to the fore? Gluck must be at least sixty, and it is only twenty-six or twenty-seven years since people began to talk of him, but you want the French public—or perhaps only the directors of the opera—to be convinced already of your ability in composition, although they have never heard anything of yours yet and only know of you from your childhood as a remarkable pianist and prodigy! Therefore you must make an *effort* to succeed and to show yourself as a composer in all *genres*. For this purpose you must look for opportunities, tirelessly seek out friends, spur them on relentlessly, revive their interest when they grow dull, and not believe that promised is as good as performed!

Leopold Mozart to his Son

31st August, 1778.

Not only has the Archbishop[1] agreed to everything, both on my behalf and yours—you are to have 500 florins—but he has furthermore expressed regret that he cannot possibly appoint you

---

[1] From 1772 Count Hieronymus von Colloredo was Archbishop of Salzburg. He had no conception of Mozart's greatness. Mozart did not take leave of him before his journey to Augsburg and Munich because the Archbishop had refused him leave to go. Leopold's efforts now brought about a renewal of relations, which Mozart finally broke off in 1781.

kapellmeister at present; but you are to take my place if I am tired or indisposed and he had always intended you should have a better salary, etc. In a word, I was astonished—but more particularly by the courteous regrets! He has raised Paris's salary by five florins so that he is to do most of the work, and you are to be accepted as concertmeister, just as formerly. We shall receive, then, a yearly official salary of 1000 florins a year as I have already told you! All depends now on whether you believe I am still in possession of my mental faculties, whether you think I have served your best interests—and whether you want to see me dead or alive! I have thought everything over. The Archbishop declares that he will give you leave to travel where you like for the purpose of writing opera; he said, in excuse for having denied us leave last year, that he could not tolerate people going about the country begging! In Salzburg you will be midway between Munich, Vienna and Italy. It will be easier for you to get an opera commission in Munich than to get an appointment there, for where are there German composers to be found? And how many?

Leopold Mozart to his Son

3rd September, 1778.

How, in Heaven's name, is the Elector to make up his mind to take you as his Court composer when he has *heard* nothing of yours? You must conduct your business from here, and it will be the easier for you to get an opera commissioned since the Italians are excluded. The matter will go of itself then. And now, at last, I solemnly swear to you that I have only remained tied to Salzburg so that, whatever happened, your poor dear mother might have been secure of a pension. That need is now past, and consequently we need put up with no tyranny—we can be up and away. In your last letter you say: "My heart laughs when I think of the happy day when I shall once again have the joy of seeing you and embracing you with all my heart!" Well, my dear Son, that day approaches, and I hope God may permit me to live to see it. You will scarcely know your poor father. On both occasions when I was summoned to the Archbishop he was so horrified at my appearance that he spoke of it to everyone. I was ill when you left a year ago—and what have I not had to go through in this year? I have a constitution of iron or I should be dead already; only if you will not lift this black burden from my heart by your presence it will crush me utterly. Heart-strengthening medicines are powerless to heal a disease of the spirit. You alone can save me from death, and no one will help you more loyally to your happiness by all possible human effort than the father who blesses you, loves you, kisses you, and desires with all his heart to hold you in his arms.

56. *To his Father*

PARIS, *ce* 11 *sept*, 1778.

Mon trés cher Pére!

I have safely received your three letters of August 13th, 27th and 31st, but I will reply to the last only as that is the most important. When I read it through (M. Heina, who sends his compliments to you both, being beside me) I trembled for joy—for soon I shall be in your arms! True, I admit it to myself, there is no great fortune awaiting me there, but when I think how I shall kiss my dearest father, my dear sister, I feel *that* is fortune enough for me. This indeed is the only real excuse I can offer people here who are deafening me with petitions to remain; for I can always answer at once, "What will you, then? I am satisfied and that settles it. There is just this one place where I can say I am at home, where I can live in peace and quiet with my dearest father, my beloved sister, where I can do as I like, where I am my own master, apart from the duties of my post, where I have a permanent income and yet can go when I will, travel every year or two—and what more can I desire?" To tell you my real feelings, the one thing which I dislike about Salzburg is the lack of agreeable society, the low estimation in which music is held—and—that the Archbishop places no confidence in sensible travelled folk; for I protest that without travel (at least for those who cultivate the arts and learning) a man is but a poor creature! I assure you that if the Archbishop had not given me leave to travel every two years I could not possibly have accepted the appointment. A man of mediocre talent remains a mediocrity whether he travels or not, but one of superior talents (such as I cannot disclaim for myself without impiety) will do no good if he is tied ever to one place. If the Archbishop would trust me I would soon make his music famous—no doubt of that. I can assure you that this journey has not been in vain—for my composition, it goes without saying, for I play the clavier as well as I ever shall. But there is one thing I would like to beg off in Salzburg, which is this: I will no longer be a fiddler as formerly. I will conduct at the clavier and accompany arias. To be sure, it would be a good thing if I could get a written promise of the kapellmeister's post, for otherwise I may perhaps have the honour of filling two posts and being paid for one—and in the end he may put some stranger over my head! My dearest father! I must confess that were it not for the joy of seeing you both again I could hardly decide to accept — and yet of course I am glad to get away from Paris, which I detest, although my affairs here are beginning to improve steadily, and I do not doubt that if I could make up my mind to endure a few years here I should make my way very well. For I am becoming fairly well known now—I am not getting to know these people, but they are hearing of me. I have made a name for myself by my two symphonies (the last of which was performed on the 8th of this month). I ought to write an opera now (having said that I am going away), but I said to Noverre, "If you will guarantee me its production as soon as it is finished and will tell me exactly what you will pay me for it, I will stay another three months and write it." (For I could not simply reject the plan, or people would have thought I did not trust my ability to carry it through.) They did not agree to these terms, however, and I knew beforehand that they would not and could not, since they are not according to usage here. Here, as perhaps you know, an opera is examined on its completion, and if the "stupid Frenchmen" do not approve it, it is not given and the composer has written in vain. If they do approve it, it is produced and paid for in proportion to its success with the public. It is all very uncertain, but I will keep these matters to discuss when we meet. For the rest, I can say sincerely that my prosperity is beginning. Matters will not be hurried — *chi và piano, và sano*. I have won friendship and

patronage by my *complaisance*. If I were to tell you all — my
fingers would ache! Well, I shall be able to tell you by word of
mouth and make plain to you that M. Grimm is fit to help
children, perhaps, but not grown men, and—but no, I will
not write of it—and yet I must! Only do not imagine that
this man is what he used to be. If Madame d'Epinay were not
here I should not be in this house. And he need not be so proud
of his hospitality, for I could have stayed in any one of four
houses and received board and lodging. The good man is quite
unaware that, had I been remaining here, I should have left
his house next month and gone to a less primitive and stupid
household than his, a house where they can do one a favour
without constantly casting it in one's teeth! Really, such conduct brings me near to forgetting that I have received a
favour, but I will be more generous than he. Only I regret that
I cannot remain here to show him that I do not need him—
and that I can do as well as his Piccini, although I am only
a German! The greatest kindness he has shown me consists in
the loan of fifteen louis d'or which he advanced me bit by bit
during the time of my sainted mother's illness and death. I
wonder if he is anxious about this? If he has any doubts about
it he really deserves kicking, for it means he doubts my honour
(the one thing which can make me angry) and also my talent
—yet I know that the latter is so, for he once told me himself
that he did not believe I was fit to write a French opera. I shall
return the fifteen louis d'or when I leave with thanks and a
few very courteous words. My sainted mother often said to
me, "I do not know how it is, but he seems to me to be quite
changed." I used always to take his part although I was secretly
convinced of the same thing. He spoke of me to no one—or if
he did, it was always very stupidly and awkwardly done—dis-
paragingly. He wanted me to be for ever running after Piccini,
and Caribaldi too, for there is a wretched *opera buffé* on here
now, and I have always said I would not go a single step to see
it. In a word, he is of the Italian faction—he is false and is
trying to keep me down. It is incredible, is it not? But it is
true for all that, and here is the proof. I have bared my whole

heart to him as to a true friend—and good use he has made of it! He has given me bad advice knowing I should follow it; but he was only successful two or three times with that, for I ceased to question him, and when he offered me advice I did not take it, although I said yes to avoid his insolence. Well, enough of this. I will tell you more when we meet.[1]

Wolfgang Amadé Mozart.

57. To his Father

NANCY, ce 3 octob., 1778.

Mon trés cher Pére !

I beg your pardon for not having announced my departure to you from Paris, but the whole business was hurried so much beyond any conjectures, opinion or wishes of mine as I cannot describe to you! At the last moment I almost had my baggage conveyed to Count Sückingen's instead of to the *burreau* of the diligence, and thought to remain a few more days in Paris —and on my honour I *should* have done so had I not thought of you—for I did not wish to cause you any anxiety. We shall have opportunity to speak of this matter in Salzburg. Only this much—can you conceive that M. Grimm actually pretended to me that I was to travel by the diligence and should get to Strassburg in five days, and that it was not till the last day that I knew that it was another coach altogether which travels at walking pace, never changes horses, and takes ten days! You may imagine my wrath! However, I only expressed my feelings to my best friends and showed myself perfectly happy and contented to him. When I got into the coach I heard the pleasant news that we should be twelve days on the road. Now you can see the great wisdom of Baron von Grimm! He sent me by this slow conveyance simply to save money, not considering that the actual expense would nevertheless be greater, because one would have to stay at so many more inns! Well, that is over and done; but what displeases me most in the whole business is the fact that he was not open with me. Of course he has spared his pocket, but not mine, for he

---

[1] This letter is not printed in full for considerations of space.

paid for the fare but not for board and lodging! If I had stayed another week or ten days in Paris I should have been able to arrange for my journey more fitly myself. Well, I have endured a week in this coach, but I could endure no more, not because of the shaking, for the vehicle is well hung, but for want of sleep. We are on the road every day by four o'clock and so have to rise at two. Twice I have had the honour of rising at one in the night, as the coach was to leave at two o'clock! You know that I cannot sleep in a coach, and consequently I could not go on like that without some danger to health. Moreover, one of our fellow-travellers was very taken up with the French. He made no secret of it and so—well, I have had enough of it and I would rather, should it come to the point, travel post. That, however, is not necessary, for I have had the good fortune to fall in with one man whom I like—a German merchant who lives in Paris and deals in English wares. We exchanged a word or so before we entered the coach and from that moment remained together. We did not eat with the company, but in our own room, and we slept together. I am glad of this man's society for he has travelled much and consequently understands the matter. He, too, grew weary of the coach, so we have both left it and to-morrow have a fortunate and not costly opportunity of reaching Strassburg. There I hope to find a letter from you and to learn thereby of my further journey. I hope you have received my letters; I have safely received yours. I beg pardon for being unable to write much, for I am never in a good humour when in a town where I am little acquainted. But I think if I could become acquainted here I should like to live here, for the town is indeed *charmante*—fine houses, fine broad streets and superb squares. I have one thing more to ask you. May I have a great coffer in my room so that I can have all my possessions by me? I should very much like it if I could have the little clavier which used to belong to Fischetti and Rust upon my desk, for it suits me better than Stein's little one. I am not bringing you many new compositions of my own as I have made very few. I have not got the three quartets and the flute concerto for M. de Jean, for he put it into the wrong chest when he went to Paris and consequently it remained behind in Mannheim. But he has promised me to send it as soon as he gets to Mannheim and I will commission Wendling to send it on. The result is that I am bringing no finished work with me save my sonatas—for Le Gros bought the two overtures and the symphony *concertante*. He thinks he has them all to himself, but it is not so—they are still fresh in my head and as soon as I am home I shall write them out again! The Munich players are playing now, of course? Are they popular? Do people go? Of musical pieces I suppose Piccini's *Fisher-Maiden* (*La pescatrice*) or Sacchini's [1] *Peasant Girl* (*La contadina in corte*) will be the first? The *prima donna* will be Mme. Keyser—that is the girl I wrote of to you from Munich. I do not know her—I have only heard her sing. It was then her third appearance on the boards and scarcely three weeks since she studied the music. And so, fare you well. I shall not have one quiet hour till I behold again all I hold dear in this world! I embrace my dear sister with all my heart, kiss your hand a thousand times, and am

> Your most obedient son,
> Wolfgang Amadé Mozart.

My compliments to all good friends, particularly to our true and dear friend Bullinger.

58. *To his Father*

STRASBOURG, *The 15th octobre*, 1778.

Monsieur, mon trés cher Pére !

I have safely received your letters of 17th and 24th September and 1st October, but it was impossible for me to answer them till now. I hope you have safely received my last from Nancy. I rejoice with all my heart and thank God that you are both sound and well. I too, I thank God, am well —very well. I will now reply as far as I can to the most important points in your three letters. As regards what you write

---

[1] Sacchini, Antonio (1734–86), composer, chiefly operatic. *Œdipe à Colonne* is his best-known work.

of M. Grimm, I naturally know all that even better than you do. There has been no lack of politeness and civility—I know that—for were it otherwise I would not have made so much ceremony. I owe M. Grimm no more than 15 louis d'or, and it is his fault that I have not repaid them—as I told him. But what is the use of writing all this—we shall soon be able to discuss it in Salzburg. I am very much obliged to you for having commended the matter so warmly to the interest of Father Martini—and also for having written to Mr. Raff. Indeed, I never doubted but that you would do so, for I know that you are glad to see your son happy and content—and that *you* know I can be so nowhere better than in Munich because it is so near Salzburg that I can often visit you. I am as delighted as is to be expected of one who took so great an interest in the matter, that Mademoiselle Weber—or I should rather say my dear Miss Weber—is getting a salary and that accordingly justice is being done her at last. I commend her once more to you most warmly—but unfortunately I no longer dare to hope for the fulfilment of my wish to get her a post in Salzburg, for the Archbishop would not give her what she is getting up there. At most she might come for a time to Salzburg to sing in an opera. I have had a letter from her father written in great haste the day before their departure for Munich in which he also told me the following piece of news. The poor things had all been in the gravest anxiety about me. They believed me dead, not having heard from me for a month as my last letter but one had gone astray—and they were further confirmed in this fear because it was being said in Mannheim that my sainted mother had died of some contagious illness. They had already been praying for my soul. That poor girl went every day to the Capuchin chapel. You laugh, perhaps? Not I! I am touched, whether I will or no. Well, to proceed. I believe I shall certainly go to Augsburg by way of Stuttgart, because, as I see from your letter, there is nothing, or at most times very little, to be done in Donaueschingen. Still, I shall ascertain about this by letter before leaving Strassburg.

Dearest father! I assure you that were it not for the joy of embracing you so soon I should certainly not come to Salzburg, for, apart from this praiseworthy and really beautiful reason, to do so is the greatest piece of folly in the world. Rest assured that this is my own opinion and has not been borrowed from others. Indeed, when people heard of my intention to leave, they confronted me with valid arguments against which my only efficient weapon was my true and tender love for the best of fathers. Thereupon, of course, they could do nothing but commend my action, but they added that, if my father knew of my present circumstances and excellent prospects (and had not received false information through a certain "good friend"), he would certainly not have written to me in such a manner that—opposition to him was out of the question! I, for my part, felt that, had I not had so much vexation to endure in the house where I was lodged and had affairs not followed one upon another like a series of thunder-claps, I should have had time to think the matter out in cold blood —and should certainly have implored you to have patience a little longer and leave me in Paris, where, I assure you, I was in the way to achieve name, fame and money—enough to release you from your debts. Well, things are *as* they are. Only do not imagine that I regret the course they have taken, for you alone, dearest father, can sweeten the bitterness of Salzburg for me—and you *will* do so, I am sure of that! Still, I must frankly confess that I should arrive in Salzburg with a lighter heart did I not remember that I am to be in the Court employ. I find this one thought insupportable. Consider it yourself—put yourself in my place! At Salzburg I shall not know what my position is—I am to be everybody and yet —at times—nobody! I ask neither so much—nor so little— I want *something*—just to be *something*! I see it is so everywhere else—the man who has an appointment as violinist remains a violinist—the same with the clavier, etc.—Still, that can all be arranged, no doubt. I hope all will turn out fortunately and happily for me. I rely wholly on you. Times are poor here, but the day after to-morrow, Saturday, I am giving a subscription concert (all by myself—for if I had a band it would cost me, with lighting, over three louis d'or, and who knows if I shall make that sum?) to please a few good friends, amateurs and connoisseurs. I am obliged to you for having made such excellent arrangements as to the money for my journey. I do not think I shall need it—even did I give no concert, but all the same I mean to make a few louis d'or either here or in Augsburg out of prudence—for one cannot tell what may happen. Meanwhile, fare you well. I shall write further soon. My sonatas cannot have been engraved yet, although they were promised me for the end of September—that is what happens when one cannot see to a thing oneself. That again is the fault of Grimm's obstinacy. They will very likely appear full of mistakes because I have not been able to look through them myself and have had to get another to do so. And I shall probably be without the sonatas in Munich. These seemingly trivial matters often make the difference between fortune, fame and money on the one hand—and disgrace on the other! And now, farewell! I embrace my dearest sister with all my heart and I kiss you, dearest, best father, in the flattering hope of being able soon to embrace you and kiss your hand.

I am your most obedient son,

Wolfgang Amadé Mozart.

My compliments to all Salzburg, but particularly to our dear and true friend Herr Bullinger.

59. *To his Father*

MANNHEIM, *le* 12 *novbre*, 1778.

Mon trés cher Père !

I arrived here safely on the 6th and pleasantly surprised all my good friends! Thank God I am in my dear Mannheim once more! I am sure you would say the same if you were here. I am staying with Madame Canabich who, with her family and all our circle, was almost beside herself with joy to see me again. We have not finished talking yet, for she is relating to me all the events and changes which have occurred during my absence. Since I have been here I have not once dined at home—there is a regular scramble for me. In a word, Mannheim loves me as I love Mannheim. I do not know, but I believe I may yet get an appointment here! Here, not in Munich —for the Elector would, I believe, be very ready to take up his residence here once more, as he can no longer support the insolence of the Bavarians! Do you know that the Mannheim company are in Munich? The two leading actresses (Madame Toscani and Madame Urban) have already been hissed off the stage there, and there was such an uproar that the Elector himself leaned out of his box and said, "Sh!" When not a soul took any notice he sent someone down to put a stop to it, but when Count Seau asked certain officers to make less noise, the answer he got was that they had paid for their seats and were answerable to no one! But, what a fool I am! You must have heard all this long ago through our — * * * (sic). Now comes something important. I have a chance of making forty louis d'or here! True, I should have to stay here six weeks—or a couple of months at most. The Seiler company is here; you will know of them by repute. Herr von Dallberg is their manager. He refuses to let me go until I have composed a duo-drama for him,[1] and, as a matter of fact, it did not take me long to make up my mind, for I have always wished to write a drama of this kind. I cannot remember if I told you anything about this type of piece when I was here on the first occasion. At that time I saw such a piece performed on two occasions and was greatly delighted. Really—I was never so surprised in my life! For I had always supposed such a piece would be quite ineffective! You probably know that these things are not sung but declaimed, the music being a recitative obligato. From time to time, too, dialogue accompanies the music with the most magnificent effect. The one I saw was Benda's [2] *Medea*. He has made yet another, *Ariadne in Naxos*—and both are really excellent. You know that Benda was always my favourite

[1] See note, page 93.

[2] Georg Benda, formerly chamber-musician in the Court band of Frederick the Great, had become famous through his melodramas. Mozart's subsequent reference is to his melodramatic setting of von Gemmingen's *Semiramis*.

among the Lutheran kapellmeisters. I am so fond of these
two works that I carry them about with me. Now imagine my
joy at having to do just the sort of work I wished for! Do you
know what I think? I think most of the recitative to opera
should be treated in the same way—and should only be *sung*
occasionally when the words can be suitably expressed to music.
An *accademie des amateurs* is being set up here, as in Paris,
at which Herr Fränzel conducts with the violin; and I am just
writing them a concerto for violin and clavier. I found my dear
friend Raff still here, but he is to leave on the 8th. He has been
singing my praises here and has interested himself on my behalf.
I hope he will do the same in Munich. Do you know what that
damned scoundrel Seau has been saying here?—that my
opera buffa was hissed off the boards at Munich! Unfortunately
for him he said it in a place where I am very well known. I
am simply amazed by his impudence, for people have only
to go to Munich to learn the exact opposite! There is a whole
regiment of Bavarians here and with them is Fräulein de Pauli
—what she calls herself now I don't know. But I have been to
see her for she sent for me at once. Oh, what a difference there
is between Palatines and Bavarians! What a language! How
coarse! And their whole manner of life as well! How I long to
hear once more the familiar "*hoben,*" "*olles mit einonder,*" and
"*gestrenge Herr*"! Now fare you right well, and write to me
soon—address me by name only, for the post knows well
enough already where to find me! Listen to this and you will
see how well my name is known here — indeed no letter for
me could possibly go astray. My cousin wrote to me, putting
Franckischenhof instead of Pfälzischenhof, but mine host at
once sent on the letter to Herr Councillor Serarius, where I
formerly lodged. I am writing to her by this post to tell her to
send on the letters that are waiting for me at her address.

The thing which pleases me best in the whole of this Mannheim and Munich incident is the success of Weber's affairs.
They are now getting some 1600 florins—for the daughter
alone has 1000 and the father 400, with an additional 200 as
prompter. This is due more to Canabich than to anyone —

it was a long story. As to Count Seau—well, if you do not know about it, I will tell you soon.

Meanwhile, farewell my dearest, best of fathers I kiss your hands a thousand times, embrace my dear sister with all my heart, and am your most obedient son,

Wolfgang Amadé Mozart.

Pray, dearest father, turn this matter to account at Salzburg by speaking of it to the Archbishop with sufficient flourish to make him think I might not come after all and resolve to better my salary. For, listen, I cannot contemplate this business with any equanimity! The Archbishop can never pay me enough to compensate for the slavery of Salzburg! As I have told you I am full of joy when I think of visiting you—but full of vexation and anxiety when I see myself again at that beggarly court! The Archbishop had better not begin to play the high and mighty with me as is his custom! It is not at all impossible that I shall pull a long nose at him!—indeed it is very likely. And I know that you will share my pleasure in so doing! *Adieu*. And if you should care to send me 10 kreutzers, address your letters to Mannheim always thus:

à

Monsieur
Monsieur Heckmann Registrateur,
de la Chambre des finances de S.A.S.
Elec: Palatine
à
Mannheim.

Adieu—farewell. Take care of your precious health.

My compliments to all good friends of both sexes, particularly to our true friend Bullinger.

Leopold Mozart to his Son

19th November, 1778.

Really, I know not what I should write. I shall go mad or die of a decline. The very recollection of the numerous projects which you have formed and communicated to me since you left Salzburg

is enough to drive me demented! It has all been a matter of pro-
posals, empty words, ending in nothing whatever. And now, having
rejoiced ever since September 26th in the comforting hope of
seeing you in Salzburg on your name-day, I have had deadly
anxiety to endure, for on the 3rd you wrote from Nancy that you
were going to Strasburg next day, the 4th, while on the 9th
I heard from the brothers Frank that you had not yet arrived
there! Then I get no letter from you from Strasburg till the 14th!
And so you were making ducks and drakes of your money in
Nancy to no purpose, when you might have laid it out in hiring a
conveyance of your own and so getting more quickly to Strasburg!
Then you sat in Strasburg till the rain-storms began, although I had
previously told you to leave at once if there were nothing to be
made and not throw your money away; and although you yourself
had told me that times were poor and that you would leave at
once after the little concert you were giving on the 17th! But
people flattered you—and that is always enough for you! There
you sat, without writing me a line, and so gave me my second taste
of deadly anxiety (for we too had rain and floods here), and the
burden on our hearts was not lifted till the 10th November by a
letter written on the 2nd. Had you travelled on the 19th and 20th
after your concert on the 17th, you would have been safely in
Augsburg before the floods, we should have been out of anxiety,
and the wasted money would have been still in your purse. Then
Herr Scherz wrote that you were to leave on the 5th. Every post-
day I hoped for news from Augsburg that you had arrived, but it
was always "he is not there yet," and a letter of November 13th
actually averred that you would not come at all! And so, having
had no line from you till to-day, the 19th, I was quite naturally in
my third state of panic, for I could not possibly entertain the mad
idea that you would stay in Mannheim where there is no Court,
and consequently thought you must have been in Augsburg long
before the 10th! Nay, I believed this with the greater certainty
that I supposed you would lose no time in getting to Munich,
where, as I imagined, you would apply for work in connection with
the carnival the moment you left Nancy. Was all your prudence
in making eight louis d'or in Strasburg simply for the purpose of
idling in Mannheim? You hope to receive an appointment in
Mannheim? An appointment? What does that mean? You must
not dream of an appointment at present, either in Mannheim or

anywhere else in the world. I will not hear the word—appointment!
If the Elector were to die to-day, a whole host of musicians in
Munich and Mannheim could go about the world begging their bread!

Leopold Mozart to his Son

23rd November, 1778.

I hope you will leave *forthwith* or else I shall write to Madame
Canabich. I desire, if God will, yet a few more years of life in
which to discharge my debts. Then, if you like, you may run your
head against the wall.—But no! You have too good a heart! There
is no evil in you! You are only irresponsible and time will cure that!

60. *To his Cousin*

KAISERSHEIM, 23rd December, 1778.

Ma très chère Cousin !

In the greatest haste, with the deepest regrets and apologies
and the sternest resolve, I write to tell you that I am leaving
for Munich to-morrow. Now dearest *coz*, don't be a *tease*!—
I should have much liked to come to Augsburg, only—his
Grace the Prince-Bishop has not given *leave*, and hate him
I dare not, however I *grieve*, for to do so would be to break
Nature's and God's *law*, and she who thinks otherwise is
naught but a *wh—e*. Consequently, so it is! Perhaps I shall
make an excursion from Munich to Augsburg, but that is far
from certain. If you care to see me as much as I care to see
you, come to the noble city of Munich. See that you get there
before New Year. I will then look you up and down, will
escort you everywhere, and, if need be, criticise you. But I
am sorry for one thing—I cannot give you lodging, for I am
not to stay at an inn but to lodge with—well, whom? I
should very much like to know! Well, joking*ggg* apart, that is
the very reason why I shall need your presence so much! Perhaps you may find you have a great part to play. Come, and
come *quick*, or I shall be *sick*. I shall then be able to pay you
my respects in my own exalted person, *ihnen den Arsch pet-
schiren*, kiss your hand, *mit der hintern Büchse schiessen*, embrace you, quiz you up and down, pay every farthing I owe

you * * * and perhaps too——? Well, *adieu* my angel, my darling; I can scarce await your coming.

Voltre sincere Cousin,

W. A.

Only write to me at once, at Munich, *poste restante*—just a short note of some two dozen pages, but do not say where you will lodge in case I should find you and you me. P.S.— Dirty Dibitari, the parson at Rodempl, has *seine Köchin in Arsch geleckt* as an example to others. *Vivat—Vivat.*

61. *To his Father*

MUNICH,[1] 31st *December,* 1778.

I have this moment received your letter through our friend Beccké. Yesterday, at his lodgings, I wrote to you—such a letter as I never wrote before, for this friend said so much to me of your tender paternal love, of your care for me, of your self-effacement and discretion where my future happiness is to be furthered, that my heart melted within me! But now, from your letter of the 28th, I see only too clearly that Beccké exaggerated somewhat in what he said to me.

Frankly and plainly then:

I shall leave as soon as the opera (*Alceste*) is on the boards, whether the diligence goes the day after the opera or even the same night. Had you only spoken to Frau von Robinig I might have been able to travel home with her! Well, as you like. The opera comes on on the 11th, and on the 12th I shall leave here (if the diligence goes). It would be to my interest to remain a little longer, but I will sacrifice that for your sake and

[1] It was at Munich about this time that Mozart's love-affair with Aloysia Weber came to an end. On reaching Munich, Mozart went at once to the Webers' house, but Aloysia seemed scarcely to know him. An eyewitness has described the scene. The composer, who was in mourning for his mother, wore a red coat with black buttons according to the Parisian fashion. Seeing the change in Aloysia he at once sat down at the clavier and sang *Ich lass das Mädel gern, dass mich nicht will,* thus expressing his readiness to resign a girl who did not love him. It may have been an extempory composition or a happily selected song! The Weber family spent some part of 1779 in Salzburg, where Mozart cultivated the friendship of a younger sister, Constance. She became his pupil at the clavier. The friendship ripened to love subsequently in Vienna, and led to their marriage.

in the hope of being doubly rewarded for it in Salzburg. As to
the sonatas, your idea is not very happy! Do you think that,
not having them, I ought to leave forthwith? Or that I ought
not to show myself at Court at all? But as a man well known
here I am bound to do that! Have no fear, however.—I got
my sonatas in Kaisersheim and as soon as they are bound I
shall present them to his Electoral Highness. *Apropos* — what
do you mean by "gay dreams"? I shall not cease to dream, for
there is not a mortal on the face of this globe who does not
sometimes dream! But *gay* dreams?—peaceful dreams, sweet,
refreshing dreams! That is what they are—dreams, which were
they not dreams but realities, would make this life of mine,
with its much sadness and little gaiety, less intolerable!

This moment, being the 1st, I receive through a Salzburger
viturino a letter from you which at first reading really staggers
me! In God's name, do you really believe that I can fix the day
of my departure now?—or is it that you imagine I would
rather not come at all? I should have thought one might be
at ease now that we are so near together. When the fellow
spoke to me of his journey a great desire came upon me to go
with him, but I *cannot* do so yet. I shall not be able to present
my sonatas to the Elector before to-morrow or the next day,
and then (do what I will) I shall probably have to wait some
days for a present. I give you my word of honour that for
your sake I will make up my mind not to see the opera at all,
but to leave the very day after receiving the present; but I
confess I find it hard. Still, if a few days more or less matter
to you, so be it! Answer me soon on this point.

I am writing abominably for I am in great haste, as the
fellow is leaving at once.

The 2nd. I look forward to conversing with you when we
meet; then you will hear properly for the first time of how
my affairs stand here. Do not be vexed with or mistrustful of
Raff. He is the most honourable man in the world, though he
is certainly no lover of letter-writing. That is largely because
he is unwilling to make premature promises and yet likes to
give encouragement. For the rest, he has gone diligently to

work (as also has Canabich). And now, fare you right well. My compliments to all good friends. I embrace my dear sister with all my heart, kiss your hands, dearest father, a thousand times, and am till death,

Your most obedient son,

Wolfgang Amadé Mozart.

Leopold Mozart to his Son

11th January, 1779.

I hope you may have ordered your affairs according to the injunctions contained in my letter of the 7th, so that nothing more will hold you back. You can deliver such baggage as is not immediately necessary to you to the diligence on the 13th and travel yourself with Herr Geschwendner, who will certainly not refuse you the favour. Well, you understand me now. The Elector's present cannot hinder you as, the sonata having been presented on the 7th, everything, if one is willing to press it a little, *must* be concluded within a week. You can find no quibble here. You have also seen the opera and so have done everything you wished to do. I expect you with Herr Geschwendner without fail.

62. *To his Cousin*

SALZBURG, 10*th May*, 1779.

Dearest, best
   Most beautiful, most amiable,
      most charming,
         justly-incensed-by
            an-unworthy-male-cousin
               little *Bäss* [1]
            (or rather little violoncello)
               Give me a tune!
                  It's a good one! Thank you!

Whether I, Joannes Christosomus Sigismundus Amadeus Wolfgangus Mozartus, am in a position to calm, assuage or pacify the rage which has heightened your enchanting beauties (*visibilia* and *invisibilia*) by at least the measure of a slipper-heel is, no doubt, a question which—I am prepared to answer!

[1] Bässchen = "little cousin." The pun is thence on "little bass-viol," or "double-bass" and "violoncello."

Imprimo—besänftigen [to assuage] means a great deal—as, for instance, to carry a person *sanft* [softly] in a *Sanfte* [litter or chair]—and I am moreover very *sanft* [mild] by nature and like eating *senf* [mustard], particularly with beef, consequently all is now well with Leipzig, notwithstanding that Mr. Feigelrapée insists on *up*holding, or rather on laying *down*, that nothing will come of this kettle of fish—a thing I cannot bring myself to believe, and besides it would not we worth the trouble of bending over it! Nay, were it a whole purseful of *convensions* kreutzers, one could scrape such a thing together, have them or get them ultimately, and on that account, as I have said, I could make no other offer! That is the very lowest price, and being no hussy, I'll have no bargaining. And so—hallo! Yes, my dear little violoncello, that is the way of the world—one has the purse and another the money and he who has not both has nothing, and nothing is as much as to say very little, and little is not much, consequently is nothing even less than little, and little even more than not much, and—well, so it is, was and ever will be!

Finish the letter, seal it up and dispatch it to its destination and goal—*Feigele.*

Latus hinüber V.S.[1]

        Your most obedient and submissive servant.

P.S.—Has the Bohemian troop left? Tell me, my dearest, I beg, for Heaven's sake! Ah! They are practising now, are they not? Oh, convince me of this, I conjure you by all that's holy! The gods know I mean it sincerely. Is "door-Michael" still alive? Whisper in my ear! How has Prost been getting on with his wife? Are they not already at loggerheads? Idle questions!

         Ein zärtliche Ode !

      Dein süsses Bild o Bäschen
      schwebt stets um meinen Blik
      allein in trüben Zähren
      dass du—es selbst nicht bist
      Ich seh' es wenn der abend

---

[1] That is, "Over the other side, turn quickly" (*V*[*olta*] *S*[*ubito*]).

mir dämmert, wenn der Mond
mir glänzt seh ichs und—weine
dass du—es selbst nicht bist.
Bei jenen Thales Blumen
die ich ihr lesen will
bei jenen Myrthenzweigen
die ich ihr flechten will
beschwör ich dich, Erscheinung
auf und verwandle dich
Verwandle dich Erscheinung
und werd—o Bäschen selbst.[1]

[*A Tender Ode*
Thine image sweet, fair cousin,
Floats still before my eyes;
Yet salt tears veil it ever
For—it is not *thyself*!
I see it when the twilight
Deepens, and when the moon
Rises, I gaze, still weeping
For—it is not *thyself*!
Oh, by those valley flowers
I seek and pluck for her,
And by this crown of myrtle
I weave and wreathe for her,
I conjure thee, fair Image,
Rise, turn and change thyself!
Change thyself, bloodless Image,
Become—my darling's self!]

Finis coronat opus   S. U.
                               P. T.   Lord of Sowstail

My and all our compliments to your male and female progenitors, particularly — — — — — — — —. *Adieu*, Angel. My father gives you his avuncular blessing, my sister a thousand cousinly kisses, and your cousin Wolfgang gives you—what he dare not give. *Adieu—Adieu*—Angel!

[1] A transcript almost word for word of Klopstock's ode *Edone*, published in 1773.

Mit nächster Ordinaire werde ich mehr schreiben und zwar was recht vernünftiges und nothwendiges und bei diesem hat es sein Verbleiben bis auf weitere Ordre. Adieu — Adieu — Engel —

Fig. I Kopf

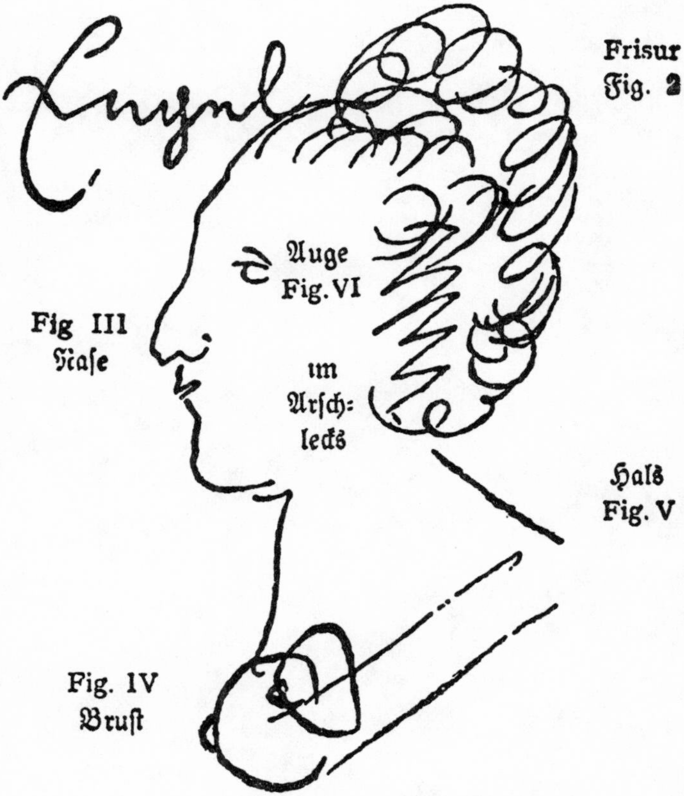

Engel
Frisur
Fig. 2
Auge
Fig. VI
Fig III
Nase
im
Arsch-
lecks
Hals
Fig. V
Fig. IV
Brust

hier ist's — — leer

63. *To his Father*

Mon trés cher Pére !

I have your letter—or rather the whole parcel. Many thanks for the money order. Up till now I have not dined once at home and consequently have had no expenses save for *friseur, balbier* and laundry—and breakfast. The aria is excellent so. There is one other alteration for which Raaf is responsible; but he is in the right about it, and even if he were not something is due to his grey hairs. He was with me yesterday. I trotted out his first aria for him and he was very much pleased with it. Well—the man is old. He can no longer make a hit with such an aria as *Fuor del mar hò un mare in seno*, etc., in Act II. and so, since he had no aria in the third act and that in the first act cannot be *cantabile* enough for him owing to the meaning of the words, he wanted to sing a pretty aria (instead of the quartet) after his last speech *O Greta fortunata ! ò me felice !* By this means, too, a useless piece drops out and the third act will now go much better. In the last scene of Act II. Idomeneo has an aria, or rather a sort of cavatina, between the choruses. It will be better to substitute for this a mere recitative with strong orchestral accompaniment, for in this scene, which will be the finest in the whole opera (on account of the action and grouping which we recently discussed with Le Grand)—there will be so much noise and confusion on the stage that an aria would cut but a poor figure at this particular juncture; and in addition there is the thunderstorm, which can scarcely be expected to stop for the sake of Herr Raaf's aria, can it? The effect of a recitative between these choruses will be incomparably better. Little Lise

145

Wendling, too, has already sung through her two arias about half a dozen times and is very well pleased. I have it from a third party that the two Wendlings have both spoken very highly of their arias. Raaf, moreover, is my best, my dearest friend!

But I shall have to teach my *molto amato castrato* del Prato the whole opera. He has no notion how to approach an aria worthy of the name and his voice is very unequal! He is only engaged for a year, and as soon as the year ends, which will be in September next, Count Seau will get another. That might be an opportunity for Ceccarelli [1]—*serieusement.*

I had almost forgotten my best news. Last Sunday, after divine service, Count Seau presented me *en passant* to his Electoral Highness the Elector, who was very gracious to me and said, "I am glad to see you here again." When I replied that I would do my best to retain his Highness's esteem he clapped me on the back and cried, "Oh, I have not the least doubt we shall do very well!"—*à Piano piano, si và lontano.*—

Pray do not forget to answer on all points touching the opera, as, for instance, that in my previous letter about a translator. I am to make a contract. The deuce! Again I cannot write all I want to write! Raaf has just been to see me. He sends you his regards, as also the whole of the Canabich and Wendling households, and Ramm, too. And now farewell. I kiss your hand a thousand times. The post is just going. Adieu. I embrace my sister,

I am for ever,

Your most obedient son,

Wolf. Am. Mozart.

My sister must not be idle, but practise well, for her playing is already a pleasure.

My *logis* is at Mr. Fiat's in the Burggasse, but there is no need to put the address as I and my dwelling-place are known at the post.

Adieu.

Eck and his son and Beecké send their compliments.

[1] A singer in the service of the Archbishop of Salzburg.

Leopold Mozart to his Son

30*th November*, 1780.

You say that I must not write you any sad news. I have written you none except to say that your sister was ill and *that* I had to tell you. For the rest, deal frankly and as far as I am concerned you may be without anxiety for the present. But should you fall sick (which God forbid!) do not conceal it from me so that I can come at once and take care of you.

64. *To his Father*

MUNICH, *ce* 1 *Decembre*, 1780.

Mon trés cher Pére!

The rehearsal [1] has gone remarkably well. There were only six violins in all — but the requisite wind-instruments. No listeners were admitted except Seau's sister and young Count Sensheim. We are to have another rehearsal to-day week, when we shall have twelve violins—double the present number —for the first act, and the second act will also be rehearsed (as the first on the previous occasion). I cannot tell you how amazed and delighted everyone was. But I did not expect anything else, and I assure you I went to this rehearsal with as easy a mind as if I were going to a dinner-party. Count Sensheim said to me, "I assure you that though I expected much of you I really did not expect this!" The Canabich household and all who frequent it are truly friendly to me. On reaching home with Canabich after the rehearsal (for we still had much to talk over with the Count) I was met at the door by Madame Canabich who embraced me, delighted that the rehearsal had gone so well. And then Ramm and Lang came in beside themselves with joy! The good lady—a true friend of mine—had spent the time alone at home with her invalid daughter Rose, absorbed in a thousand anxieties on my behalf. Ramm said to me—if you knew him you would call him a true German, his face so plainly expresses what he thinks— he said, "I must confess that I have never yet heard music which made so much impression on me, and I assure you I

---

[1] Of *Idomeneo*.

thought fifty times of your father and of his delight when he hears this opera."

But enough of this. My cold became somewhat worse at the rehearsal. When fame and honour are at stake one grows heated, however cold-blooded one may be at first. I have used all your prescriptions, but it is a slow business and very inconvenient to me at the moment, for writing prolongs the catarrh and yet I must write. I have begun to-day to take fig-juice and a little oil of almonds and notice some alleviation already. I have kept within doors again, another two days.

Yesterday forenoon Mr. Raff called on me again to hear the aria in the second act. The man is as much enamoured of his aria as a young ardent lover of his fair one, for he sings it at night before falling asleep and on waking in the morning! As I heard first from a reliable source and now from his own lips, he said to Herr von Vierreck, the principal equerry, and to Herr von Castel, "Hitherto I have always had to adjust my parts, both in recitatives and arias, but now everything remains as it was written—there is not a note which does not suit me," etc. *En fin!* he is happy as a king. It is true he wanted to alter the new aria a little with me. He also objects to the *era* and then—if we could have here a peaceful quiet aria — even if it were only a part—so much the better.

In the *Achile in Sciro* there is such an air—

> *Or che mio figlio Sei*
> *o fido il destin nemico*
> *sento degl'anni miei*
> *il Peso à lagierir.*[1]

In the meantime I suppose Herr Sieger has been to see you and given you a letter of mine? Please send the *sordini* [mutes] soon for the horns and trumpets.

Many thanks to my sister for the list of comedies she sent me—and the comedy. *Rache für Rache* [*Revenge for Revenge*] is a strange thing. It has been given here often with great success—once quite recently, but I did not see it. My most

---

[1] Alleggerir.

humble regards to Fräulein Therese von Barisani.[1] If I had a brother I would beg of him to kiss her hand with the deepest respect—but since I have a sister I can do much better, for I beg her to embrace her most warmly in my name!

Pray convey my regards to Fräulein Babette von Mölk, and as she knows my many activities she will forgive me, I am sure, for not having yet written to her as I promised.

My heartiest good wishes for your name-day! Well, *adieu.* I kiss your hand a thousand times, embrace my sister with all my heart, and am for ever your

P.S.—Pray send me the   most obedient son, recipe for cooking sago—for a good friend.   Wolfgang Amadé Mozart.

A thousand compliments to all—all. *Apropos.* Do write to Canabich some time. He has deserved it and it will please him uncommonly. What does it matter, after all, if he does not answer! It is not intentional. He is the same with everyone— one only has to know him.

Leopold Mozart to his Son

4th December, 1780.

We are delighted to hear that the rehearsal went so well. I have no sort of doubts or anxieties about your work if only it is well produced—that is, if you have capable performers. And you have them. So I am not anxious. But your music will always lose with a mediocre orchestra, for it is composed with so much discernment for the various instruments, and not just all on one level like most Italian music.

Leopold Mozart to his Son

11th December, 1780.

I recommend you to think when at work not only of the musical but also of the unmusical public. You know that for ten true connoisseurs there are a hundred ignoramuses! Do not neglect the so-called popular, which tickles long ears.

[1] A Dr. Sigismund Barisani was a Viennese physician of standing, a musical amateur, and Mozart's doctor. He died in the autumn of 1787, to Mozart's grief, and, perhaps, to the subsequent detriment of his health.

Leopold Mozart to his Son

I was told so by Herr Fiala,[1] who came to see me and showed me a letter from Herr Becke[2] full of praise of your music in the first act. He wrote that this music brought tears of joy and pleasure to his eyes when he heard it, that everyone asserted it was the most beautiful music they had ever heard, that it was all new and strange, etc., that you were now in course of rehearsing the second act, that he would write to me himself later and that I must forgive him for not having written as he had been rather unwell. Well, thank God, all goes right! I cannot think, knowing your work, that these are empty compliments; for I am convinced that your composition must have its effect if only it is adequately performed.

65. *To his Father*

Mon trés cher Pére !

I have safely received the last aria for Raff (who sends his regards to you), the two trumpet mutes, your letter of the 15th, and the pair of under-hose. The last rehearsal went as well as the first. The orchestra and audience discovered to their delight that the second act has actually succeeded in being more expressive and original even than the first. Next Saturday both acts are to be rehearsed again. But the rehearsal is to be held in a big room at Court, a thing long needed, for there is not nearly room enough at Count Seau's. The Elector is to listen (incognito) in a neighbouring room. "We must rehearse, then, for our very lives!" said Canabich to me— though he was drenched with sweat at our last rehearsal. *Apropos*, speaking of sweating, it is my opinion that both means must have worked together in that same comedy—did my sister deliver the compliment?—

Herr Esser also heard my rehearsal—he was to have dined with Canabich on Sunday, but took occasion to go to Augs-

---

[1] One of the most celebrated oboe-players of the eighteenth century He entered the service of the Archbishop of Salzburg.

[2] Joint music-director and Groom-of-the-Bedchamber to the Prince von Oettingen-Wallerstein. Mozart called him "the father of all pianoforte-players" (Edward Holmes).

burg—and off he went! *Bon voiage!*—He came to take leave of me, so they tell me, but I was not at home; I was calling on the Countess Baumgarten!

Herr Director Canabich, whose name-day it is to-day and who was with me this moment, sends you his very kindest regards, scolded me for not finishing my letter and left at once so that I might do so.

As to Madame Duschek—it is frankly impossible at the moment—but it will be a pleasure when the opera is finished. Meantime pray send her my compliments. As to the debt, we shall settle that at once when she comes back to Salzburg. I should be pleased indeed if I could have a few *cavallirs* like old Czernin—that would be a little help yearly—but not less than 100 florins a year. I should not mind what sort of music it was then.

You are now, I hope, and thank God for it, quite well again? Indeed, if one has oneself rubbed by such an one as Therese Barisani, it cannot well be otherwise! You will see by my letter that I am well — and happy! One *is* glad to be rid at last of so great and laborious a piece of work, glad too, of the honour and glory it brings. And I am almost rid of it, for only three arias, the last chorus of Act III. and the overture are still wanting, and then—*adieu partie!* As to those arias for Heckmann which have no words as yet, there are two only which you do not know. The rest of mine comprise one from *Ascanio in Alba,*[1] or rather two—that for Mme. Duscheck, which you can send me without the words as I have them here and can write them in myself. There is also one by Anfossi and one by Salieri with oboe solo—both Madame Haydn's—I forgot to copy the words before as I did not think I should have to leave so hastily—I do not know them by heart.

Apropos—to come to the most important point of all—for I must hurry. I hope to receive the first act at least, with the whole of the translation, by the next diligence. The scene between father and son in Act I. and the first scene in Act II. between Idomeneo and Arbace are both too long. They would certainly prove tedious, particularly as both act badly in the

---

[1] Mozart's *Ascanio in Alba*. Dramatic Serenata, Milan, 1771.

first scene and one of them in the second, while the whole contents of both amount to no more than a narrative of what the audience has already witnessed with its own eyes. These scenes were printed as they stand. But I wish Herr Abbate would show me how they may be shortened—as drastically as possible, too—for otherwise I must do it myself; they cannot remain as they are—when set to music I mean, of course.

I have just received your letter which, my sister having begun it, is of course without a date! A thousand compliments to my little Therese. I can well believe that Katie would like to come to Munich—if she is allowed to take my place at table here (apart from the journey)—*eh bien*, I shall be able to manage! She can share a room with my sister. *Apropos*. Pray let me know at least a week in advance when you are to arrive, so that I can have my stove moved into the other [room]. *Adieu*. [What] beautiful handwriting! [I kiss your hand] a thousand times, [embrace] my sister heartily, and am ever your

Most obedient son,

Wolf. Amdé. Mzt.

Mes compliments à tous nos amis et amies. A longer and better letter next time!

Leopold Mozart to his Son

25th December, 1780.

But you should do your best to keep the whole orchestra in good humour; flatter them and cultivate all-round attachment to yourself by judicious praise! For I know your style of composition—it requires unusually close application from the players of *every* type of instrument, and to keep the whole orchestra at such a level of industry and alertness for three hours at a stretch is no laughing matter. Everyone, even the worst of viola players, may be deeply stirred by personal praise and becomes by so much the more zealous and attentive, while a little courtesy of that kind costs you no more than a word or two. However—you know all this yourself, and I merely mention it because rehearsals afford few opportunities of the kind and so one is likely to forget it till the opera is staged, when one first really notices any want of cordiality and zeal in the members of the orchestra.

FIRST YEARS IN VIENNA, AND *FIGARO* (1781-5)

66. *To his Father*

VIENNE, *ce* 17 *de mars*, 1781.

Mon trés cher amy!

Yesterday, being the 16th, I arrived here safely, thank God, all by myself in a post-chaise—I almost forget the hour, but it was about nine o'clock in the morning. I travelled by the diligence as far as Unter-Haag, but by that time I was so sore in the seat and surrounding parts that I could endure it no longer! I intended to proceed by the *ordinaire*, but a certain Herr Escherich, a government official, had also had enough of the diligence and gave me his company as far as Kemmelbach. In Kemmelbach I proposed to wait for the *ordinaire*, but the post-master assured me that he could not possibly allow me to travel by it, as there was no head post-office in that place. Accordingly I was forced to go *per extra poste*. On Thursday the 15th I arrived in Pölten dog-tired, slept till two in the morning and then came straight on to Vienna.—Where do you think I am writing this? In the Messmers' garden in the Landstrasse! The old lady is not at home, but the erstwhile Fräulein Franzl, now Frau von Bosch, is here and desires me to send you and my sister very many kind regards. Do you know that, 'pon my honour, I should hardly have known her, she has grown so stout! She has three children, two young ladies and a young gentleman. The elder girl is called Nannerl and is four years old, though one would swear she was six. The boy is three, but one would swear he was seven, and one would take the nine months old baby for two at least, so strong and well grown are they all! Now about the Archbishop. I have a delightful apartment in the same house in which the Archbishop lodges!—Brunetti and Ceccarelli lodge elsewhere. *Che distinzione!* My neighbour is a certain Herr von Kleinmayer, who loaded me with civilities on my arrival and is, indeed, a

charming man. We dine about midday, unfortunately somewhat too early for me. At our table sit down the two valets,
body (and soul) servants, the Controller, Herr Zetti, the con
fectioner, two cooks, Ceccarelli, Brunetti and—my insignificant
self! N.B.—The two valets sit at the head of the table, but I
have at least the honour of sitting above the cooks! Well, I
could fancy myself in Salzburg! There is much coarse joking
at table, but none with me, for I speak hardly at all and, when
necessary, with the greatest gravity. When I have finished my
own dinner I go my way. There is no evening meal, but each
person receives three ducats—which will go a long way! My
Lord Archbishop is most gracious, glorifies himself through his
dependants, robs them of their service and pays them nothing
for it! We had music yesterday at four o'clock, and there were
present at least twenty persons of the highest *noblesse*. Ceccarelli has already had to sing at Balfi's. To-day we are to go
to Prince Gallizin's; he was at the party yesterday. I shall now
wait to see whether I get anything. If not I shall go to the
Archbishop and tell him quite frankly that if he will not allow
me to earn anything he must pay me, for I will not continue
to live at my own expense. I must write no more, for I mean
to hand this letter to the post in passing as I have to go
straight on to Prince Gallizin's. I kiss your hand a thousand
times, embrace my sister warmly, and am ever your

Most obedient son,
Wolfgang Amadé Mozart.

P.S.—Rossi, the comedy singer, is here. I have been at the
Fischers'. I cannot describe how glad they were to see me.
The whole household sends its compliments. I hear there are
concerts in Salzburg? Think what I am losing! *Adieu*. My
address is The German House, Singerstrasse.

67. *To his Father*

VIENNA, *24th March*, 1781.

Mon trés cher Pére !

I have safely received your letter of the 20th of this month
and read therein with pleasure of the safe arrival and sound

health of you both. You must put it down to my bad ink and pen if you have to spell out this letter rather than read it. *Basta !* It must, nevertheless, be written, and this time it is the gentleman who mends my pens (Herr von Lirzer) who has ordered me to do so! I can only describe this man (for you will probably get to know him yourself) as being, to the best of my belief, a Salzburger. I do not think I ever saw him in my life except once at Robinig's at the so-called "Eleven o'clock music." He called on me at once, however, and seems to me to be a very pleasant and (because he cuts my pens for me) a very civil person. I take him to be a secretary. Another who surprised me with a visit was Gilovsky, Katie's brother. Why "surprised"? Well, because I had entirely forgotten that he was in Vienna. What an effect a strange place can have on a man! He will no doubt prove a most excellent and honest man, both within and without his profession. Meantime you will have received the letters from the Emperor and Prince Kaunïtz. As to what you write me of the Archbishop, it is perfectly true that his vanity is tickled by possessing my person—but what use is all this to me? One cannot live on it! And I assure you he acts as a screen to keep me from the notice of others! With what "distinction" am I treated? Herr von Kleinmayer and Beneckè have a special table with the illustrious Count Arco; it would be some "distinction" if I sat at that table. But there is none in sitting with these valets, who, beside taking the head of the table, light the candles, open the doors and have to wait in ante-rooms! And with the cooks, too! Moreover, when we are called upon to attend a concert anywhere, Herr Angelbauer has to stand waiting till the Salzburg gentlemen come, when he sends a lackey to tell them they may enter. So Brunetti himself told me in conversation. I thought to myself, "Just wait till I come!" Accordingly, when recently we were to go to Prince Gallizin's, Brunetti said to me in his courteous manner, "*Tu, bisogna che sei qui sta sera alle sette, per andare insieme dal Prencipe gallizin. L'Angelbauer ci condurrà.*" Hò risposto "*Va bene—ma—se in caso mai non fossi qui alle sette in punto, ci andate pure, non*

serve aspettarmi—sò ben dovè stà, e ci verrò sicuro." [1] I therefore
took care to go alone, for I am ashamed to go anywhere with
them. When I reached the top of the stairs, there stood Herr
Angelbauer to tell the servants to lead me in. I took no notice
of either the valet or the footman, but went straight through
the apartments into the music-room, for all the doors stood
open, walked to the Prince at once, paid him my respects,
and stood there talking with him. I had quite forgotten about
my Seccarelli and Brunetti for they were not at all visible,
but stood leaning against the wall right behind the orchestra,
whence they did not venture a step into the open! If a gentleman or a lady speaks to Ceccarelli he invariably titters, while
if anyone speaks to Brunetti he flushes up, and makes the
driest answers. Oh, I could fill sheets if I were to describe all
the scenes which have taken place between the Archbishop
and Ceccarelli and Brunetti since I came, and before! I only
wonder that Brunetti is not ashamed of himself—but I am
ashamed for him. And yet how the fellow hates it here! It is
all far too grand for him. I think he spends his happiest hours
at table. To-day Prince Gallizin sent to ask Ceccarelli to sing.
Next time it will probably be my turn. This evening I am to
go with Herr von Kleinmayer to Counsellor Braun's, a good
friend of his and a very great amateur of the clavier, so everyone
tells me. I have already dined twice with the Countess Thun [2]
and go there almost every day. The Countess is the most charming and amiable lady I have ever met and I am in high esteem
with her. Her husband is still the same eccentric yet right-
minded and upright gentleman. I have also dined with Count
Cobenzl at the instigation of his aunt, the Countess von Rumbeck, a sister of the Cobenzl in the *Pagerie* who was at one time
in Salzburg with her husband. My principal object here is

[1] "Take care that you are here this evening at seven, that we may go
together to Prince Gallizin's. L'Angelbauer will take you there." "Very
well," replied I, "but—if I should not be there precisely at seven, you go on
nevertheless—it is no use waiting for me. I know quite well where he lives;
I shall certainly find my way there."
[2] The Countess Thun had discovered Haydn living in poverty and had
become his pupil and patroness. She was one of the chief favourites of the
Emperor Joseph.

to introduce myself favourably to the Emperor's[1] notice, for I am absolutely determined that he shall get to know me. I should like to run through my opera to him and then play some good fugues, for those are what he likes. Oh, had I but known that I should be in Vienna in Lent I should have written a little oratorio and performed it at the theatre for my benefit, as is the custom here! It would have been easy for me to write it beforehand, for I know all the voices. How gladly would I give a public concert, as is usually done here, but—I know I should never get permission to do so, for listen to this! You know that there is here a society which gives concerts for the benefit of the widows of musicians, at which everyone who has any inkling of music plays *gratis*. The orchestra is 180 strong, and no virtuoso with the least spark of charity refuses to play when asked by the society, for to do so wins him favour with both Emperor and public. Starzer was commissioned to invite me, and I agreed at once, saying, however, that I must first get the consent of my Prince, which I had no doubt of obtaining as it was for a good work, a religious work of a kind, and gratuitous. Yet he refused me permission! All the nobility here took it very ill of him. My sole regret is on this account. I should have played no concerto, but (the Emperor being present in the proscenium box), I should have preluded quite alone, and played a fugue and the *Je suis Lindor* variations on the Countess Thun's beautiful Stein *pianoforte* which she was to have lent me. Wherever I have played these things publicly I have always received great applause, for they serve as admirable foils to each other, and each person in the audience has something to his taste. But *pazienza!*

I think two thousand times better of Fiala for refusing to play for less than a ducat. Has not my sister been asked to play yet? She, I hope, will demand two, for I should not like it

[1] The Emperor Joseph (born 1741, reigned 1780–90), succeeded to the Imperial throne on the death of his mother, the Empress Maria Theresa. He was an enlightened ruler, but cold and ungenerous in personal relations. Mrs. Piozzi describes him as "a stranger on principle to the joys of confidence and friendship," though his manner was often easy and good-natured. He won Mozart's loyalty and even affection by his manner and traded upon it, but never paid him adequately. See note 1, page 232.

at all if we, who are so different in every way from the ordinary
Court musician, were not different in this matter also! They
can take it or leave it, but if they want her, let them pay, in
Heaven's name!

I am to go to see Madame Rosa to-day, and you may rest
assured you will be satisfied with your envoy's subtlety! I will
handle the matter as tactfully as the wise man when they tolled
the bell for his wife's mother!

Herr von Zetti has offered to convey my letter. He will
dispatch it with the parcel.

I do not need the two quartets nor the Baumgarten aria.

Apropos. What of the Elector's present? Has anything
been sent yet? Did you see Mme. Baumgarten before leaving?

Pray give my regards to all good friends of both sexes,
particularly to Katherl, to Schachter and Fiala. Herr von
Kleinmayer, Zetti, Ceccarelli, Brunetti, the Controller, the
two valets, Leitgeb and Ramm, who leaves on Sunday, send
their compliments to all. *Apropos*, Peter Vogti is here. Now
fare you well. I kiss your hands a thousand times, embrace
my sister warmly and am ever

Your most obedient son,

Wolfg. Amadé Mozart.

Rossi the comedian is also here.

March 28th. I did not conclude the letter because Herr
von Kleinmayer came and carried me in his coach to a concert
at Baron Braun's. Accordingly I can now add that the Archbishop has given me permission to play at the Widows' Concert,
for Starzer went to Gallizin's concert, and he and the whole
noblesse so plagued the Archbishop that he gave the permission. I am so glad. Since I came here I have dined at home
but four times. The hour is too early for me—and the company
too ill. Only when the weather is very bad, as to-day *par
exemple*, I remain at home.

Write and tell me the news of Salzburg, for I have been
exhaustively cross-examined about it. These gentlemen are
more eager for Salzburg gossip than I am.

Madame Mara [1] is here and gave a concert in the theatre last Tuesday. Her husband dared not show himself, or the orchestra would have refused to accompany; for he published in the newspapers that there was not a man in Vienna fit to accompany him. *Adieu.* Herr von Moll waited on me yesterday, and I am to breakfast with him to-morrow or the day after, taking my opera with me. He sends his regards to you both. As soon as the weather improves I shall go to see Herr von Auerhammer and his plump mademoiselle daughter—by which you may observe that I have received your last of the 24th. Old Prince Colloredo gave us each five ducats for a concert at his house. The Countess Rumbeck is my pupil. Herr von Mesmer (inspector of the *Normal* College), with his wife and son, send their compliments. His son plays *magnifique,* only he is idle because he fancies he is competent enough already. He has also much talent for composition, but is too indolent to pursue it, which vexes his father. *Adieu.*

68. *To his Father*

Vienne, *ce* 4 *avril,* 1781.

Mon très cher Père !

My letter to-day must be short, but Brunetti goes home on Sunday and then I shall be able to write more.

You want to know how things are going with us in Vienna —or rather with me, more particularly, I hope, for I do not class myself with the other two! I told you in a recent letter that the Archbishop stands very much in my way here. I am now the worse through him by one hundred ducats at least, for I could make that sum without a doubt by a concert in the theatre—the ladies themselves having offered to dispose of tickets. I may say that I was very well pleased with the Viennese public yesterday. I played at the Widows' Concert at the Kärtnerthor Theatre and had to begin all over again, so interminable was the clapping. Then how much do you suppose I should make if I gave a concert of my own, now that

---

[1] Mara, Gertrude (*née* Schmeling, 1749–1833), a famous singer who in 1773 married Johann Mara, 'cellist and composer.

the public has got to know me? But this arch-clown of ours
will not permit it—would rather see his dependants worse off
than better! Still, he will not altogether succeed in bringing
this about in my case, for with two pupils I am better off here
than in Salzburg. I can dispense with his board and lodging.
Now listen to this! At table to-day Brunetti told me that
Arco had said he had been instructed by the Archbishop to
tell us that we were to receive money for our coach fares and
to be off before Sunday! However, anyone who wished to
remain (O wisdom!) might remain, but must live at his own
charges, for he would no longer get either board or lodging
from the Archbishop! Brunetti's mouth watered at the idea,
for *il ne demande pas mieux*. Ceccarelli would like to stay, too,
but he is not so well known here and does not understand
social usages as I do. He will try to get something, but if he
does not succeed go he must, in God's name, for there is not
a table nor a bed in all Vienna which he can have without
payment. When they asked me what I intended to do, I replied,
"I shall ignore the matter till the day of leaving, for I will
not believe it until Count Arco tells me himself—and then I
shall have my answer ready for him." Benecke was present and
smirked. Oh, how I shall enjoy pulling a long nose at the
Archbishop—with extreme *politesse*, of course! For he cannot
get rid of me. Enough. In my next letter I shall be able to tell
you more. Be assured that if my status here is not really good
and if I do not see my advantage plainly I shall certainly not
stay. But if I do see my advantage, why should I not profit
by it? Meanwhile you are drawing two salaries and have not
me to keep. If I stay here I can promise you that I shall soon
be able to send money home. I am speaking seriously, and if
things turn out otherwise than as I hope I shall come back.
Well, *adieu*. You shall have the full story in my next. I kiss
your hand a thousand times, embrace my sister warmly, and
hope she has replied to Mademoiselle Hepp.

   Adieu. Ever

Your most obedient son,

Wolfg. Amadé Mozart.

My compliments to all—all—all.

P.S.—I assure you this is a magnificent place, the best place in the world for my profession. Everyone will tell you the same. Moreover, I like being here and consequently am making all the profit out of it that I can. I promise you that my one object is to make as much money as possible, for after health, etc., it is the thing most worth having. Think no more of my follies. I have long repented of them from the bottom of my heart. Misfortunes teach one sense, and my head is now full of quite other thoughts. *Adieu*. A full account in my next.

Adieu.

69. *To his Father*

VIENNE, *ce 9 de mai*, 1781.

Mon trés cher Pére !

I am still seething with bitter resentment which you, my best and dearest father, will no doubt share, for my patience, long tried, has at last given out! I am no longer so unfortunate as to be in Salzburg service—to-day was a happy day for me! Listen!

Twice already this—I do not know what to call him!—has given me violent abuse and impertinence to my face—insults which, to spare you, I did not tell you of and which I should have revenged upon the spot if I had not had you, my dearest father, ever before my eyes. He called me knave and slovenly rascal, told me to take myself off and I—endured it all—felt that not only my honour but yours too was involved, and yet held my peace, for such was your wish. But now listen! A week ago a footman appeared unexpectedly and told me I must begone that instant. The others had all been warned of the day, but not I. So I threw everything into my trunks with all speed, and Madame Weber was good enough to open her doors to me. I have a charming room in her house, and am among helpful people who see that I have ready to hand all the things which one sometimes needs in a hurry (and cannot have when living alone). I arranged to leave by the diligence on Wednesday (that is, to-day, the 9th), but as I could not collect the money still due to me within that time, I postponed my journey till Saturday. When I presented myself this morning, the valet told me the Archbishop wished to place a packet in my charge to be carried with me. I asked if it were urgent. They told me, "Yes, it is of the greatest importance." "Then," said I, "I am very sorry I cannot have the privilege of serving his Grace, for (on account of aforementioned reasons) I do not leave before Saturday. I am not in the household. I live at my own expense and consequently, as is natural, I cannot travel till I have funds to enable me to do so—no one has the right to ask me to ruin myself." Kleinmayer, Moll, Benecke and the two valets all said I was quite in the right of it. Well, when I came into the presence—N.B. I must tell you first that it had occurred to me to make excuse that the diligence was already full—a reason which would have greater weight with him than the true one—well, as I came into the presence his first words were, "Well, when are you going, fellow?" I "I had intended to go to-night, but all the places were taken." Then he began without a pause for breath—I was the most slovenly fellow he knew—no one served him so ill as I—I had better leave to-day or he would write home and have my salary stopped. It was impossible to get a word in edgeways, for he raged on like a conflagration. I listened to it all passively. He lied to my face that my salary was 500 florins, called me a scoundrel, a lousy rascal, a vagabond—oh, I cannot write it all down! At length, my blood boiling, I could no longer keep silence, and said, "Then is your Grace dissatisfied with me?" "What! you would threaten me, would you? Oh, you idiot! There is the door! I will have no more to do with such a wretch, do you hear?" At last I got in, "Nor I with you!" "Well, go!" And I, in going, said, "This is final. To-morrow you shall have my resignation in writing." Tell me now, dearest father, did I not say the word too late rather than too soon?—For my honour, as you know, is above everything precious to me and I know that it is so to you also!

Do not be in the least anxious about me. I am so secure of my position here that I would have resigned even without an occasion, and now that I have the occasion—and that thrice over—I cannot make a virtue of it. *Au contraire* I had twice played the coward and I could not do so a third time.

I shall give no concert as long as the Archbishop remains here. You are altogether mistaken if you suppose that I shall have got myself into ill-odour with the nobility and the Emperor, for the Archbishop is hated here and most of all by the Emperor. In fact he is enraged just because the Emperor did not invite him to Luxemburg! Next post I shall send you a little money to convince you that I am not starving here. For the rest, pray be easy, for my good luck is just beginning and I hope my good luck may also be yours. Write and tell me privately that you are glad about it (and, indeed, well you may be)—but in public give me a thorough scolding so that no one can throw the blame on you! If, however, the Archbishop should, notwithstanding, offer you the slightest impertinence in this matter, come at once with my sister to Vienna. There is enough for us all three to live upon, that I assure you on my honour. Still, I would prefer it if you could hold out one more year. Do not address any more letters to the German House. I will hear no more of Salzburg—I hate the Archbishop to madness!

Adieu. I kiss your hand a thousand times, embrace my sister with all my heart, and am ever your most obedient son,

W. A. Mozart.

Write to me "To be delivered at the *Peter im Aug-gottes,* 2nd story." Let me hear soon that you are content, for that is the only thing wanting to my present happiness. *Adieu.*

70. *To his Father*

VIENNE, *ce* 12 *de May,* 1781.

Mon très cher Père!

My last letter will have informed you that I have asked the Archbishop for my discharge—he himself having bid me go, for at two previous audiences he said to me, "You can take yourself off if you will not serve me properly!" True, he will

deny it, but it is nevertheless as true as that God is in heaven.
What wonder then if, after being roused to fury with "knave,"
"scoundrel," "rascal," "slovenly rogue," and such like decorous
expressions in the mouth of a prince, I at last took "Be off
with you!" literally? On the following day I gave Count Arco
a petition for presentation to his Highness, at the same time
returning the money for my travelling expenses, which consisted of 15 florins, 40 kreutzers for the diligence and two ducats
for other travelling needs. He would accept neither, and
assured me I could not resign without my father's consent.
"That is your duty," said he. I told him at once that I knew
my duty to my father as well as he, and perhaps better, and
that I should be sorry if I had to learn it first from him.
"Very well, then," said he, "if he is satisfied you may ask for
your discharge, and if not, you can ask for it all the same."
A pretty distinction! The Archbishop's many edifying remarks
to me during my three audiences, particularly the last, and
subsequent communications from this wonderful man of God,
have had such an excellent effect upon my health that I was
obliged to leave the opera in the middle of the first act and lie
down at home. For I was quite feverish, trembled in every
limb and reeled like a drunkard in the street. I also spent the
whole of the following day, yesterday, in the house, the morning
in bed, drinking tamarind water.

The Count has also had the kindness to send his father a
very laudatory account of me which you have probably had
to swallow by now! It probably contained a certain number
of fabulous passages, but if one is writing a comedy and hopes
to obtain applause, one must exaggerate a little and not stick
too closely to the true facts. Also you must remember this
gentleman's active benevolence in his favour.

I will now do no more than set down leisurely (for I value
my health and my life and am sorry enough when circumstances
force me to jeopardise them), the chief accusation brought
against me in respect of my service. I had no sort of idea that
I was supposed to be a valet in attendance, and that proved
fatal to me. I ought to have idled away a couple of hours each

morning in the ante-chamber. Indeed, I had often been told I ought to present myself, but I could never recollect that this was part of my duty, and merely came punctually whenever the Archbishop sent for me.

I will confide to you my inflexible determination in this affair very briefly, though I have no objection to the whole world knowing of it. Should I be offered a salary of 2000 florins by the Archbishop of Salzburg and a mere 1000 florins by someone else, I would—take the second offer; for in place of the 1000 florins I should have health and peace of mind! I trust, therefore, by all the love you have ever lavished upon me so richly from childhood and for which I can never be sufficiently thankful (though I can show it least of all in Salzburg), that if you wish to see your son well and happy you will say nothing to me at all of the affair, but let it be buried in the deepest oblivion; for one word of it would be enough to fill me with renewed bitterness and—admit it—to embitter even you yourself!

Now fare you well, and be glad that you have not a coward for a son. I kiss your hands a thousand times, embrace my dear sister with all my heart, and am ever

Your most obedient son,

Wolfgang Amadé Mozart.

71. *To his Father*

Vienne, *ce* 16 *de may*, 1781.

Mon trés cher Pére !

I could hardly have supposed otherwise than that you would, in the heat of the moment, write just such a letter as I have just now been constrained to read, for at the time the surprise was too great for you, especially as you were actually expecting my arrival![1] Now, however, you have reflected more thoroughly on the matter and, as a man of honour, are more acutely conscious of the insult; you realise, too, that this is not something which is about to happen, but which has happened already. It is necessarily harder to break away in

---

[1] No letters from Leopold Mozart to his son are extant of later date than January 1781.

Salzburg itself. There *he* is wholly master, whereas here he is another's servant, just as I am his. Moreover, be assured I know you and I know my own affection for you! The Archbishop would have given me another few hundred gulden, perhaps, and I—I should have submitted—and there would have been the old story all to do again! Believe me, my dearest father, it takes all the manliness I possess to write to you as common sense bids me write. God knows how hard I find it to leave you, but if I had to beg my bread I would never serve such a lord again; for it is a thing I shall never forget all my life long. And—I beg you, I beg you by everything sacred, strengthen me in this resolution rather than seek to dissuade me from it! You would only stultify me—for my heart is set on winning fame and money for myself, and I have good grounds for hoping that I can be more helpful to you in Vienna than in Salzburg. The way to Prague is less firmly closed against me here than if I were in Salzburg. As to what you write about the Webers, I can assure you that it is not so. I was a fool, it is true, about Madame Lang,[1] but of what is one not capable when one is in love? But I did love her truly, and I feel that even now she is not a matter of indifference to me. Therefore it is fortunate for me that her husband is a jealous fool and lets her go nowhere, so that I seldom have an opportunity of seeing her. I assure you that old Madame Weber is a very obliging woman and that, having so little time at my disposal, I really cannot show her courtesy enough in return for her good offices. I long to receive a letter from you, dearest, best of fathers! Cheer your son, for it is only the thought of displeasing you that can render him unhappy in the midst of his rising fortunes. *Adieu.* A thousand farewells. I kiss your hand a thousand times, and am ever

Your most obedient son,

W. A. Mzt.

[1] Aloysia Weber married Lang, a tragedian. The marriage was unhappy. "Conversing on the subject of her youthful rejection of Mozart some years since at Vienna with a friend of the author's, Mme. Lang observed that she knew nothing of the greatness of his genius—she saw him only as a *little man*" (Edward Holmes).

P.S.—Should you incline to believe that mere hatred of Salzburg and irrational affection for Vienna keep me here, pray take steps to inform yourself better. Herr von Strack,[1] a good friend of mine, will, as a man of honour, write you the whole truth of the matter.

72. To his Father

VIENNE, ce 19 de may, 1781.

Mon trés cher Pére !

I do not know how to begin this letter, my dearest father, for I cannot recover from my astonishment, and never shall be able to do so if you continue to think and to write as you do! I must confess that there is not a single trait in your letter by which I could have recognised my father! *A* father indeed, but not that best, that dearest of fathers, ever careful for his own honour and for that of his children—in a word *my* father! Still, that was all no more than a bad dream. You are awake now and need no answer from me to your points to *more* than convince you that—now more than ever—I can never abandon my resolve. Yet in certain passages my honour and my character are so rudely assailed that I must after all answer upon these points! You say you can never think it right that I tendered my resignation in Vienna? I should have thought that, if one desired to do this (although at one time I did not wish to, or I should have done so on the first occasion), it would be most rational to do it in a place where one had a good standing and the finest prospects in the world. That it was not the right thing in the eyes of the Archbishop I can well believe! But you cannot call it otherwise than right from my point of view. You say that the only way to save my honour is to abandon my resolve? How can you conceive such a contradiction? You surely did not consider when you wrote this that I should show myself the most abject fellow in the world by

---

[1] Von Strak was one of the principal gentlemen-in-waiting to the Emperor. See Letter No. 84. Later (1787), when consulted by the Emperor as to a suitable salary for Mozart, von Strak, though he had repeatedly enjoyed the composer's hospitality, named the paltry sum of 800 florins for fear of alarming the parsimonious monarch (Edward Holmes).

such a recantation! All Vienna knows that I have left the
Archbishop, and all Vienna knows why—knows that my honour
was insulted, and insulted for the third time! And am I publicly
to testify the contrary?—make myself out a poltroon and the
Archbishop a noble prince? No man has power to do the first,
I least of all, and, as to the second, God only can do it, if He
should be pleased to enlighten him! And so I have shown no
love towards you? Must it be shown for the first time now?
Can you really say that I "will sacrifice none of my pleasures
for your sake"? What kind of pleasures have I here, pray?
The pleasure of taking trouble and pains to fill my purse!
It seems to me that you fancy I am plunged in gaieties and
amusements. Oh, how can you so deceive yourself!—That is,
as to the present! At present I have barely enough to live on.
But the subscription for the six sonatas is in train and then I
shall get money. It is also already settled about the opera;
in Advent I am to give a concert and then things will go from
good to better, for in the winter season there is much to be
made here. If you call it "pleasure" to be free from a prince
who does not pay one and plagues one to death, then it is
very true, "pleasure" is mine. For if I was forced to do nothing
but think and work hard from morning till night, I would do
it gladly merely to avoid living upon the favour of such a ——.
I can scarcely call him by his right name! I have been forced
to take this step, and I cannot retreat from my position by a
hair's breadth. Impossible! All that I can say to you is this—
that on your account—solely on your account, my father,—I
am very sorry that they drove me to this point, and that I
could have wished the Archbishop had been more reasonable
merely that I might have been able to dedicate my whole life-
time to you! To please you, my dearest father, I would sacrifice
my happiness, my health and my life—but my honour—that
is precious to me above all things, and it must also be so to you.
Read this to Count Arco and to all Salzburg. After this insult,
after this threefold insult, were the Archbishop to tender me
1200 florins in his own person I would not accept them. I am
no lackey, no menial, and had it not been for you I would not

have waited for him to tell me to take myself off a *third* time
without taking him at his word! Waited! *I* would have said
the word and not he! I am only surprised that the Archbishop
should have behaved so indiscreetly in a place like Vienna!
Well, he will see how he has given himself away! Prince
Breiner and Count Arco need the Archbishop, but not I! And
should it come to extremities, should he forget every duty of
a prince, and a prince of the Church, come and join me in
Vienna! You have your 400 florins—how do you think he
would stand with the Emperor, who hates him already, if he
were to do that! My sister, too, would have better prospects
here than in Salzburg. In many gentlemen's houses they are
chary of taking a male tutor, but a female would be very well
paid. Well, all these things may come to pass! At the next
opportunity, when Herr von Kleinmayer, Benecké or Zetti go
to Salzburg, I will send you the sum to settle the matter in
question. The Herr Controller, who leaves to-day, will bring
my sister the lawn. Dearest, best of fathers, ask what you will
of me, only not that—anything else—the mere thought makes
me tremble with rage! *Adieu.* I kiss your hands a thousand
times, embrace my sister with all my heart, and am ever

Your most obedient son,

Wolfgang Amadé Mozart.

73. *To his Father.*

VIENNE, *ce 2 de juin*, 1781.

Mon trés cher Pére !

You will have gathered from my last letter that I have
myself spoken with Count Arco. God be praised and thanked
that everything has passed off so well! Do not be afraid, you
have nothing to fear from the Archbishop, for Count Arco
said no word to me about taking care lest ill should befall
you. When he told me that you had written to him and complained bitterly of me, I took him up at once with "And did
he not write to me, too? I tell you he wrote to me so that I
often thought I should go distracted. But reflect on the matter
as I will I cannot, *cannot* possibly," etc. He also said to me, "You

are allowing yourself to be unduly dazzled in this city, believe me. A man's fame here is but short. At first, it is true, he hears compliments on all hands and makes much money as well—but how long does that last? After a few months or so the Viennese crave some new sensation." "You are right, Count," replied I, "but do you suppose I shall remain in Vienna? Oh, by no means! I know where I mean to go. However, the Archbishop, not I, is the cause of this incident having occurred in in Vienna rather than elsewhere. If he knew how to deal with people of talent it would never have happened. I am the most good-natured fellow in the world, Count, if only people show good will to me." "Yes," said he, "the Archbishop takes you to be a particularly civil person!" "That I can well believe," I replied, "and indeed I was so to him. I treat other people as they treat me. If I see that someone scorns and despises me I can be as proud as a peacock." Among other things he asked me if I did not realise that he, too, often had to swallow abuse. I shrugged my shoulders and said, "You, no doubt, have your reasons for putting up with it and I—have my reasons for not putting up with it." You know all the rest from my previous letter. Do not despair, my dearest, best father! It will certainly be for my good and consequently for yours. It is perfectly true that the Viennese are very ready to turn one off, but that only applies to the stage, and my particular branch of music is so popular that there can be no question but that I shall be able to hold my own here. This indeed is Clavier-land! And then, suppose we concede the point, the case would not arise for several years at least, and in the meantime I should have made money and fame. This is not the only place in the world, and who can tell what opportunity may not offer before then? Meanwhile, I have already spoken to Herr von Zetti, and he will remit you something. This time you must pray be content with very little—I cannot send you more than thirty ducats. Had I foreseen these events I would have accepted the pupils who were offered me; but I thought then I should be leaving in a week, and now they are all gone into the country. The portrait, too, will follow. If he cannot take it with him, it shall be sent by the diligence. Now fare you well, dearest, best of fathers. I kiss your hands a thousand times, embrace my dear sister warmly and am ever

Your most obedient son,

Wolfgang Amadé Mozart.

My compliments to all good friends of both sexes. I will answer Ceccarelli very shortly.

74. *To his Father*

VIENNE, *ce* 20 *de juin*, 1781.

Mon trés cher Pére !

I have safely received the package, and hope that by now you will have got the portrait and ribbons. I do not know why you did not pack everything together in a trunk or chest, for it costs more to send things one by one and pay for each little article separately, than to send one big package. I am not surprised that you are looked at askance by these smooth-spoken courtiers, but what have you to do with such wretched menials? The more hostile these people are to you, the greater the pride and scorn with which you should regard them!

As regards Count Arco, I cannot but trust solely to my own feelings and judgment, and accordingly need the help of no lady or person of quality to do what is just and right, not too much and not too little. It is the heart which ennobles the man, and though I am not a count my honour is as valuable, perhaps more valuable than that of many a count. Count or lackey, if he abuses me he is a scoundrel! To begin with, I shall tell him quite reasonably how badly and clumsily he has done his business—but to conclude, I shall be constrained to assure him, in writing, that he may confidently expect to feel my boot in his hinder parts, and a box on the ear in addition! For when I am insulted I will have my revenge, and if I do no more than was done to me, it were mere repayment and not punishment! Besides, I should put myself on an even footing with him, and I protest I am too proud to level myself with such a stupid booby.

Unless I have anything of special import to tell you, I shall write only once a week as I am very busy just now. I will close now, for I have to prepare some variations for my pupil. *Adieu.* I kiss your hands a thousand times, embrace my sister with all my heart, and am ever—

75. *To his Sister*

VIENNE, *ce* 4 *de juillet*, 1781.

Ma très chère Sœur !

I am very glad that the ribbons were to your taste. I will find out the price of the ribbons, both the painted and the unpainted. At present I do not know it, since Frau von Auerhammer, who had the kindness to procure them for me, refused to take any payment, but begged me to give you all possible civil messages from her, unacquainted though you are, and to say that she would be very glad at any time to be able to do you any favour. I have already conveyed to her your kind regards in return. Dearest Sister! I recently wrote in a letter to our dear father that if you would like anything from Vienna, be it what it might, it would be a real pleasure to me to serve you. I now repeat it, with the addition that I should be very grieved if I heard that you had given your commissions to anyone else in Vienna. I am heartily glad that you are well. I, too, thank God, am well and happy. My sole entertainment is the theatre. I wish you could see a tragedy acted here! I do not know any theatre where all kinds of plays are really well performed; but here every rôle, even the least, is well cast and understudied. I should very much like to know how things are going between you and a certain good friend you wot of? Do write to me about it! Or have I lost your confidence in this matter? In any case, pray write to me often, when you have nothing better to do, be it understood, for I should be so very glad of news sometimes, and you are the living protocol of Salzburg, for you write down everything that occurs, and so to please me you might write it all down a second time! But you must not be angry if, from time to time, I leave you long without an answer.

As regards something new for the clavier, I may tell you that I am about to have four sonatas engraved. Those in C and B flat are among them, and the other two only are new. Then I have written three arias with variations which I could send you, of course, but I think it is hardly worth the trouble, and would rather wait till I have more. I suppose the marksmen's club dinner will soon be held. I beg you *solemniter* to drink the health of a true marksman! Should the talk turn on me, write to me of it and I will have a target painted!

Now fare you well, dearest, best of sisters, and be assured that I shall ever remain

Your

true friend and brother,

Wolfgang Amadé Mozart.

76. *To his Father*

VIENNE, *ce 25 de julliet*, 1781

Mon trés cher Pére !

Once more I may tell you that I have long had it in mind to take another lodging, and that solely because people are gossiping. I am sorry to be obliged to do this on account of foolish chatter in which there is not one word of truth. I should much like to know what pleasure certain folk can find in spreading utterly baseless reports abroad. I live with them,[1] therefore I am to marry the daughter! There has been no talk of our being in love; they have taken a leap beyond that; I lodge in the house and am about to marry! If ever in my life I have put aside all thoughts of marriage it is just now! For there is nothing I want less than a rich wife, and even if I could really make my future by marrying now, I could not possibly pay court to any lady, for I have quite other matters to occupy me. God has not given me my talent that I might dance attendance on a woman, and consequently waste my young life in inactivity. I am just beginning to live, and am I to poison my life for myself? Indeed, I have nothing against matrimony, but for myself, at present, it would be an

---

[1] He lodged with the Weber family, who had moved to Vienna. Fridolin Weber had died in the meantime.

evil. Well, there is no other way; untrue as it is I must at least avoid all appearance—even though this appearance rest on nothing but my living here. People who do not come to the house cannot even tell whether I have as much intercourse with her as with the rest of God's creatures, for the children seldom go out, and then to no place but the comedy, where I never go with them, for I am usually from home at the hour for the comedy. Once or twice we went to the Prater,[1] when the mother was also with us, and I, being in the house, could not refuse to go with them. At that time, moreover, I had heard nothing of this fool's talk. I may tell you, too, that I paid for nothing but my own share of the entertainment— and that when the mother heard this talk herself, and also heard it from me, she herself advised me to move elsewhere in order to avoid further annoyance; for she said she would not like to be the innocent cause of any misfortune to me. That, then, is the sole reason why (since the gossip began) I have thought of leaving. Actually, I have no reason to go, but this chatter drives me to it—most unwillingly, I confess, for although I could easily get a pleasanter room, I could hardly find so much comfort and such friendly and pleasant people. Moreover, I will not say that I am on bad terms at home with this mademoiselle whom they have already married to me, or that we never exchange a word—but we are not in love. I play and joke with her when time permits (and that is only in the evening when I sup at home—for in the morning I write in my room, and after noon I am seldom in) and—that is all! If I had to marry all the ladies with whom I have jested, I should have two hundred wives at least! Now to come to money. My pupil has been in the country for three weeks. Consequently no money has been coming in, and expenses continue as usual. I could not, therefore, send you thirty ducats, though I could send twenty. As I was in hope of subscriptions, however, I intended to wait, and so be able to send you the promised sum. Now, however, Countess Thun tells me it is useless to think of subscriptions before autumn,

[1] A public garden in Vienna.

as all the people with money are out of town. She could find no more than ten people, and my pupil only seven just at present. Well, meanwhile I am having six sonatas engraved which I had already discussed with Arteria [1] (the music-engraver), and as soon as they are sold, and I get money, I will send it to you. I must beg my dear sister to forgive me for not having sent her congratulations by letter for her name-day. The letter is lying by, half-written. When I was beginning it on Saturday, Countess Rumbeck's servant appeared to tell me that they were all going into the country, and to ask me if I would like to go with them. As I do not wish to refuse anything to Cobenzl, [2] I left the letter lying, hastily collected my things and went with them. I thought my dear sister would not take it ill of me. Accordingly, within the octave, I wish her every possible good and salutary blessing that a true and most loving brother could wish, and I kiss her most tenderly. I drove back here with the Count yesterday, and to-morrow I drive out with him again. Now fare you well, dearest, best of fathers! Believe and trust your son, who cherishes the warmest sentiments towards all right-minded people—why not, then, towards his dear father and sister? Believe him and trust him more than do certain people—who have nothing better to do than to slander honest folk. Well, *adieu.* I kiss your hands a thousand times, and am ever your

Most obedient son,
Wolfgang Amadé Mozart.

77. *To his Father*

VIENNE, *ce* 1 *d'aout*, 1781.

Mon trés cher Pére !

I have at once fetched the sonatas for four hands, for Frau von Schindl is just opposite the *Aug-Gottes.* Should Madame Duscheck be in Salzburg at any time, pray give her my kindest regards, and ask her whether, before she left Prague, a gentle-man waited on her with a letter from me? If not, I shall write

---

[1] Artaria, the publisher.
[2] The Prince de Cobentzel, Mozart's advocate with the Emperor Joseph.

to him at once to forward it to Salzburg. The man is Rossi, of Munich. He begged me to assist him with a letter of recommendation. He took several excellent letters with him to Prague—and if my letter had concerned his recommendation alone, I should have left it at his own disposition; but in it I also asked Madame Duscheck to help me with my subscriptions for the six sonatas. I was especially glad to do Rossi a favour, since he prepared for me the poem of a cantata which I am to give at my benefit concert in Advent.

The day before yesterday young Stephani gave me a libretto to compose. I must confess that, badly as he may be capable (for all I care!) of treating other people, of which I know nothing, he has been a very good friend to me. The libretto is quite good. The subject is Turkish and is called: *Bellmont und Constanze*, or *Die Verführing aus dem Serail*. I shall employ a Turkish style of music for the symphony, the chorus in the first act, and the closing chorus. Mlle. Cavalieri, Mlle. Teyber, M. Fischer, M. Adamberger, M. Dauer and M. Walter will sing in it. It gives me such joy to compose on the libretto that I have already finished Cavalieri's first aria, and that of Adamberger, and the terzett which closes Act I. The time is short, it is true, for it is to be performed in the middle of September, but the circumstances connected with the date of performance, and all other considerations generally, inspire me to such a degree that I hasten to my desk with the greatest eagerness, and sit there in the most absolute content. A Russian grand duke is to come here, and that is why Stephani begged me, if possible, to compose the opera in so short a space of time. Moreover, the Emperor and Count Rosenberg are to come shortly, and it will be asked at once whether anything new is in train. He will then have the satisfaction of saying that he has at last concluded his search for a composer (for he has long had the opera by him), and that I am composing it for him—and he will certainly count it as a favour from me that, for this reason, I have undertaken to write it in this short time. No one knows of it yet but Adamberger and Fischer, for Stephani begged us to say nothing as Count Rosenburg is still absent, and it might lead to all kinds of gossip. Stephani does not even wish it to appear that he is any too friendly with me, but rather that he is doing all this because Count Rosenburg wishes it, and indeed the Count, on his departure, did actually order him to look round for a libretto, no more.

I can think of nothing else to tell you for I have heard no news. The room to which I am removing is being got ready. I am now going to borrow a clavier, for I cannot move into my room till I have one there, as I have now to compose without wasting a moment. Nevertheless, I shall lack many comforts in my new lodging—particularly as regards meals. When I really had to write they delayed the meal for me as long as I liked; and I could write on without dressing, and simply step out of one door and into another to my meal, both morning and evening. Now, when I wish to avoid spending money in having a meal sent to my room, I waste at least an hour in dressing (which I used not to do till afternoon) and going out—particularly in the evening. You know that I usually write fasting. The good friends with whom I might take my supper sit down to table at eight o'clock, or nine at latest. *There* we never did so before ten o'clock.—Well, *adieu*, I must close, for I have to look round for a clavier. Farewell. I kiss your hands a thousand times, embrace my dear sister with all my heart, and am ever your

Most obedient son,
Wolf. Amdé. Mozart.

P.S.—My compliments to all Salzburg.

78. *To his Father*

VIENNE, *ce 22 d'aout*, 1781.

Mon trés cher Pére !

I cannot yet let you know the address of my new lodging, for I still have none. I am, however, in negotiation for two, of which I shall certainly take one, as I cannot stay here next month and so must move out. It appears that Herr von

Auerhammer wrote to you, and told you I actually had a room!
It is true, I had one, but such a one!—fit for rats and mice,
but not for'human beings. At twelve o'clock midday one had
to mount the stairs with a lantern. My room was a mere
closet, reached only through the kitchen. In the door there
was a little window, and although they promised me to curtain
it, they asked me in the same breath to draw it back as soon
as I was dressed as otherwise they could see less well in the
kitchen than in the other adjoining room. The woman of the
house herself called it a rats' hole; in a word, it was a horrible
place to look at. It would have made a splendid dwelling for
me in which to receive the visits of various persons of quality!
The good man thought of no one but himself and his daughter,
who was the worst *seccatrice* [bore] I have ever known. As I
read in your last letter Count Daun's praises of this house,
I, too, must give you some account of it. Otherwise, I should
have passed over all this in silence as something neither here
nor there, and merely a private *seccatura* [worry] of my own.
As, however, I perceive from your letter that you have a
somewhat high opinion of this household, I feel constrained to
tell you frankly both the good and the evil of it. *He* is the
kindest man in the world—too kind, indeed, for his wife, the
most foolish and ridiculous gossip in the world, wears the
breeches! When she speaks he does not venture a word. On
our frequent walks together he begged me not to mention in
his wife's presence that we took a *fiacre* or a glass of beer
together. Well, I can put no confidence in such a man—he is
too insignificant a factor in his own household. He is honest,
and a good friend of mine. I could dine with them frequently
at midday, but it is not my habit to allow people to pay me
for my favours. True, they would not be adequately paid for
by a midday repast—but people of that type think they are!
I was in their house for their advantage, not for my own. I
see no profit in it for myself, and I never met a single person
there who was worth my setting his name on this paper. Decent
people, indeed, but no more—people who have sense enough
to perceive how useful was my acquaintance for their daughter,

who, as everyone says who knew her previously, has entirely changed since I began to teach her. I will not attempt to describe the mother. Enough that it was an effort to prevent myself laughing at her at table. *Basta!* You know Frau Adlgasser, and this is a worse case of the same sort, only *medisante* into the bargain—stupid *and* malicious. The same with the daughter. If a painter should want to portray the devil to the life, he should have recourse to her face! She is as fat as a farm-wench, sweats in a way to make one sick, and goes so scantily clad that one can read as plain as print: "Pray, look here!" True, to look is enough to strike one blind, but it is pain enough for one day if one is so unlucky as to turn one's eyes upon her—tartar is the only remedy! So loathsome, dirty and horrible! Pah, the devil! Well, I told you she plays the clavier, and I told you why she persuaded me to help her. I am very pleased to do people favours, but I hate importunity. She is not content if I spend a couple of hours with her daily —she wants me to sit beside her all day long—and then she will do well! But more yet! She is *serieusement* in love with me! I thought it a joke, but I now know it is true. When I perceived it—for she took liberties—for example, made me tender reproaches if I appeared somewhat later than usual, or could not stay so long, and the like, I was forced, not to make a fool of the girl, to tell her the truth very civilly. That, however, was no use. She became more loving than ever! I took to treating her at all times with great courtesy, save when she began her nonsense, and then I was rough. Then she would take my hand, and say, "Dear Mozart, pray do not be so angry. You may say what you like, I love you all the same." The whole town began to say we were to marry, and the only wonder was that I would take such a face! She told me that when anything of the kind was said to her she simply laughed, but I know, through a certain person, that she confirmed the rumour with the addition that we should then travel together. That enraged me! Recently, I boldly told her my mind, and that she was not to abuse my kindness. Now I no longer go there every day, but every other day only, and

I shall gradually drop it altogether. She is no more than a love-sick fool. For before she knew me she said, when she heard me in the theatre: "He is coming to see me to-morrow, and I shall play him his variations with the same *gusto*," that being a boastful speech and a lie, for I had never heard that I was to visit her next day, and I did not go at all! Well, *adieu*, my paper is full. The first act of the opera is now complete. I kiss your hands a thousand times, embrace my dear sister with all my heart, and am ever your

Obedient son,

W. A. Mozart.

79. *To his Father*

VIENNE, *ce 5 de 7bre*, 1781.

Mon très cher Père !

I am now writing to you in my new room—*Auf dem Graben*, No. 1175, 3rd story. From the way you have taken my last letter, I am sorry to see that—as if I were an arch-scoundrel, a blackguard, or both at once!—you place more reliance on the gossip and idle scribblings of others than you do in me—in fact you have no trust in me whatever! But I assure you that all that is nothing to *me*—they can write the eyes out of their heads if they like—but I shall not change by a hair, and shall remain the same honest fellow as ever. And I swear to you that if you had not wanted me to change my quarters I should never have moved away—for it is like changing from one's own commodious private carriage into the diligence. But silence on that subject—it is useless to talk of it, for the maggots put into your head, by whom, God only knows, always outweigh any reasons of mine! Only, when you write to me of anything you disapprove in me, or that you think might be improved, and I reply with my ideas on the subject, I beg you always to regard it as a matter between father and son alone, as confidential, and not for the ears of others. Therefore, please let it rest at that, and do not apply to other people, for, by God, I will not be answerable for one moment to others as to what I do or leave undone; no, not to the Emperor himself! Trust me, for indeed I deserve it. I have trouble and worry enough here getting my livelihood, and vexatious letters are not at all good for me. Since first I came here I have had to live entirely on my own resources, on what I can earn. The others have always had their salaries to draw on as well. Ceccareli has earned more here than I, but has made ducks and drakes of it all. If I had done the same I should never have been in a position to resign. It is no fault of mine, dearest father, but of the present bad season that I have sent you no money yet. Have patience—I, too, have to cultivate it. By God, I am not likely to forget it! During the affair with the Archbishop, I wrote for clothes. I had nothing then but my black suit. The time for mourning was past—the weather grew warm—no clothes came—and so I had to have some made. I could not go about Vienna like a tramp! Then, my underlinen was a pitiful sight. No lackey here had such coarse linen shirts as I had—and surely that has the worst effect on a man's appearance! That meant more expense. I had a single pupil. She was away for three weeks—more losses for me. One dare not make oneself cheap—that is a cardinal point here—or one is lost for ever. The man with the most assurance of bearing has the best chance here. In every one of your letters I see that you fancy I do nothing but amuse myself here. You are very greatly deceived. Indeed, I may say that I have no pleasures here—none at all—save the single one of being away from Salzburg! In the winter I hope all will go well, and then, dearest father, I shall certainly not forget you. If I see that good will come of it, I shall remain here, if not, I think of making a bee-line for Paris. Please tell me what your opinion is. And now, farewell. I kiss your hands a thousand times, embrace my dear sister with all my heart, and am ever

Your most obedient son,

W. A. Mzt.

P.S.—My compliments to the Duschecks. Pray, when you have occasion, send me the aria I made for Madame Baumgarten, the rondo for Madame Duscheck, and Ceccarelli's. *Adieu.*

80. *To his Sister*

VIENNE, *ce* 19 *de* 7*bre*, 1781.

Ma tré chere sœur !

I gather from our dear father's last letter that you are ill, and this causes me no little sorrow and anxiety. I see that you have been taking the water-cure for a fortnight, so you must have been ill some time—and I knew nothing of it! Well, I will be quite frank with you about these constantly recurrent indispositions of yours. Believe me, dearest sister, quite seriously, the best cure for you would be a husband—and just because it would have so great an effect upon your health, I could wish that you might marry soon. In your last letter you scolded me, but not so much as I deserved. I am ashamed when I think of it, and the only excuse I have to offer is that I began to write to you the moment I received your last letter but one, and then—left it unfinished! In the end I tore it up, for it is too early yet to give you any really reassuring news, although I hope to be able to do so soon. Now listen to what I think.

You know that I am writing an opera. Those parts which are already completed have won extraordinary praise on all hands, for I know these people—and I hope it will be a great success. If so I shall be as popular here as a composer as I am as a pianist. Well, after this winter, I shall know my circumstances better, and no doubt they will be good. For you and D' Yppold there are scarcely any—indeed, I may say *no*—prospects in Salzburg; but could not D' Yppold do something for himself here?

Ask him about it—and if he thinks the thing at all practicable, I will certainly perform prodigies, for I take the strongest interest in this affair! If we could bring it off, you two could safely marry, for, believe me, you could earn money enough yourself here, by playing at private concerts and by giving lessons, for example. You would be besieged with applications —and you would be well paid. Then my father would have to resign his post and come, too—and we could live happily together again. I see nothing else for it—and even before I

knew that matters were really serious between you and
D' Yppold, I had some such plan in mind for you—only the
difficulty was with our dear father, for I wished him to be able
to come with a quiet mind, and not have to vex and plague
himself. By this scheme, however, that might well be, for we
could manage easily upon your husband's income, your own,
and mine, and enable him to live in peace and comfort. Only
talk it over soon with D' Yppold and send me instructions, for
the sooner one begins to move in the matter the better. I
can do most through the Coblenzls—but he must let me know
how and what.—

M. Marchall sends you his regards, and he also wants you
to remember him to M. D' Yppold, whom he thanks very
warmly for the very friendly service he did him when he was
setting out on his journey. Now I must close, for I have still
to write to Papa. Farewell, dearest sister! I hope to get better
news of your health in Papa's next letter—and to have it
confirmed soon by your own hand. *Adieu.* I kiss you a thousand
times, and am ever your inalterably most loving brother,

W. A. Mozart.

81. *To his Father*

Mon trés cher Pére !

VIENNE, *ce* 15 *de Decbre*, 1781.

I have this moment received your letter of the 12th. Herr
von Daubrawaick will bring you this letter, the watch, the
Munich opera, the six engraved sonatas, the sonata for two
claviers, and the cadenzas. It is all off between the Princess
of Würtemburg and myself. The Emperor has stood in my way,
for he cares for no one but Salieri.[1] The Archduke Maximilian
recommended me to her and she replied that, had it rested
with her, she would have taken no one but me, but that the
Emperor had recommended Salieri to her on account of the

---

[1] Salieri, Antonio (1750–1825), composed some forty operas, among them
Armida, Semiramide and *Falstaff*. He was so much a rival that he was actually
accused of having brought about Mozart's death by poison and felt it necessary to make a solemn declaration to the contrary on his own deathbed
(Edward Holmes). For a time he instructed Beethoven.

singing; she was very sorry about it. As to what you write about the house of Würtemburg and yourself, it is not impossible that it may prove useful to me.—

Dearest father! You challenge me to explain certain words I wrote at the end of my last letter!—Oh, how gladly would I have opened my heart to you long since; but the thought of the reproaches you might have made me for considering such a matter so unseasonably kept me from it—although *consideration* can be at no time unseasonable. I am bent, first on making sure of some small regular income—for it is easy to live here with the help of windfalls — and then — on marrying! You are horrified at this idea? I beg you, dearest, best of fathers, give me a hearing! I have been obliged to disclose my wishes to you—now permit me to reveal my reasons for those wishes —my very well-grounded reasons. The voice of nature speaks as loud in me as in others, louder, perhaps, than in many a big strong lout of a fellow. I cannot possibly live as do most young men in these days. In the first place, I have too much religion; in the second place, I have too great a love of my neighbour, and am too honourably-minded to seduce an innocent maiden; while, in the third place, I have too much horror and disgust, too much fear and loathing of disease, and too much care for my health, to consort with whores. Hence, I am able to swear to you that I have never had relations of that sort with any female—for if such a thing had occurred, I would not have concealed it from you; for to err is natural enough to man, and to err *once* were no more than mere weakness — nevertheless I could not trust myself to stop short at one error only if I once went astray in this matter. But I would stake my life on the truth of what I have told you! I know very well that *this* reason (powerful as it is) is not cogent enough. But I can think of nothing more necessary to my disposition, more inclined as I am to quiet domesticity than to revelry (and from youth up I have never been accustomed to looking after my own effects, clothes, washing, etc.), than a wife! I cannot tell you how much I am often obliged to spend because I do not look after these matters, and I am quite convinced that I should do better with a wife (upon the same income on which I live alone) than I do by myself. And how many useless expenses does not one cut down! True, one incurs others in their stead, but one knows what they are, and can govern oneself accordingly—in a word, one lives a well-ordered life. A bachelor, in my opinion, is only half alive. Those are my views and I cannot help it. I have pondered and considered the matter enough, and I shall not change my mind. But who is the object of my love? Again, do not be horrified, I beg you! Not one of the Webers? Yes, one of the Webers—but not Josepha, not Sophy—Constance, the middle one. In no other family have I ever met with such differences of temperament. The oldest is a worthless, gross, perfidious person, not to be trusted. Madame Lang is insincere and ill-disposed and a *coquette*. The youngest—is still too young to be anything—an amiable but feather-headed little creature. May God protect her from seduction! But the middle one, my good, dear Constance, she it is who suffers from all this, and who, perhaps for that very reason, is the best-hearted, the cleverest, in a word, the best, of them all! She makes herself responsible for the whole household, and yet she can never do right! Oh, my dearest father, I could fill whole sheets with descriptions of the scenes between us two in that house! If you ask for them, I will give you them in my next letter. But before I cease to plague you with my chatter, I must make you better acquainted with the character of my dearest Constance! She is not ugly, but no one could call her a beauty. Her whole beauty consists in two little black eyes and a graceful figure. She has no wit, but wholesome common sense enough to fulfil her duties as wife and mother. She is *not* inclined to extravagance—that is an absolute falsehood. On the contrary, she is used to being ill-dressed, for what little her mother was able to do for her children she did for the two others, and never for *her*. True, she would like to go neat and clean, but not *fine*. And most things that a woman needs she is able to make for herself. She dresses her own hair every day—understands housekeeping, has the kindest heart in the world, and—I love her and she me with all our hearts! Tell me whether I could wish myself a better wife?

One thing more I must tell you, which is that I was not in love at the time of my resignation. It was born of her tender care and service when I lodged in their house.

Accordingly, I wish for nothing but a small secure income (of which, thank God, I have well-founded hopes) and then I shall ask your leave to save this poor girl—and myself with her—and I think I may say—make us *all* happy. You are happy, are you not, that I should be so? And you shall enjoy half my fixed income. My dearest father! I have opened my heart to you and explained those words of mine. Now pray explain yours in your last letter. You say you will not believe that I could know of a proposal made to you and to which you, as I understand, made no reply! I do not understand a word of this—I know of no proposal! Have compassion on your son! I kiss your hands a thousand times, and am ever

Your most obedient son,

W. A. Mozart.

82. *To his Father*

Vienne, *ce* 22 *Xbre*, 1781.

Mon trés cher Pére !

I am still full of rage and fury over the shameful lies of that arch-scoundrel Winter—yet calm and composed because they have left *me* untouched—and well satisfied, delighted with my inestimable, dearest, best of fathers! But I could have expected nothing else from your sound judgment, and from your love and affection for me. You will by now have learned from my last letter of my acknowledged love and my intentions. You will also perceive from it that I am not so foolish in this, my twenty-sixth year, as to marry off-hand without any certain income; that I have good reason for marrying as soon as possible, and that my girl, as I have portrayed her, will be a very suitable wife for me. For as I have described her, so she is—not one whit better or worse. I shall also be quite open with you about the marriage contract, fully convinced that you will pardon me this latest step, for, had you found yourself in my case, you would, I am convinced, have acted as I did. Only, as regards this step, I must ask pardon for not having let you know of it long since. But my excuses on this point have been made already in a previous letter, together with the reasons which held me back. Accordingly, I hope you will forgive me, for no one has suffered more by it than I—and even if you had not given me occasion in your last letter, I should have written and disclosed all to you. For, by God, I *could* not keep silence any longer!

Now, however, to come to this marriage contract, or rather the written assurance of my honourable intentions towards the girl. You know, of course, that they have a trustee,[1] the father (unhappily for the whole family and for myself and my Constance) being dead. Certain officious and impertinent persons like Herr Winter must needs fill this man's ears (he knew nothing of me) with all sorts of stories about me—how there was need to beware of me—that I had no certain prospects—that I was perpetually with her—that I might jilt her, and that then the girl would be ruined, etc. The trustee swallowed all this—for the mother, who knows me and knows me to be honourable, let things take their course, and said nothing to him of the matter.—For all our intercourse consisted in the fact that I lodged with them, and afterwards visited the house daily. No man ever saw me with her outside the house. This gentleman filled the mother's ears with his representations till she told me of it, and begged me to speak to him myself as he was to come that very day. He came. We talked—the result (as I could not give him as clear an account of myself as he wished) was that he told the mother to forbid me all intercourse with her daughter until I had settled the matter with him in writing. "They see nothing of each other except when he comes to my house," she replied, "and—I cannot forbid him my house; he is too good a friend, and a friend to whom I am under many obligations. My mind is quite at ease. I trust him. You must settle it with him yourself."

[1] Johannes Thorwarth. Cf. Letter No. 88.

Accordingly he forbade me to see her until I had settled with
him in writing. What other course was open to me? I had
either to give my written promise, or—agree not to see the
girl! What man who loves with truth and constancy can absent
himself from his beloved? Might not the mother, might not
the beloved one herself, place the most dreadful interpreta-
tion upon it? That was my position. I accordingly drew up a
document, promising to wed Mademoiselle Constance Weber
within the space of three years; in the unlikely event of my
changing my mind she should have a claim on me of 300
florins a year. Indeed, it was the easiest thing in the world
for me to write this, knowing I should never have to pay
those 300 florins, for I shall never forsake her, and even should
I be so unfortunate as to be capable of changing my mind,
I should be glad enough to be free for 300 florins, while Constance, if I know her, would be too proud to let herself be
bought and sold! But what did that divine girl do as soon as
the trustee was gone? She asked her mother for the document,
and said to me, "Dear Mozart! I need no written assurance
from you—I trust your word—thus!" and she tore up the
paper! This act made my dear Constance yet more precious
to me, and, the writing having been destroyed, and the trustee
having given his *parole d'honneur* to keep the matter to himself, my mind was set almost completely at ease, my dearest
father, on your account. For I had no fear but that you would
give your consent to the marriage (the girl lacking nothing
but money) when the right time came, knowing well your
good judgment as regards this subject. Will you forgive me?
Indeed, I hope so—I do not despair! And now, repugnant as
it is to me, I will speak of that swindler. I believe that Herr
Reiner's only disease was that he was not quite right in the
head! I saw him by chance in the theatre, where he gave me
a letter from Ramm. I asked him where he lodged, but he said
he could not tell me either the name of the street nor of the
house, and expressed irritation at having allowed himself to
be persuaded into coming here. I offered to take him to the
Countess, and to introduce him wherever I had the *entrée*.

I also assured him that if he should be unable to give a concert I would present him to the Archduke. All he replied was, "Pshaw! There is nothing to be done here. I shall leave again at once." "Only have a little patience," said I, "and if you cannot tell me where you lodge, I can give you my address and it is easy to find." I saw nothing of him, however, and by the time I had made inquiries and tracked him down he had left. So much for this gentleman. As to Winter, I do not know if he deserves to be called a man (though he is a husband [1]), but I suppose he is at least human—as to Winter, I may say that he has ever been my worst enemy on Vogler's account! As, however, he is a beast in his manner of life, and in all his business dealings a child, I should be ashamed to write a single word about him! He deserves the utter contempt of every honourable man, and so I will not write, instead of infamous lies, infamous *truths* about him, but—give you instead some account of my own manner of life.

Every morning at six o'clock my *friseur* arrives and wakes me and by seven I am fully dressed. I then write till ten o'clock. At about ten o'clock I have to give a lesson at Frau von Trattner's, and at eleven at the Countess Rumbeck's, each of whom pays me six ducats for twelve lessons. I go there every day, unless they send to stop me, which I do not like at all. I have an agreement with the Countess that she will never send, and if I find her from home I have my *billet* at least, but Frau von Trattner is too economical for that. I do not owe a single kreutzer to any man. I have heard no whisper of any amateur concert at which two persons played the clavier very finely. And I may tell you candidly that I do not think it worth the trouble to reply to all the filth which such a lousy rascal and wretched bungler may have spread about me; he merely renders himself ridiculous by it. If you are capable of supposing that I am hated by all the *grande* and *petite noblesse*, do but write to Herr von Strack, the Countess Thun, the Countess Rumbeck, Baroness Waldstätten,[2] Herr von

---

[1] In German the same word denotes "man" and "husband."
[2] See Letters Nos. 86, 88, 91, 93, 94, 95, 98.

Sonnenfels, Frau von Trattner, *enfin*, to whom you will, and in the meantime I may merely inform you that the Emperor lately spoke a great eulogy upon me at table, accompanied by the words, "*C'est un talent decidé!*" and that yesterday, the 24th, I played at Court! Another clavier-player, an Italian named Clementi,[1] has arrived here. He, too, was in attendance. I received fifty ducats yesterday for my playing, and indeed I stand in need of them at the moment.

My dearest, best of fathers! You will see that my circumstances are gradually improving. What use to make a great commotion—rapid fortune is not lasting. *Che và piano và sano.* One must cut one's coat according to one's cloth. Among all the cowardly slanders uttered by Winter, the only one which enrages me is his calling my Constance a hussy. I have portrayed her to you as she is. If you wish for other people's opinions, write to Herr von Auerhammer, whose house she visited several times, and she once dined there. Write to Baroness Waldstätten, who had her with her, though, unfortunately, for a month only, when she—the Baroness—was ill. And now her mother will not let her leave her again. God grant I may be able to marry her soon!

Ceccarelli sends his regards. Yesterday he sang at Court. There is one more thing I must say to you about Winter. Among other things he once said to me, "You are very unwise to marry. Keep a mistress—you can do it, you earn enough. What holds you back, then? Some —— religious scruple?" *Now* believe what you will! *Adieu.* I kiss your hands a thousand times, embrace my dear sister with all my heart, and am ever your

Most obedient son,

W. A. Mzt.

The Baroness's address is:

A Madame
Madame La Baronne de Waldstätten
née de Scheffer

à   *Vienne*

Leopoldstadt, No. 360.

[1] The well-known clavier virtuoso and composer, Muzio Clementi.

83. *To his Sister*

Ma tres chere sœur!

Thank you for sending me the little book, which I really have awaited with the greatest longing! I hope that by the time you receive this letter you will have our dear good father with you once more. You must not deduce from my failure to answer you that I find the receipt of your letters burdensome! It will ever be a very great delight to me, dear sister, to be honoured with a letter from you, and if the necessary business of making my living did not prevent me, God knows I should not fail to answer you! And have I never answered you? Well, then! Forgetfulness it cannot be—nor negligence, either, and therefore it can be nothing but actual hindrances, real impracticability! Do I not write little enough to my father? Badly enough, you would say, but, in Heaven's name, you both know Vienna! In such a place has not a man without a kreutzer of secure income plenty to think of and to do from morning till night? When father has finished with his service in the church, and you with your few pupils, you can both do what you will the livelong day, and write letters comprising whole litanies! But not so I. I recently wrote of my manner of life to my father, and I will repeat it to you. My hair is dressed at six o'clock in the morning, and by seven I am always fully dressed. I then write till nine, and from nine to one give lessons. I then dine, unless I am invited to some house where they dine at two, or even at three o'clock, as, for instance, yesterday and to-day at the Countess Zizi's and the Countess Thun's. I cannot work before five or six o'clock in the evening, and even then I am often prevented by a concert. If not, I write till nine o'clock. I then go to see my dear Constance, where our joy in seeing each other is embittered more often than not by her mother's sharp speeches. I shall explain this in my next letter to my father, and that is the reason why I hope to set her free, to save her, as soon as possible. At half-past ten or eleven I get home—it depends on the fury of her mother's bombardment and on my power of sustaining it! As

I cannot rely on getting time to write in the evening on account
of concerts, and also because of the uncertainty whether I
may not be summoned now here, now there, I am accustomed
(especially if I get home somewhat early) to write a little before
going to bed. I often write on till one o'clock—and I am up
again at six. Dearest Sister! If you imagine that I could ever
forget my dearest, kindest father, and you, then—but peace!
God knows my constancy, and that is satisfaction enough for
me. May He punish me if I were ever capable of forgetting
you! *Adieu*. I am ever

Your faithful brother,
W. A. Mozart.

P.S.—If my dearest father is back in Salzburg, tell him I
kiss his hands a thousand times.

84. *To his Father*

VIENNE, *ce* 10 *d'avril*, 1782.

Mon trés cher Pére !

I see from your letter of the twelfth of this month that
you have got all the things safely. I am glad that you like
the watch-chains and snuff-box, and my sister the two caps.
I did not buy either the watch-chains or the snuff-box, as
Count Zapara made me a present of them. I have given your
mutual kind regards to my dear Constance. She kisses your
hand in return, my dear father, and warmly embraces my
sister, whose friend she would gladly be. She was perfectly
content when I told her you liked the two caps, as she hoped
you would.—That postscript touching her mother is only true
in so far that she is more addicted to liquor than a woman
should be. Still, I have never yet seen her drunk, that I must
say. The children drink nothing but water—and although
their mother almost *forces* wine upon them, she cannot bring
them to touch it. This often gives rise to fierce disputes—
are not such disputes with a mother almost unimaginable?

The reason why I said nothing to you about this rumour
you write of, that I can be certain of entering the Emperor's

service, is that I myself know no such thing! It is true that here, too, the whole town is full of it, and a host of people have already congratulated me — and I am quite ready to believe that the subject has been mentioned to the Emperor, and that he may have the matter in mind, but up till now I *know* nothing. Things have gone so far that the Emperor is considering it, and that without my having taken a single step to that end. I have several times visited Herr von Strack (who certainly is very much my friend) to let myself be seen and because I like to be with him, but I have not gone there often, because I do not wish to be a burden to him nor to seem to have ulterior motives. As a man of honour he is bound to affirm that he has never heard a word from me which could give him occasion to think I wished to stay here, let alone approach the Emperor. Our talk was of music only. Therefore it must have been entirely of his own accord, and quite without *interesse*, that he spoke so favourably of me to the Emperor. Since things have gone so far without any action on my part, they can so proceed to their conclusion.—For if one makes any move oneself the salary drops at once, the Emperor being something of a screw! If the Emperor wants me he must pay me, for the honour of the position will not alone suffice me. You may rely upon it that if the Emperor were to offer me 1000 florins, and some Count 3000, I should take courteous leave of the Emperor and go to the Count.—*Apropos*—may I ask you, when you send me back the rondo, to enclose with it Handel's six fugues and Eberlin's [1] toccatas and fugues? I go to Baron von Suiten's [2] every Sunday at midday, where nothing is played but Handel and Bach. I am now making a collection of the fugues of Bach—not only of Sebastian, but also of Emmanuel and Friedemann Bach. I am also collecting

---

[1] Eberlin, Johann Ernst (1702-62), a prolific and able composer, for some years kapellmeister to Archbishop Sigismund at Salzburg.

[2] Baron von Swieten, a member of the Privy Council and Superintendent of the royal library of music in Vienna, was an enthusiastic and intelligent amateur and a friend and patron to Haydn, to whom he suggested *The Creation* and *The Seasons*; to Mozart, to whom he suggested the particular study of Bach; and to Beethoven. He had music performed at his house with a full orchestra. See Letters 95, 92, 118, 122.

Handel's fugues—I now have them all but these six, and I should like the Baron to hear Eberlin's as well. You have no doubt, heard that the "English" Bach is dead? What a loss to the musical world! Now farewell! I kiss your hands a thousand times, embrace my dear sister with all my heart, and am ever your

Most obedient son,

W. A. Mozart.

P.S.—May I also ask you to send, at your convenience (but the sooner the better), my concerto in C for Countess Litsow?

85. *To his Sister*

VIENNA, 20*th April*, 1782.

My very dearest Sister!

My dear Constance has at last summoned up courage to follow the impulse of her gentle heart—that is, to write to you, my dear sister! Should you be willing to favour her with an answer (and indeed I hope you will, for the joy *I* shall have in seeing the sweet creature's pleasure in it reflected in her face!), may I beg you to send your letter under cover to me? I write this merely as a precaution, and so that you may know that her mother and sisters are unaware that she has written to you. I send you herewith a prelude and three-part fugue. That is why I did not reply to your letter at once, having been unable to get it ready earlier on account of having to write all those tiresome little notes. And even now it is written very awkwardly. The prelude should come first, with the fugue following, but I had already composed the fugue, and was copying it out while meditating on the prelude. I only hope you will be able to read it, for it is written so very small, and also that you will like it. Another time I will send you something better for the clavier. My dear Constance is really the cause of this fugue's coming into the world. Baron von Suiten, whom I visit every Sunday, gave me all the works of Handel and Sebastian Bach to take home with me after I had played them through to him. When Constance heard the fugues she fell quite in love with them. She will listen to nothing but fugues now, and (in that form) to nothing but Handel and Bach. Having often heard me play fugues out of my head, she asked me if I had ever written any down, and when I said I had not, she scolded me very thoroughly for not having written anything in this most artistic and beautiful of musical forms, and would give me no peace till I made her a fugue—with this result! I have taken particular care to write *andante maestoso* upon it, so that it should not be played fast—for if a fugue is not played slowly the ear cannot clearly distinguish the new subject as it is introduced and the effect is missed. With time and opportunity I hope to compose five more, and then present them to Baron van Suiten, whose musical library is, as a matter of fact, great in quality but meagre in quantity. And for that very reason I beg you not to withdraw your promise and to let no one see my piece. Learn it by heart and play it—it is not so easy to pick up a fugue by ear. If Papa has not yet had those works by Eberlin copied I shall be well content. I got them privately, and besides I had unfortunately forgotten that they are far too slight to deserve a place between Handel and Bach. All respect for his four-part movements, but his clavier fugues are nothing but long-drawn-out *tirades*. And now, farewell! I am glad the caps suit you. A thousand kisses to you, and I remain,

Your faithful brother,
W. A. Mozart.

Tell Papa I kiss his hand. I received no letter to-day.

Constance Weber to Mozart's Sister

20th April, 1782.

Most honoured and most valued Friend!

I should never have been so bold as to follow the dictates of my heart and to write to you, most esteemed Friend, had not your Brother assured me that you would not be offended by a step undertaken on my part, solely through excess of eagerness to communicate, if only in writing, with a person unknown and yet very dear to me through the name of Mozart. You cannot, I think, be angry if I venture to tell you that, though I have not the honour of knowing you personally, I esteem you most highly as the sister of so estimable a brother, that I love you and even dare to beg for your friendship. Without pride I may venture to say that I partly deserve it and shall endeavour to deserve it wholly! May I in exchange offer you mine—that friendship which I have long since accorded you in the secrecy of my heart? Indeed I hope it may be so, and in this hope I remain, most honoured, most valued friend,

Your
most obedient servant
and friend

Constance Weber.

Pray tell your father that I kiss his hand.

86. *To Constance Weber*

29th April, 1782.

Dearest, kindest friend!

Surely you will still permit me to address you by this name? Surely you cannot hate me so much that I may be your friend no longer—you no longer mine? And even if you wish to be so no more you cannot, after all, forbid me to take thought for you, my friend, for it has become a habit with me! Think well over what you said to me to-day. In spite of all my prayers you thrice gave me my dismissal, and told me to my face that you did not care to have anything more to do with me. I, who am less indifferent than you to the loss of the beloved object, am not so hasty as to accept my dismissal unreflecting and unreasoning! I—love you too well for that! And so I beg you to reflect once again on the cause of the whole trouble, and to consider what it was I found fault with when you were so pert, and so ill-judged as to say to your sisters— in my presence be it noted—that you had let a young man measure the calves of your legs![1] No woman who cares for her honour can do such a thing. It is quite a good maxim to do as

---

[1] In the game of forfeits.

one's company does, but at the same time there are many
questions to be considered—as, for instance, "whether there
are none but good friends and acquaintances present," "whether
I am a child or a marriageable girl," or, more particularly,
"whether I am a promised bride." But the *chief* thing is
"whether all the company present are my equals," or "whether
my inferiors—and even more particularly—my social superiors
are among them." Even though the Baroness [1] herself allowed
it to be done to her, that is still quite a different matter, for
she is a woman past her bloom, who could no longer by any
possibility excite desire. — And in any case is very promiscuous
with her favours! I hope, dearest friend, that you will never
wish to lead such a life as hers, even if you refuse to be my
wife! If you were obliged to take part in the game (although
it is not always wise for a man to do so, still less for a woman)
—but if you could not possibly refuse to do so, you might, in
Heaven's name, have taken the ribbon and measured your
calves yourself (as self-respecting women have always done in
like circumstances in my presence), and not have allowed a
man——! Why I, I myself, would never have done such a thing
to you in others' presence—I would myself have put the
ribbon in your hands! Still less, then, should you have permitted it to be done by a stranger—a man I know nothing of.—
But it is all past and done with now, and the least acknowledgment of your somewhat ill-considered conduct on that occasion
would have set the matter right—and can yet set it right, my
dearest friend, if you will cease to be angry! That will show
you how much I love you—I do not flare up like you, I think,
I reflect—and I feel! Do but surrender to your feelings also,
and I am sure that, even to-day, I shall be able to say
that Constance is still the virtuous, the self-respecting, the
prudent and loyal sweetheart of her upright and devotedly
loving,

Mozart

[1] Von Waldstäden? See Letter No. 82.

87. To his Father

VIENNE, *ce* 20 *de juillet,* 1782.

Mon trés cher Pére !

I hope that you have by now safely received my previous letter informing you of the good reception of my opera.[1] It was given for the second time yesterday. Can you believe it?—there was an even stronger cabal yesterday than on the first evening! The whole first act was accompanied by hissing, but they could not prevent the loud cries of *"bravo!"* during the arias. I had set my hopes on the closing terzett, but unluckily Fischer was away, Dauer (Pedrillo) also, and Adamberger alone could not make up for their absence. The consequence was that the whole effect was lost, and—this time—it will not be repeated. I was so angry—that I scarcely knew myself, as also was Adamberger—and I said at once that I would not let the opera be given again without holding a short rehearsal (for the singers). In the second act the two duets were encored as on the first night, and in addition Belmont's rondo, *"Wenn der Freude Thränen Fliessen."* [2] The theatre was fuller, if possible, than on the first night, and on the preceding day no reserved seats were to be had in the stalls or third circle, and no boxes. The opera has brought in 1200 florins in the two days. I send you herewith the original, and two libretti. You will find many passages struck out. The reason is that I knew the score would be copied here at once, and consequently gave free rein to my ideas, making alterations and cuts here and there before sending it to the copyist. It was given just as you have it there, except that the parts for trumpets, kettle-drums, flutes, clarinets and Turkish music are occasionally lacking, as I could not get paper ruled with so many lines. They were written as extra leaves and the copyist has probably lost them, for he could not find them. When I was sending the first act somewhere or other—I have forgotten where—it unfortunately fell in the mud, which accounts for its dirty condition.

---

[1] *Die Entführung aus dem Serail (The Abduction from the Seraglio).*
[2] " When tears of joy are flowing."

I have no little work in front of me. By Sunday week my opera must be orchestrated for a band, or someone will step in in front of me and take the profit. In addition, I am to compose a new symphony! How to do all this, I know not! You cannot imagine what hard work it is to orchestrate such a thing to make it fit for wind-instruments without sacrificing the whole effect. Well, I must just spend the night over it—and to you, dearest father, be the sacrifice! You shall hear from me every post-day. I shall work as fast as possible and, as far as haste permits, I shall do good work.—

Count Zitchi has this moment sent to invite me to go with him to Luxemburg, so that he can present me to Prince Kaunitz. I must therefore leave off to dress, for when I do not expect to go abroad I spend my time in *déshabille*. The copyist has just sent me the remaining parts. *Adieu*. I kiss your hands a thousand times, embrace my dear sister with all my heart, and am ever your

Most obedient son,

W. A. Mozart.

P.S.—My dear Constance sends her regards to you both.

88. *To the Baroness von Waldstädten*

July 1782.

Most esteemed Ladyship![1]

Madame Weber's maid-servant has just brought me my music, for which I had to give her a written receipt. The maid-servant also told me something which, though I do not believe it could occur as it would expose the whole family to shame, yet seems possible when one remembers Madame Weber's folly and consequently gives me anxiety. Sophy, it appears, came to the maid-servant crying, and when the latter asked her the reason, she said, "Tell Mozart secretly to arrange for Constance's return home, for my mother is determined to have her fetched by the police." Is it possible for the police here to have immediate entry into any house?

---

[1] The Baroness von Waldstädten, who befriended Mozart in motherly fashion, had taken Constance into her household.

Perhaps the whole thing is merely a trap to get her home. But if it could be done, the best plan I can think of is that I should marry Constance early to-morrow—or to-day if that is possible. For I would wish not to expose my betrothed to this scandal—and it could not occur to my wife! One thing further. Thorwath has been ordered away to-day. I beg your lady-ship's grace for your friendly counsel, and that you will give us two poor creatures your support! I may be found at home all day. I kiss your hands a thousand times, and am your

most obliged Servant,

W. A. Mozart.

In the greatest haste. Constance knows nothing of this as yet. Has Herr von Thorwarth been to see you? Is it necessary for us two to visit him after dinner to-day?

89. *To his Father*

VIENNE, *ce* 27 *juillet*, 1782.

Mon très cher Père !

You will open your eyes wide when you see that this contains nothing but the first allegro. But—I could not help it! I have had to spend one night in rapid composition, but solely in orchestration (otherwise I could have used it for *you* too). On Wednesday, the 31st, I am sending off the two minuets, the andante and the last piece. If I can I will also send a march, but if not you must simply use the one of Hafner's which is very little known:

I have put it in D as I know you prefer it.

My opera was given yesterday for the third time in honour of all Nannerls [1] amid great applause. The theatre was again full to bursting despite the fearful heat. Next Friday it is to be given once more, but I have protested against this, for I do not wish it to become hackneyed. I may say that the populace are quite crazy over this opera. It does one good to hear such applause. I hope you have received the original of the work safely. Dearest, best of fathers, I must now entreat you, by all that is sacred, to give me your consent to my marriage with my dear Constance! Do not suppose that I am thinking only of the marriage—I would willingly wait for that, but I see that, for my own honour and for that of my girl, for the sake of my health and spirits, it is now indispensable! My heart is restless, my head confused, and how can one think and work to any purpose thus? What is the reason for this? Most people believe we are already married. Her mother is provoked by the rumour and the poor girl herself is plagued to death. The remedy is so easy. Believe me it is as easy to live in dear Vienna as elsewhere. It all depends on economy and good management, which are impossible for a young bachelor, particularly for one very much in love. A man who gets such a wife as awaits *me* cannot but be happy. We shall live very modestly and quietly and yet we shall be happy! And so do not be anxious, for should I, which God forbid, fall ill, I could wager that (particularly were I married) some of the most exalted among the *noblesse* would give me their protection.—I can say that with confidence. I know what Prince Kaunitz has said of me to the Emperor and the Archduke Maximilian. I eagerly await your consent, my dearest father. I also await it with confidence, for my honour and fame depend upon it. Do not postpone too long the joy of embracing your son and his wife! I kiss your hands a thousand times, and am ever

Your most obedient son,
W. A. Mozart.

[1] Nannerl. A South German diminutive of Anne and Mozart's sister's name. July 26th is St. Anne's Day.

P.S.—I embrace my dear sister with all my heart. My
Constance sends you both her regards. *Adieu.*

90. *To his Father*

Mon trés cher Pére !

You see that my intentions are good—only what one
cannot do one *cannot.* I do not want to scrawl inferior work.
Accordingly I cannot send you the whole symphony till next
post-day. I could have sent you the last movement, but I
would rather send all together, as it will mean one payment
only. What I have sent has already cost me three gulden. I
have to-day received your letter of the 26th—a cold, indifferent
letter, such as I could never have expected in reply to my
news of the good reception of my opera! I thought (judging
by my own feelings) that you would scarcely be able to open
the packet for eagerness and haste to see your son's work,
which, far from falling flat, has made so great a stir in Vienna
that the people will hear nothing else and the theatre is constantly filled to the doors! Yesterday it was given for the fourth
time and is to be played again on Friday. But you—had not
time enough — — —. And so "the whole world" is saying, is
it, that my boasting and criticisms have made me enemies
among the professors of music and others? What sort of a
world? Probably the world of Salzburg—for everyone in *this*
place can see and hear enough to convince them of exactly the
contrary! And that shall be my reply. In the meantime you
will have received my last letter, and I have no doubt at all
that you will give me your consent to my marriage in your
next. You can have no objection to make—indeed you have
none! Your letters show me that; for Constance is a respect-
able, good girl of good parentage. I am in a position to support
her—we love each other—and want each other! All you have
written as yet—all you might yet write—is no more than
mere well-meaning advice which, however fine and good in
itself, is no longer applicable to a man whose feelings for a
girl have gone so far as have mine. In such a case there must

be no further delay—he must rather put his affairs in order and act like an honest man! God will ever reward him. I mean to have nothing with which to reproach myself! Now fare you well. I kiss your hands a thousand times, and am ever your

Most obedient son,

W. A. Mozart.

P.S.—I embrace my dear sister with all my heart. *Adieu.*

91. *To his Father*

VIENNE, *ce* 7 *d'août,* 1782.

Mon très cher Père !

You are much deceived in your son if you can suppose him capable of acting dishonestly. My dear Constance, now (I thank God) actually my wife, knew my circumstances, and long since heard from me what I had to expect from you. But her affection and love for me were so great that she willingly, most joyfully, consecrated her whole future life to—sharing my fate! I kiss your hands and thank you with all the tenderness a son ever felt for a father for the consent and paternal blessing so kindly bestowed upon me. But I could safely rely upon it—for you know that I could not but see for myself only too well all possible *objections* to such a step! But you also know I could not act otherwise than as I did without injury to my honour and my conscience. Consequently I could build on your consent! For this reason, having waited in vain for an answer over two post-days, and the ceremony having been fixed for a day by which I expected to have received your reply, I plighted troth to my dear one before God and in the comforting certainty of your consent. Next day I got your two letters together. Well, it is over! I have now nothing to do but to beg your forgiveness for my perhaps over-precipitate reliance in your paternal affection. In this frank admission you have a fresh proof of my love of truth and hatred of a lie. Next post-day my dear wife will beg her dearest father-in-law for his paternal blessing and her beloved sister-in-law for the continuance of her much-prized friendship.

No one was present at the wedding save her mother and youngest sister, together with Herr von Thorwarth as trustee and guardian to both, Herr von Zetto (Landrath) as friend of the bride, and Gilofsky as my friend. When we were joined together both my bride and I shed tears. All present, even the priest, were much moved, and all wept at witnessing these tokens of our deep emotion. The marriage-feast consisted in a supper given for us by the Baroness von Waldstädten, and which, as a matter of fact, was *princely* rather than baronial! My dear Constance is now a hundred times more delighted at the prospect of a visit to Salzburg! And I wager—I wager— you will rejoice in my good fortune when you come to know her!—that is if you agree with me that a right-minded, upright, virtuous and amiable wife is a blessing to her husband.—

I send you herewith a short march! I only hope it will arrive in good time and prove according to your taste. The first Allegro should go with considerable fire. The last—as fast as possible. Yesterday my opera was given again—and that at Gluck's request. He complimented me upon it very warmly. I am to dine with him to-morrow. As you will see, I write in great haste. *Adieu.* My dear wife and I kiss your hands a thousand times, and we both embrace our dear sister with all our hearts.

I am ever
Your most obedient son,

7th *August*, 1782.   W. A. Mozart.

92. *To his Father*

Mon trés cher Pére !

I forgot to tell you recently that on Portiuncula Day my wife and I together paid our devotions at the church of the *Theatiners*. If genuine devotion had not moved us to do so we should nevertheless have gone on account of the banns, without which our marriage would not have been possible. For some time, too, we have gone together to Mass, confession and communion, and I have found that I never prayed so earnestly, or confessed and received communion so devoutly, as when by her side. It is the same with her. In a word, we are made for each other, and God, who orders all things and has accordingly ordained this also, will never forsake us! We both thank you most submissively for your paternal blessing. By now, I hope, you will have received a letter from my wife.

As regards happiness, I think just as you write to me in your letter, my dearest father.—But I must tell you one thing more. These Viennese gentry (by which I chiefly mean the Emperor) must not imagine that I am in the world purely for the sake of Vienna! There is no monarch in the globe I would sooner serve than the Emperor—but I will not be a mendicant for any post. I believe I am capable of bringing honour to any Court—and if Germany, my beloved Fatherland, of which, as you know, I am proud, will not take me up—well, let France or England, in God's name, become the richer by another talented German—and that to the disgrace of the German nation! You know well that it is the Germans who have always excelled in almost all the arts, and yet where have they ever found fame and fortune? Certainly not in Germany! Even Gluck—is it Germany which has made a great man of him? Alas, no! Countess Thun, Count Zitschy, Baron von Suiten, even Prince Kaunitz himself, are all very displeased with the Emperor because he does not value persons of talent more, and lets them leave his realms. The latter recently said to the Archduke Maximilian, when the talk turned on me, that such people only come into the world about once a century, and that they must not be driven out of Germany, especially when by good fortune they are actually to be found living in the capital! You cannot imagine with what kindness and courtesy Prince Kaunitz treated me when I went to visit him. When I took leave, he said, "I am very much obliged to you, my dear Mozart, for having taken the trouble to visit me." You would also scarcely believe what efforts Countess Thun, Baron von Suiten and others are making to keep me here. But I cannot wait indefinitely, and indeed I will not be so dependent on

their charity. Moreover, I am not so desperately in need of
their favours, not even of the Emperor's own! My idea is to
go to Paris next Lent—of course not without previous inquiry.
I have already written to Le Gros on the subject and await
his reply. I have mentioned it here, too, especially to people
of position—just in the course of conversation. One can drop
a hint or so which is more effective than any definite declaration. I might be able to secure engagements for the *concert
spirituel* and the *concert des amateurs*, and it would not be
impossible for me to take pupils. Now that I have a wife I
can arrange that more easily and in a more business-like manner.
I could compose, but should rely chiefly on opera. I have been
practising my French daily, and have now taken three lessons
in English. In three months I hope to be able to read and understand English books with fair ease. Now fare you well. My
wife and I kiss your hands a thousand times.

I am ever

Your most obedient son,

W. A. Mozart.

P.S.—What does Luigi Gatti say?

My compliments to Perwein.

I hope my dear sister's indisposition will not have serious
consequences. My dear wife and I kiss her a thousand times,
and hope she may soon be well again. *Adieu.*

93. *To his Father*

VIENNE, *ce* 31 *august*, 1782.

Mon trés cher Pere!

You wonder how I can flatter myself that I could be
maestro to the Princess! Salieri is certainly not equal to in-
structing her in the clavier—all he can do is to try to injure
me with Someone Else in this matter! Very likely! But the
Emperor knows me—and the Princess liked my lessons on a
former occasion. I know, too, that my name is in the book in
which are kept the names of all who are in any way suitable
for her service.—*Le Chevalier* Hypolity has not been to see me

yet. You say I never told you on which floor I am lodging? The information must have got stuck at the end of my pen! Well, I tell you here and now that I live on the second floor. But I cannot understand how you got the notion that my venerated mother-in-law lodged here too! Really, I did not marry my girl in such haste in order to live a life of vexations and quarrels, but for the sake of getting a little peace and happiness! The only way to attain these was to cut oneself off from that household. We have visited her twice since our marriage, but on the second occasion the scolding and quarrelling began again so that my poor wife began to cry. I put an end to the strife at once by telling her it was now time for us to go, and we have not been there since; nor shall go, except to celebrate the birth- or name-day of the mother or one of the two sisters. But you also say that I did not tell you on what day we were married! I must, indeed, beg your pardon—but either your memory has this time betrayed you, in which case you have only to take the trouble to look among my letters for that of August 7th, where you will find it quite clearly stated that we confessed on Friday, Portiuncula Day, and were married on the following Sunday, the 4th, or else you never received this letter; though I cannot see how that may be as you got the *March*, and also answered various other points in the letter. Now I have a petition to make. Baroness Waldstätten is leaving here and would like a good, small *pianoforte*. I have forgotten the name of the clavier-maker in Zweybrücken, and I should like to ask you to order one from him. It would have to be ready, however, within a month, or six weeks at the most; the price the same as the Archbishop's. May I also ask you to send me some Salzburg tongues at the next opportunity, or by post (if the duty does not make it impossible). I am very much indebted to the Baroness, and the conversation turning on tongues, she said she would like to try one, and I offered to get one for her. If you could think of any other delicacy, and would send it me, I should indeed be much obliged to you. I should much like to give her some such little pleasure. I could repay you through Peisser or leave it till

our next meeting. Could I not get *schwarzreuter*? [1] And now
farewell. I and my wife kiss your hands a thousand times,
embrace our dear sister with all our hearts, and ever remain,

Your { most obedient daughter,
{ most obedient son,

Wolfgang and Constance Mozart.

P.S.—Should you be writing to my cousin, pray give her
kind regards from us both. *Addio*.

94. *To the Baroness von Waldstädten*

VIENNE, 28*th September*, 1782.

Most esteemed Ladyship!

When your Ladyship had the kindness yesterday to invite
me to dine with you to-morrow, Sunday, I had forgotten that
I had engaged myself a week ago to dine at the Augarten.[2]
Martin,[3] who fancies himself obliged to me in several matters,
is determined to treat me to a *diné*. I thought yesterday that
I could accommodate the matter in accordance with my
wishes, but found it impossible, since Martin has already
ordered and arranged everything, and consequently would be
put to useless expense. Consequently, and on this account, your
Ladyship will be so good as to excuse me this time, and if your
Ladyship will permit it, we two will have the honour of waiting
upon you next Tuesday—to render you our *homage*, and to
do Fräulein von Auerhammer some *damage*, if to secure her
door more firmly she cannot *manage*!—But now, joking apart,
as regards the concerto I played in the theatre, I really should
not like to surrender it under six ducats. On the contrary, I
would be ready to bear the cost of copying myself.—As regards
that beautiful red coat which took my fancy so vastly, pray,
pray let me know where it is to be had, and at what price—
for *that* I have quite forgotten, having been unable to take in

---

[1] A local table delicacy.
[2] A public resort in Vienna.
[3] "In the spring of 1782 Mozart entered into a speculation with one Martin,
who had received the Emperor's permission to give twelve concerts in the
Augarten, and four grand serenades in the principal squares" (Edward Holmes).

FACSIMILE OF A LETTER TO HIS FATHER
(By kind permission of the Mozart Museum, Salzburg.)

anything at the time but its splendour! Indeed, such a coat I must have—one which will really do justice to certain buttons with which my fancy has long gone pregnant! I saw them once, when I was choosing buttons for a suit, in the Kohlmarkt at Brandau's button-shop, opposite the Milano. They are made of mother-of-pearl, with some sort of white stones round the edge and a fine yellow stone set in the centre of each. I should like to have all my things of good quality, workmanship and appearance! How is it, I wonder, that those who have not the means would be prepared to spend any amount on such articles, while those who *have* the means—do not do so! Well, I believe it is high time I made an end of my scrawl.

J kiss your hands, and hoping to see you in good health the Tuesday, j am,

Your most humble servant,[1]

Mozart.

Constance, my other self, kisses your Ladyship's hands a thousand times, and gives Fräulein Auerhammer a kiss. But I am not to know a word of that, or I should be seized with horror!

95. *To Baroness von Waldstädten*

Dearest, best, loveliest,
  gilded, silvered, sugared,
    Most esteemed and treasured
      Gracious Lady
      Baroness!

Herewith I have the honour to send your Ladyship the rondo in question, together with the two volumes of the *Comedies* and the little book of stories. I made a terrible blunder yesterday! I felt all the time I had something more to say, yet could cudgel nothing out of my dull brains. It was this— I ought to have expressed my gratitude to your Ladyship for your kindness in taking so much trouble about the fine coat—and for your graciousness in promising me such a one!

[1] Mozart's English.

And yet I never thought of it, which is just what is constantly happening to me. I often regret that I did not study architecture instead of music, for I have often heard it said that the best architect is a man who never has an idea! I may say with truth that I am a very happy—and at the same time, a very unhappy—man! Unhappy since the day when I saw your Ladyship so beautifully *coiffée* at the ball—for that made an end of all my peace of mind! Naught since then but sighs and groans! During the rest of the time I spent at that ball I did not dance—I leapt! Supper was already ordered, but I could not eat—I fed! At night, instead of enjoying soft and sweet repose—I slept like a dormouse and snored like a bear! And (without building too much upon it) I would almost be prepared to wager that it was much the same with your Ladyship! You smile? You blush? You do! I am indeed happy! My future is made! But ah! who is this that takes me by the shoulders? Who peeps into my letter? Oh, oh, oh—my wife! Well, well, *nom de Dieu*, I love her and must keep her! What else is there to do? I must praise her—and pretend to myself that my praises are deserved! I am fortunate in needing no Fräulein Auerhammer as a pretext to write to your Ladyship like Herr von Taisen, or whatever his name is (I would he had no name!), for I have something to send your Ladyship's self. And, moreover, apart from this, I should have had occasion to write to your Ladyship—and yet when it comes to the point I dare not say it! Yet why not? Well, then, *courage!* May I entreat your Ladyship to—the deuce! that would be too gross! *Apropos.* Does not your Ladyship know the little rhyme?

> *Ein frauenzimmer und ein Bier*
> *wie reimt sich das zusamm' ?*
> *Das frauenzimmer besitzt ein Bier,*
> *Davon schickt sie ein' Bluzer mir*
> *So reimt es sich zusamm' !*

> [A woman and a pint of beer
> How do they rhyme together?

The woman has a barrel of beer,
A pint therefrom she sends me here,
And so they rhyme together!]

I brought that in very neatly, did I not? But now *senza burle*. If your Ladyship could send me a pint this evening you would be doing me a great favour. For my wife is—is—is—and she has longings—but only for beer prepared in the English manner! Now, bravo, little wife! I see at last that you are good for *something*! My wife, who is an angel of a wife, and I, who am a model of a husband, both kiss your hands a thousand times, and am ever your

faithful vassals,
Mozart magnus, corpore parvus
et
Constantia omnium uxorum pulcherrima et prudentissima.

VIENNA, *2nd October*, 1782.

My compliments, pray, to Fräulein Auerhammer.

96. *To his Father*

VIENNE, *ce 22 de janvier*, 1783.

Mon trés cher Pére !

You need have no fear that the three concertos are too dear. I think, after all, I deserve a ducat for each concerto—and then I should much like to see who would have it copied for himself for a ducat! They cannot be copied, however, for I will not let them out of my hands until I have a certain number of orders. They have now been advertised for the third time in the Viennese daily papers. The subscription tickets can be had from me from the 20th of this month for four ducats cash, and the concertos may be collected from me during the month of April on presentation of the tickets.

With my next I will send the cadenzas and preludes for my dear sister. I have not yet altered the preludes in the rondo, for when I play the concerto I always put in whatever occurs to me. Pray send the symphonies I asked for as soon as you can, for I really need them. And now, one more request, for my wife leaves me no peace! You know, of course, that it is now Carnival, and there is much dancing here just as in Salzburg and Munich. I should very much like to go as Harlequin (but unknown to everyone), as there are so many— indeed nothing but—asses at the masquerades! So may I ask you to send me your Harlequin dress? But it must be very soon, and we shall not attend the masquerades till it comes, although they are now in full swing. We prefer private balls. Last week we gave a ball in our own rooms. But of course the men had each to pay two gulden. We began at six o'clock in the evening and ended at seven. What! Only an hour? Oh no,—seven o'clock next morning! But you will wonder, I expect, how we could make room? Yes, and it has just occurred to me that each time I have written to you I have forgotten to tell you that we have been in new lodgings for the last six weeks or so— but still on the Hohenbrücke and not many doors away. So our address is *In kleinen Herbersteinischen Hause*, No. 412, 3rd floor, at Herr von Wezlar's—a rich Jew's. Well, I have a room there (1000 paces long and one wide!), a bedroom, an ante-chamber and a fine big kitchen. Then there are two more fine big rooms next to ours which still stand empty, so I used these, too, for the dance. Baron Wezlar and his wife were there, the Waldstättens, Herr von Edelbach, Gilofsky, Windmacher, young Stephani *et uxor*, Adamberger and his wife, M. and Madame Lang, etc.—I cannot possibly tell you them all. Now I must close as I still have a letter to write to Madame Wendling at Mannheim about my concertos. Pray remind that ever-ready opera composer, Gatti, about the operatic libretti. I should have liked to have them by now. And now, *adieu*. We kiss your hands a thousand times, embrace our dear sister with all our hearts, and remain ever your

Most obedient children,
W. *et* Co. Mozart.

97. *To his Father*

Mon très cher Père !

I have your last letter safely, and hope that in the mean-time you will have got my last letter and my request for the Harlequin dress. I renew it again here, begging you to be so very kind as to dispatch it with all possible speed. Also will you please send the symphonies, especially the last, as soon as may be, for my concert is to take place on the third Sunday in Lent, that is on March 23rd, and I still have much revision work to do upon it. So I thought that, if it is not copied already, you might send me back the original score just as I sent it to you—but send the minuets with it.

Is Cecarelli no longer in Salzburg, then? Or was he given no part in Gatti's cantata? For I see you do not include him among the wranglers and brawlers!

Yesterday my opera [1] was given for the seventeenth time —as usual to a full house and amid universal applause.

Next Friday, that is the day after to-morrow, a new opera is to be given, the music (which is gibberish) by a young fellow living here, a pupil of Wagenseil, which is as much as to say *gallus cantans, in arbore sedens, gigirigi faciens.* [2] Probably it will not be much liked, though more so than its predecessor, an old opera by Gasman (*La notte crittica*, in German *Die unruhige Nacht* [*The Unquiet Night*]), which with difficulty survived three performances. This in its turn was preceded by that execrable opera I wrote to you about, and which never achieved a third performance at all. In any case the German opera season is over at Easter, yet it almost seems as if they were trying to bring it to a premature end. And this is the work of men who are themselves Germans! Oh, shame!—

In my last letter I begged you to do all you could to rouse Gatti about those Italian libretti, and I repeat my request here. Now I must tell you of my plan. I do not think the Italian opera season will last long, and besides, I side with the German!

[1] *Die Entführung aus dem Serail.*
[2] "A crowing cock, sitting in a tree, uttering cock-a-doodle-doos."

I prefer it even if it costs me more trouble. Every nation has its own opera, why not Germany? Is not German as singable as French and English? Is it not more so than Russian? Very well, then! I am now writing a German opera on my own initiative. I have chosen Goldoni's [1] comedy *Il servitore di due Padrone* for my purpose, and the whole of the first act has now been translated. Baron Binder is the translator. But it must be kept secret until all is ready. Well, what do you think of it? Do you not think I shall do very well over it? But I must make an end of my letter. Fischer, the bass singer, has called to see me. He has asked me to write about him to Le Gros in Paris, as he means to go there this very Lent. The people here are committing the folly of letting a man go who can never be replaced! My wife and I kiss your hands a thousand times, embrace our dear sister with all our hearts, and remain ever your

Most obedient children,

W. *et* C. Mozart.

gaetano Majorani (Caffarello)
Amphion Theba
ego Domum.

98. *To the Baroness von Waldstädten*

Most esteemed Ladyship!

Here am I in a pretty pickle! Herr von Tranner and I recently bargained for an extension, agreeing to pay up at the expiration of a fortnight. As this is a thing every merchant does unless he is the most imprudent man in the world, my mind was quite at ease, and I hoped that, by then, even if I could not produce the sum myself, I should be able to borrow it! Now Herr von Tranner lets me know that the other party is determined to wait no longer, and if I do not pay before to-morrow morning he will bring an action. Now let your Ladyship imagine what an awkward business that would be

[1] The Venetian playwright.

for me! I cannot pay—not even half the sum! If I could have
foreseen that the subscriptions for my concertos would come
in so slowly, I should have borrowed the money on a longer
period! In Heaven's name, I beg your Ladyship help me to
save my good name and my honour! My poor little wife feels
a little out of sorts so I cannot leave her, otherwise I would
have come myself to ask in person for your ladyship's aid. We
kiss your ladyship's hands a thousand times, and remain
Your Ladyship's
Most obedient children,
W. A. and C. Mozart.

At home, 15*th Feb.*, 1783.

99. *To his Father*

VIENNE, *ce* 29 *de mars*, 1783.

Mon trés cher Pére !

I do not think it can be necessary for me to write you
much about the success of my concert, as you will probably
have heard of it already. Enough—the theatre could not
possibly have been fuller and all the boxes were taken. What
pleased me most, however, was that his Majesty the Emperor
was present, was delighted and applauded me loudly. It is
his custom to send money to the box-office before he enters
the theatre, otherwise I should have had every reason to expect
more from him, for his satisfaction knew no bounds. The sum
he sent was twenty-five ducats. The items were as follows:
(1) The new Hafner symphony; (2) the aria, accompanied by
four instruments, from my Munich opera, *Se il padre perdei*,
sung by Madame Lang; (3) the third of my subscription concertos, played by myself; (4) Countess Baumgarten's *scena*, sung
by Adamberger; (5) the little *concertante* symphony from my
latest *final musique*; (6) the favourite concerto in D with which
I have incorporated the variations rondo played by myself;
(7) the *scena* from my last Milanese opera, *Parto, m'affretto*,
sung by Mademoiselle Täuber; (8) I played a little fugue
(the Emperor being present) and variations on an aria from
an opera called *The Philosophers*. I was recalled, and played

variations on an aria "*Unser dummer Pöbel meint,*" etc., from *The Pilgrims from Mecca* [1]; (9) my new rondo, sung by Madame Lang; (10) the last movement of the first symphony.

To-morrow Mademoiselle Täuber is giving a concert at which I also am to play. Next Thursday Herr von Daubrawaick and Herr von Gilowsky leave for Salzburg and will take with them the Munich opera, the two copies of my sonatas, a few variations for my sister, and money in settlement of my debt for the copying of the opera. I safely received the parcel of music and thank you for it. Pray do not forget about the *Lauda Sion*, and we should also very much like to have some of your best church pieces, my dearest father, for we like to play and listen to all possible masters, both ancient and modern. So please send us soon something of your own. Now I must end my letter. My wife and I kiss your hands a thousand times, embrace our dear sister with all our hearts, and ever remain your

Most obedient children,

W. A. Mozart.

100. *To his Father*

VIENNE, IN THE PRATER,[2] *ce* 3 *de mai,* 1783.

Mon très cher Père!

I cannot possibly make up my mind to go back into the town so early. The weather is far too lovely, and it is far too pleasant here in the Prater to-day. We have taken our meal out of doors, and shall stay on till eight or nine o'clock this evening. My company consists solely of my pregnant wife and her—not pregnant—but fat and flourishing husband! I went straight to Herr Peyser, got the banker Schefler's address from him, and I then went at once to the banker, but there they know nothing of any merchant's son named Rosa who might have an introduction to them. For further security I have left my address there. I shall now wait and see what happens. I fear I must ask you to wait patiently for a longer letter and the aria variations—for, of course, I cannot accomplish them in the Prater, and I cannot miss this beautiful weather for my

---

[1] By Gluck.　　　　　　　　[2] A park in Vienna.

dear little wife's sake! Change and exercise are good for her
health. So I write merely a few words to-day to say that we
are both, thank God, well, and have safely received your last
letter. Now fare you well. We kiss your hands a thousand times,
embrace our dear sister warmly, and are ever your
                    Most obedient children,
                              W. A. and C. Mozart.

101. *To his Father*   VIENNE, *ce 18 de juin,* 1783.

Mon très cher Père !

I congratulate you, you are a grandpapa! Early yesterday
morning, the 17th, at half-past six, my dear wife was happily
delivered of a fine, big, sturdy, fat boy! The pains began at
half-past one in the morning, so it was over with all rest or
sleep for either of us that night! At four o'clock I sent for my
mother-in-law—and then for the midwife. By half-past six
all was over. My mother-in-law has now fully atoned by her
kindness for all the ill she did her daughter in her single state.
She spends the whole day with her.

My dear wife, who kisses your hand and embraces my dear
sister affectionately, feels as well as the circumstances permit.
I hope to God that by taking good care of herself she will come
well through her child-bed. From the condition of her breasts,
I have some fear of milk-fever! And now against, and yet by,
my will, they have got a wet-nurse for the child! I was always
quite determined that, whether she were able to do so or not,
my wife should never suckle her child—and yet I was equally
determined my child should take no stranger's milk! I intended
to bring it up on water, like my sister and myself, only the
midwife, my mother-in-law and the majority of people here
have begged me not to think of it, simply because it is the
water which causes most of the children's deaths here, as the
people do not know how to use it. That moved me to give in,
for I should not like to have anything to reproach myself with.

Now as regards the godparents! Let me tell you what has
passed. I sent Baron Wezlar[1] (who is my good and true friend)

[1] See Letter No. 96.

immediate news of my wife's happy delivery. He came at once himself and offered to stand godfather. I could not refuse him and thought to myself, "I can still call him Leopold," but while the thought passed through my mind, he said joyfully, "Now you have a little Raymund," and kissed the child. What was to be done? I accordingly had the boy christened Raymund Leopold. I frankly admit that if you had not given me your opinion on the matter by letter I should have found myself in an embarrassing position, and I cannot vouch for it that I should not have refused his offer! But your letters comforted me with the assurance that you would not be displeased with my course of action! After all, Leopold is one of his names.—

Now I must close. I and my wife kiss your hands, send a thousand embraces to our dear sister, and remain ever your most obedient children,

W. and C. Mozart.[1]

102. *To his Sister*

Glücks Wunsch
beym Punsch!

Ich bin heut ausgegangen, du wusstest nicht warum,
Ich kann nur so viel sagen, dass es geschah darum,
um dich mit etwas kleinen ein wenig zu erfreu'n,
wobey ich weder kösten, noch fleis noch müh wollt' scheu'n.
Ich weiss zwar nicht gewiss, ob du den Punsch magst
    trinken
O sage doch night Nein, sonst möcht das Bindband stinken,
Ich dachte so bei mir, du liebst die Engeländer,
den liebtest du Paris, so gäbe ich dir Bänder,
Wohlriechende Gewässer, ein köstliches Backett
du aber, liebste Schwester, du bist keine Kokett,
Drum nimm aus meiner Hand den guten kräft'gen
    Punsch,
Und lass ihn dir recht schmecken, das ist wein einz'ger
    Wunsch.

[1] "Towards the end of July in this year Mozart and his wife visited their father at Salzburg" (Edward Holmes).

[Punch-brew
Here's to you!
To-day I went abroad, you'll never guess the cause;
All that I'm free to say is that I went because
To give you one least pleasure, however poor and small;
My time, my cash, my trouble, I grudge them not at all.
'Tis true I am not certain if Punch is your desire,
Yet pray do not deny it, or the fat is in the fire!
For, thought I within myself, you love the folk of England,
And had your choice been Paris, I would have chosen
        riband—
A bottle of sweet essences—a precious little packet;
But, dearest sister mine, you surely are no coquette!
So pray take from your brother this punch so good and
        strong, for
If you but like its flavour, I shall have all I long for!]

SALZBURG, 31st July, 1783.

W. A. Mozart,
poet-laureate.

103. *To his Father*

24th April [1784].

We now have here the famous Madame Strinasacchi[1] from Mantua, a very good violinist. There is much taste and feeling in her playing. I am just engaged upon the composition of a sonata which we are to play together on Thursday at her concert in the theatre. Some quartets have been published recently by a certain Pleyel,[2] a pupil of Haydn's. If you do not know them yet, try to get them; you will find them worth the trouble. They are very well written and most pleasing. You will also see at once who was his master. 'Twill be a happy thing for music if Pleyel is some day able to replace Haydn for us!

[1] Strinasacchi, Regina (1764–1839), for whom Mozart wrote his B-flat-major violin sonata. She married Schlick, the 'cellist.

[2] Pleyel, Ignaz Joseph (1727–1831), conductor and composer in Paris, Vienna, Rome, London, etc. He did not fulfil his promise, but declined into a server of popular taste, and eventually ceased to compose and took to music-dealing and pianoforte manufacture. Founder of the famous firm of piano-makers.

104. *To his Father*

VIENNA, 28*th April*, 1784.

I have to write in haste. Herr Richter, a clavier-player, is making a tour on his way back to Holland, his native country. I have given him a letter of introduction to the Countess Thun at Linz. As he also wished to visit Salzburg, I have given him a few lines to you, dearest father. I am writing now to say that he will appear soon after you receive this. There is a great deal of execution in his playing, but, as you will hear, it is too broad, too laboured, and without a trace of taste or feeling. Otherwise he is the best fellow in the world and without a trace of pride. He fixed his eyes on my fingers while I played to him, then said suddenly, "My God; I work at it till I sweat and yet get no success—while you, my friend, simply play at it!" "Yes," said I, "but I too had to work in order that I might be exempt from work now." *Afin* he is a man with a place among good clavier-players, and I hope the Archbishop will be the more inclined to hear him for being a clavier-player—*en dépit de moi* (although *I* am very glad to possess that *dépit*!). All is right about the violinist Menzl and he will probably set sail from here on Sunday. You will get some music from me by this means. And now, farewell . . .

105. *To his Father*

VIENNE, *ce* 26 *may*, 1784.

Mon tres cher Pere !

In your last letter I have news that you have got my letter and the music safely. I thank my sister for her letters, and as soon as time permits I shall certainly write also to her. Meanwhile pray tell her that Herr Richter is mistaken as to the key of the concerto, or else I have read a letter wrong in your writing. The concerto Herr Richter praised to her so warmly is that in B flat, the first I made and the one he praised so highly to me at the time. I really cannot make a choice between these two concertos. They both require effort, but, as regards difficulty, the B flat concerto has the advantage over that in D. For the rest, I am very curious to know which of the three concertos in B flat, D and G pleased you and my sister best. The one in E does not enter into the matter. It is a concerto of a quite peculiar kind, and is written rather for a small orchestra than for a big one—so I speak only of the three big concertos. I am curious to know whether your judgment accords with the general opinion here and also with mine. Candidly, it is necessary to hear all three well performed with all their parts. I am quite willing to wait patiently till they are returned to me as long as nobody else is allowed to lay hands on them. I could have got twenty-four ducats for one of them to-day, but I think it better to keep them by me a year or so, and then make them known by publication.

But I must tell you something about Loiserl Schwemmer! She wrote a letter to her mother, and as the address was so arranged that the post would hardly have accepted it—it went like this:

Dieser Brief zueku-
men meiner vilgeliebtisten
Frau Mutter in Salzburg
barbari schbemerin
abzugeben in der
Judengasen in Kauf
man eberl haus
in dritten Stock.

[This letter bee-
longs to my derest
Mother at Salzburg,
Mrs. barbara schbemer,
to be delivered at
Jew Street at Mer-
chant eberl's house
the third floor.]

I said I would address it afresh for her. Being inquisitive, but rather to read more of this beautiful composition than to penetrate any secrets, I opened the letter! In it she complained that she had to go to bed too late and get up too early— but I should have thought one could get sleep enough between eleven o'clock and six—that is seven hours, after all! We ourselves do not go to bed till twelve and get up at half-past five, or even five, as we go to the Augarten almost every morning early. She further complained about the food, with the impertinent remark that we should starve, all four of us, as my wife, I, the cook, and she had less to eat here than she and her mother had between them at home! You know that I took the girl at the time out of pure pity to help her when she was a stranger in Vienna. We promised her 12 gulden a year and she was quite content with it, though she now complains about it in her letter. And what is it she has to do? To clear the table, hand the dishes round and take them to the kitchen, and help my wife to dress and undress! Moreover, apart from her sewing, she is the clumsiest and stupidest creature in the world. She cannot even light a fire, let alone make coffee, things which a girl who pretends to be a parlour-maid should be able to do. We gave her a gulden and the very next day she asked for more money. I made her give me an account of her expenses, and found that beer made up the greater part of them! A certain Herr Johannes travelled here with her, but he dare not show his face at my house any longer. Twice when we were from home he came here and ordered in wine, and the girl, who is not used to drinking wine, filled herself so full that she could not walk without support, and the last time was sick all over her bed! Who in the world would keep such a person under such conditions?—

I would have contented myself with the sermon I read her on the occasion, and would have said nothing about it to you, but her impertinent letter to her mother has driven me to it. So will you pray send for the mother and tell her that I will put up with her a little longer, but that she must look about for another place? Were it not that I hate to make people unhappy I would dismiss her on the spot. There is something, too, in her letter about a certain Herr Antoni—a future bridegroom perhaps!

Well, I must finish my letter. My wife thanks you both for your good wishes respecting her condition and future

confinement, which should probably occur in the first days of
October. We both kiss your hands, embrace our dear sister
affectionately, and ever remain your

Most obedient children,

W. et C. Mozart.

P.S.—Pray do contrive to send me the buckles by the
next diligence. I am burning with eagerness to see them.

106. *To his Sister*

VIENNA, 18th August, 1784.

Ma très chère sœur !

Potz Sapperment ! [1] It is indeed time I wrote to you if I
want my letter to find you still a vestal! A few days later—
and that is past! My wife and I wish you all happiness and
joy in your change of state, and only regret most sincerely
that we cannot have the pleasure of being present at your
wedding. But we have the certain hope of seeing you as Frau
von Sonnenburg, together with your husband, in Salzburg and
in St. Gilgen next spring. Our only regrets are for our dear
father, who will now be left so utterly alone! True, you will
not be far away from him, and he can often walk as far as
your house—only he is tied to that accursed choir service
again! Were I in my father's place I would do as follows: I
would now go to the Archbishop and ask him—as a man of
long service—to allow me to retire, and then, on getting my
pension, I would join my daughter at St. Gilgen and live there
in peace and quiet. If the Archbishop refused my request, I
would ask for my discharge and go to my son in Vienna.—And
what I chiefly want to ask you is—to do your best to persuade
him to act thus! I have suggested the same thing in my letter
to him to-day.

And now I send a thousand good wishes from Vienna to
Salzburg, more especially that you two may live together as
happily as—we two! So accept a little piece of good advice
from the poetic treasure-house of my brains! Listen:

[1] An ejaculation and minced oath.

Du wirst in Ehstand viel erfahren,
was dir ein halbes Rätsel war;
bald wirst du aus Erfahrung wissen,
wie Eva einst hat handeln müssen,
dass sie hernach den Kain gebar.
Doch, Schwester, diese Ehstandspflichten
wirst du von herzen gern verrichten,
denn glaube mir, sie sind nicht schwer.
Doch jede Sache hat zwo Seiten :
der Ehstand bringt zwar viele Freuden,
allein auch Kummer bringet er.
Drum wenn dein Mann dir finstre Mienen,
die du nicht glaubest zu verdienen
in seiner üblen Laune macht :
so denke, dass ist Männergrille,
und sag : Herr, es gescheh dein Wille,
bei Tag—und meiner in der Nacht.

[In marriage you will learn to fathom
Much that before was half a riddle;
Experience soon will teach to you
What Eve herself had once to do
Ere she gave birth to Cain and Abel.
Yet, sister, those same marriage dues
Are what your heart will gladly choose,
For, trust my word, they are not heavy!
Yet every object has two faces
And wedlock, bringing many graces,
Brings also troubles in a bevy.
So, when your man an angry brow
Which, as deserved, you'll not allow,
Discloses to your sight,
Think, " 'Tis but menfolk's freakish way."
Say, "Lord, thy will be done by day
But mine be done by night!"]

Your faithful brother,
W. A. Mozart.

Leopold Mozart to his Daughter [1]

19th November, 1784.

Die Entführung aus dem Serail was fairly well performed on the 17th and very greatly applauded. Three pieces were encored. By five o'clock all the lower part of the theatre was full, and by a quarter past five the upper places were full also. The whole town is delighted with it and even the Archbishop was so very gracious as to say it was "really not bad!"

Leopold Mozart to his Daughter [2]

14th February, 1785.

On the same Friday evening we went to the first of his subscription concerts, for which a great number of persons of rank were assembled. The concert was incomparable, the orchestra most excellent. In addition to the symphonies a female singer from the Italian theatre sang two arias, and then came a magnificent new clavier concerto by Wolfgang, which the copyist was still engaged upon when we arrived, leaving your brother no time to *play* over the rondo even once, as he had to *read* over the whole copy.

On Saturday evening we had Herr Joseph Haydn and the two Barons Tindi with us, and the new quartets were played—but only the three new ones he has composed in addition to the other three we already have. They are a little easier than the first three, indeed, but excellently composed. Herr Haydn said to me, "I tell you, calling God to witness and speaking as a man of honour, that your son is the greatest composer I know, either personally or by repute! He has taste, and, in addition, the most complete understanding of composition."

Leopold Mozart to his Daughter

19th March, 1785.

I believe that if my son has no debts to pay he will now be able to place 2000 florins in the bank. The money is certainly there, and the household management, as far as food and drink are concerned, is economical in the highest degree.

---

[1] This and the following letters from Leopold Mozart to his daughter are all addressed to St. Gilgen, where she lived with her husband, Berchthold von Sonnenburg, Baron of the Holy Roman Empire.

[2] Leopold Mozart was at this time his son's guest in Vienna. Towards the end of March he returned to Salzburg and father and son never met again.

THE GREAT OPERAS (1785-93)

107. *To Professor Anton Klein, Mannheim*

Most estimable Herr Geheimrath,[1]

I am much at fault, I must confess, for not having at once acknowledged the safe receipt of your letter and the accompanying packet. As to my having received, in the meantime, two further letters from you—but it was not quite like that! The first would have instantly aroused me from my slumber, and I should have answered it as I am doing now, but I got both your letters together last post-day! I have already acknowledged my guilt in not having answered you at once, but, as regards the opera,[2] I should have been able to say as little then—as I can now! My dear Herr Geheimrath! My hands are so full of affairs that I can find scarce a minute for myself. A man of so much insight and experience as yourself will know even better than I that these things, however carefully and attentively read, need reading through not only once, but many times. Hitherto I have not had time to read it through even once without interruption! All that I can say for the present is that I should not like to part with it yet. Will you therefore pray entrust the piece to my keeping a little longer? In case I should be inclined to compose upon it, I should like to know beforehand whether its production has been arranged for anywhere, for a work like this, as regards both poetry and music, deserves better than to be completed and yet come to nothing! I shall await further information from you on this point. I cannot at present give you any news of the future

[1] Privy-councillor. A title of honour.
[2] Klein had offered Mozart an operatic libretto

German operatic stage, as, apart from building operations at
the Kärntnerthor Theatre, which is to be used for the purpose,
very little is going forward. It is to be opened early in October.
I for my part have no great hopes of its success. According
to present plans, it looks more as if they were attempting
to bring final ruin upon German opera, which at present is
suffering a perhaps only temporary eclipse, than to raise it
up and preserve it. My sister-in-law, Madame Lang, is the
only one who is to join the German opera company. Madame
Cavallieri, Adamberger, Madame Teuber, all Germans of whom
Germany may well be proud, are to stay at the Italian opera
—to compete against their own fellow-countrymen! — — —
The tale of German singers, male and female, of the present
day is soon told, and even if there are to be found among them
people as good as, or even better than, those I have named
(which I very much doubt), I cannot but feel that the directors
of our theatre will prove to be too parsimonious, and too little
patriotic, to pay large sums to get strangers to come here
when they could get better singers on the spot—or at least
as good—for nothing! For the Italian company has no need
of them—numerically speaking. It is sufficient to itself. The
present idea is to employ for the purposes of the German
opera actors and actresses who only take singing rôles when
they must. Most unfortunately both orchestral and theatrical
directors have been retained who, by a combination of ignorance
and inactivity, have done much to ruin their own enterprise.
If there were but *one* patriot on the board—the affair would
take on quite another aspect! Then, perhaps, the vigorously
sprouting German national theatre would actually begin to
flower—and what an everlasting shame it would be for
Germany, to be sure, if we Germans were seriously to begin
to think German, to act as Germans, to talk German, and
even—to sing German ! ! !

Pray do not take it amiss, my dear Herr Geheimrath, if
in my zeal I have perhaps gone too far ! Secure that I was
speaking to a true German, I gave my feelings rein, a thing
unhappily so seldom possible in these days that one might

boldly follow each such heart-outpouring with a drinking bout without danger of doing any injury to one's health!

I remain, with the deepest respect,

Most estimable Herr Geheimrath,

Your most obedient servant,

W. A. Mozart

VIENNA, 21st March, 1785.

Leopold Mozart to his Daughter

18th April, 1786.

Le Nozze di Figaro is to be performed for the first time on the 28th. It will be very significant if it succeeds, for I know there are astonishingly strong cabals against it. Salieri and all his partisans will again endeavour to move heaven and earth. Duschek said to me recently that the reason your brother has all these cabals against him is that he is held in such high esteem for his great talents and ability![1]

108. *To Sebastian Winter, Royal Groom-of-the-Chambers*

DONAUESCHINGEN.

Dearest friend! Companion of my youth!

It was with exceptional pleasure that I received your letter, and nothing but business which could not possibly be postponed has kept me from answering you before.—I am very glad that you have applied to me personally. I should long since have sent some specimen of my poor work to his Highness the Prince (to whom I beg you will say, in my name, that I lay myself at his feet and thank him most humbly for the present he has sent me) had I known whether or no my father had already sent him anything and, if so, what! Accordingly I place at the end of my letter a list of the latest-born children of my fancy, amongst which his Highness has only to choose that I may hasten to serve him. If his Highness pleases, I could in future pay him my respects with each of my pieces

[1] Salieri and Righini, being at the time ready with operas, were both competitors with Mozart for preference; and the contest between the composers was so warm that the Emperor was obliged to interpose, and he decided for *Figaro*.

as it is completed. Moreover, I venture to make his Highness a little proposal in the matter of music which I would ask you, my friend, to lay before your Prince. Since his Highness possesses an orchestra, his Highness might like to possess certain orchestrated pieces of mine for use solely at his Court— in my poor opinion a possible gratification to him. If his Highness would be so gracious as to commission me, year by year, with a certain number of symphonies, quartets, concertos for different instruments or other pieces according to choice, and if he would be pleased to endow me with a fixed yearly salary therefor, his Highness should be well and punctually served, and *I should be able to work with a more collected mind, being sure of having that work to do !* I hope his Highness will not take my proposition amiss, even should he be disinclined to accept it, for indeed it arises from an impulse of genuine zeal to serve his Highness diligently, which, in such a situation as mine, is only possible if one can be secure of at least a certain support and can consequently afford to reject work of the meaner sort.

In expectation of a speedy reply I am ever at his Highness's service,

Your sincere friend and servant,

Wolfgang Amadé Mozart.

VIENNA, *8th August,* 1786.

Leopold Mozart to his Daughter

17th November, 1786.

I have had to-day to answer a letter of your brother's which has cost me a great deal of writing, so my letter to you must be short. You will realise that I had to write to him very emphatically when I tell you that he made no less a proposition than that *I* should take charge of his two children as he wished to make a tour through Germany and England, etc., at mid-Lent! I have, however, written very explicitly and have promised him a continuation of my letter by the next post! A pretty suggestion indeed! They are to set out light-heartedly on their travels, die perhaps, perhaps stay in England—in which case I could come running after them with

SINFONIA di Wolfgango Amadeo Mozart

1. Adagio

2. Allº

3. Allº

4. Allº

Concerti per Cembalo

1. Allº

2. Allº

3.

4.

5. Allº

Sonata per Cembalo con Violino, Terzetto:
Cembalo, Violino e Violoncello

Quartetto: Cembalo, Violino, Viola e Violóncello

the children and so on!—or else, with the payment he offers me for
the children and their nurse—*Basta!* My refusal is a forcible one—
and instructive, too, if he will but profit by the lesson![1]

Leopold Mozart to his Daughter

12*th January*, 1787.

Your brother and his wife must be in Prague by now, for I hear
from him that he was to begin his journey last Monday. So successful was the performance of his opera *Le Nozze di Figaro*, that the
orchestra and an association of distinguished experts and amateurs
addressed him a letter of invitation and sent him a poem which
had been made about him.

109. *To his Father*

Mon très cher Père!

I am very displeased that my letter has failed to reach
your hands through Mlle. Storace's[2] stupidity. Among other
matters contained in it I asked you whether you had received
my last letter, but as you make no reference to it at all (it was
the second I sent you from Prague) I do not know what to think.
It is quite likely that some servant of Count Thun's took it
into his head to pocket the postage money! I would much
rather pay double the postage than suspect that my letters
have fallen into wrong hands. Ramm and the two Fishers
(a bass-singer and an oboe-player) came here this Lent from
London. If the latter played no better at the time we knew
him in Holland than he plays now, he certainly does not deserve his fame! Nevertheless, between ourselves, in those days
I was not competent to form an opinion. I can only remember
that he pleased me extraordinarily, as he did everybody. It
is comprehensible, of course, on the supposition that taste

[1] Mozart's preparation for a visit to England had proceeded so far that
everything was packed, when all his plans were changed by the receipt of an
appointment as Chamber-music Composer to the Emperor, accompanied by
a pension.

[2] Storace, Ann Selina (1766–1817), born in London of Italian parentage,
a famous *coloratura* singer, and sister of Stephen Storace, a composer of
operas and musical comedies. Mozart wrote the part of Susanna in *Figaro*
for her.

has changed extraordinarily. His playing belongs to an old
school—but no! The long and short of it is that he plays like
a bad beginner. Young André, Fiala's pupil, plays a thousand
times better. And then his concertos!—his own compositions! Each ritornello lasts a quarter of an hour. Then the
hero appears—lifts up leaden feet one after another and bangs
them down alternately on the ground! His tone is utterly
nasal—and his *tenata* is a *tremolando* on the organ! Would
you have pictured him like this? And yet it is the truth—
though I would not proclaim it to anyone but you.—I have
this moment received a piece of news which greatly distresses
me—all the more because I gathered from your last letter
that you were, thank God, in very good health. But now I
hear you are really ill! I am sure I need not tell you how
greatly I long for reassuring news from yourself. Indeed I
expect it, even though I have accustomed myself to contemplate the worst on all occasions. Since death, when we come
to consider it, is seen to be the true goal of our life, I have
made acquaintance during these last few years with this best
and truest friend of mankind, so that his image not only no
longer has any terrors for me, but suggests, on the contrary,
much that is reassuring and consoling! And I thank my God
for blessing me with the opportunity (you understand me) of
coming to recognise Him as the key to our true blessedness.—
I never lie down upon my bed without reflecting that—
young as I am—I may perhaps never see another day—and
yet not one of those who know me can say that I am morose
or sad among my fellows! For this blessing I daily thank my
Creator and wish with all my heart that my fellow-men may
share it.—I had already declared my mind to you on this
point (in the letter Mlle. Storace dispatched) on the occasion
of the death of my dearest, best of friends, Count von Hatzfeld.[1]
He was just thirty-one years old—my own age. I do not grieve
for him—but I do from my heart pity myself and all who knew
him as well as I. I hope, I wish, that while I write this you are

[1] A musical amateur of Vienna, who with others performed *Idomeneo*
privately in the winter of 1785-6.

getting better. But should you, against all expectation, be no better, I beg you will not . . . will not conceal it from me, but tell me, or have me told, the whole truth, so that I can come with all human speed to your arms! I conjure you, by all that is—sacred to both of us! Yet I hope soon to get a reassuring letter from you, and in this happy expectation, I with my wife and Carl,[1] kiss your hands a thousand times, and remain ever

Your most obedient son,

VIENNA, 4th April, 1787.   W. A. Mozart.

110. *To his Sister*

Dearest, best Sister!   VIENNA, 16th June, 1787.

I was neither astonished nor shocked that you did not yourself inform me of the sad and, to me, quite unexpected death of our dear father,[2] for I could easily guess the reason. May God take him to Himself! Be assured, my dear, that if you desire a kind and loving brother to care for you, you will find one in me on every occasion. My dearest, best Sister! If you were still without support all this would be unnecessary. As I have said and thought a thousand times, I would leave everything to you with true delight in doing so. But now, since it is, so to speak, unnecessary to you, but to me, on the contrary, a special benefit, I feel it a duty to think of my wife and child.[3]

111. *To Baron Gottfried von Jacquin, Vienna*

Dearest friend!   PRAGUE, 15th October, 1787.

You probably imagine that my opera [4] is over by now—

[1] Mozart's second child, born in 1784, died 1858. The first, Raymund, did not survive its first year.
[2] Leopold Mozart died on 28 May, 1787.
[3] During July 1787 Mozart was seriously ill.
[4] Embittered by intrigues in Vienna, Mozart wrote *Don Giovanni* for Prague. He had only succeeded in getting *The Marriage of Figaro* staged in Vienna in the teeth of violent opposition (see Leopold Mozart's letter of 18 April, 1786), whereas in Prague the opera was excellently performed and enthusiastically received (Leopold Mozart's letter, 12 January, 1787).

but if so you are *out* a little! In the first place, there is no such able *personale* here as at the theatre in Vienna, so that the opera could not be learned in so short a time. In the second place, I found on my arrival that so few preparations had been made that it would have been an impossibility, no less, to give the opera on the 14th, that is yesterday. Accordingly, yesterday, my *Figaro* was put on in a fully illuminated theatre, and I myself conducted. In this connection I have a good joke to tell you. Certain of the foremost ladies here (one, in particular, of the most illustrious) were pleased to deem it ridiculous, inept, and I know not what else, to present the Princess with *Figaro*—"that silly piece," as they were pleased to term it. They did not reflect that no opera in the world can exactly suit such an occasion unless very specially written for it, nor that it mattered not at all whether this or that opera was put on, so long as it was a good one and unknown to the Princess; and *Figaro* was certainly this last! In a word, this wire-puller actually talked the Government into forbidding the impresario to give this piece on that night! She was triumphant! "*Hò vinta*," she cried one evening from her box. She probably had no notion that the *hò* would be changed into a *sono*![1] Next day, however, Le Noble came, bringing his Majesty's command that if the new opera could not be given *Figaro must* be! My friend, if only you had seen that lady's lovely haughty nose! Oh, it would have amused you vastly, as it did me!

Don Giovanni is now fixed for the 24th.

Oct. 21*st.*

It *was* fixed for the 24th, but a further delay has been occasioned by the illness of one of the singers. As the company is so small, the impresario is obliged to take all possible care of his people, for fear lest some unforeseen indisposition should put him in the most awkward of all awkward situations—that of being unable to stage anything at all!—

There are constant delays here because the singers (being

[1] *Hò vinta*—I *have* conquered: *Sono*—I *am.*

lazy) will not rehearse for opera, and the *entrepreneur* (being anxious and fearful) will not force them to do so — — but what is this?—what vision assails my ears, what sound bombards my eyes?—a letter from — —? I may rub my eyes till they are sore, but it is—deuce take me ✠ Lord, preserve us ✠ —it actually *is* from you! If the cold weather were not so close at hand I would throw my cap over the roof! Since, however, I am in frequent need of it now and expect to need it yet oftener in the future, I will take the liberty of expressing my amazement in somewhat more moderate fashion, and merely tell you in so many words that I am extraordinarily pleased to receive news of you and your estimable family.—

25th October.

To-day is the eleventh day I have been scrawling this letter! You will see from this that there is no lack of good will to the task. Whenever I can snatch a moment I pen a few more lines, but I cannot get long at it, for I am too much at other people's disposal and too little at my own. I need hardly tell you so late in the day as this, that this is not the manner of life I would voluntarily choose.

The opera is to be performed for the first time next Monday, the 29th. The day after that you shall have an account of it from me. As to the arias, for reasons I will recount when we meet, it is unfortunately impossible for me to send you them.—

I am delighted to hear from you that little Katherl is well and manages to exist on terms of respect with the cats and friendship with the dogs. If she is fond of her papa (to whom I send kindest regards), it is already as if she never had been mine! Now, fare you well. Pray kiss your lady mother's hand on my behalf, convey my compliments to your sister and brother, and rest assured that I shall ever remain,

Your true Friend and Servant,

W. A. Mozart.

112. To Michael Puchberg,[1] merchant, of Vienna

Honourable O.B.! [2]

June 1788.

Dearest, best of Friends!

The conviction that you are indeed my friend, and that you know me for a man of honour, emboldens me to disclose all my heart to you, and to make you the following petition. In accordance with the frankness natural to me I will go straight to the point without affectation.

If you would be so kind, so friendly, as to lend me the sum of one or two thousand gulden for a period of one or two years, at suitable interest, you would be doing me a most radical service! You will no doubt yourself realise and acknowledge that it is inconvenient, nay, impossible, to live from one instalment of income to another!—Without a certain necessary capital sum it is impossible to keep one's affairs in order. Nothing can be done with nothing! If you will do me this friendly service I can *imprimo* (being in funds) more easily meet unavoidable expenses at the proper time, whereas now I have to postpone payment and then, usually at the most inconvenient time, part with my whole income at once and, *secondo*, work with a lighter heart and more care-free mind, and consequently earn more. As to security, I do not suppose you will entertain any doubts! You know, broadly speaking, how I stand, and you know my principles! You need have no anxiety about the subscription. I am now extending the time by a few months, and hope to find more patrons abroad than I do here.

I have now opened my whole heart to you in a situation of great gravity to myself—that is, I have acted *as a true brother*. But it is only *with a true brother* that one can be perfectly frank! I now look eagerly for an answer—indeed for a favourable answer. I do not know—but I think I see in you a man, who, like myself, if it is in any way possible will certainly

---

[1] Michael Puchberg was a member of the lodge of Freemasons which Mozart joined in 1785.

[2] O.B. stands for *Ordensbruder* = Brother of the Order.

help his friend, if he be a true friend, his brother, if he be
indeed a brother. If you should perhaps be unable to spare
so large a sum at such short notice, I beg you to lend me a
few hundred gulden at least till to-morrow, as my landlord in
the Landstrasse was so importunate that, in order to avoid
trouble, I was obliged to pay him on the spot, and this has put
me to great embarrassment! We are to sleep to-day for the
first time in our new quarters, where we shall remain summer
and winter. I consider this will do equally well, if not better,
for I have little to do in the town, and without the hindrance
of numerous visitors I shall have more time for work. If I have
business to transact in the town, which will certainly be seldom,
any *fiacre* will take me there for ten kreutzers, while these
rooms will be cheaper and pleasanter, too, during spring,
summer and autumn, as I have a garden. Our rooms are in
the Waringergasse, at the Three Stars, No. 135. Now pray
accept my letter as a true sign of my entire confidence in you,
and remain ever my friend and bro., as I shall remain, till the
grave,

Your true, most devoted friend and bro.,

W. A. Mozart.

P.S.—When are we to have a little music at your house
again?—I have written a new trio!—

113. *To Michael Puchberg*

Most honourable O.B.,

Dearest, best of Friends!

I have been expecting to come to town to-day and to be
able to thank you in person for the kindness you have shown
me. But now I have not the heart to enter your presence as
I am obliged to tell you frankly that I cannot possibly pay
back so soon the sum you lent me, and must beg you to have
patience with me! I am very sorry that as things are you
cannot help me as I could wish. My circumstances are such
that I must absolutely get money. But, good God!—in whom

am I to put my trust? In no one but you, my best friend! If you would only be so kind as to get me the money through some other channel! — I am quite willing to pay interest, and whoever lends to me is, I think, secure enough by reason of my character and my salary.[1] I am sorry enough to be in this situation, but that is the very reason why I want a fairly substantial sum for a fairly long period, as I can then prevent its recurrence. If you, my most worthy Brother, will not help me in my predicament, I shall lose honour and credit, which of all things I dearly wish to preserve. I build securely on your genuine friendship and brotherly affection, and confidently expect you will stand by me in word and deed. If my wish is fulfilled I can breathe freely again, for I shall then be able to get my affairs in order and keep them so. Do come to see me! I am always at home. I have done more work in ten days since I came to these rooms than in two months at any other lodgings, and were I not visited so frequently by black thoughts (which I *must* forcibly banish), I should do still better, for I live here pleasantly, comfortably, and—cheaply. I will not detain you longer with chatter of my affairs, but will hold my tongue—and hope!

Ever your grateful Servant,
true friend and O.B.,

27th June, 1788.   W. A. Mozart.

114. *To Franz Hofdemel, Judge in Chancery, Vienna*

[*Before April* 1789.]

Dearest Friend!

I take the liberty of writing without ceremony to ask you a favour. If you could and would lend me 100 florins till the 20th of next month I should be very much obliged to you. On the 20th I receive my quarter's salary, and I shall then be able to return the loan with thanks. I have relied too much on a sum of 100 ducats due to me from abroad. Not having

---

[1] In December 1787 Mozart had received a definite appointment as Imperial Chamber-musician with a yearly salary of 800 florins.

received it up to the present hour (though expecting it daily) I have left myself too short of cash, and as I need ready money at the moment, I throw myself on your goodness, being convinced of your friendship.

We shall soon be able to congratulate ourselves!—Your affair is nearing completion!—

Mozart.

115. *To his Wife*

8th April, 1789, BUDWEIS.

Dearest Little Wife! [1]

While the Prince is engaged in bargaining for horses, I joyfully seize the occasion to write you a few lines, little wife of my heart! How goes it with you? Do you think of me as often as I do of you? Every moment I look at your portrait and weep, half for joy, half for sorrow! Look after your precious health, which means so much to me, my dear, and farewell!— Do not be anxious on my account, for I am suffering no hardships or inconveniences on this journey, save that of *thy* absence, which, since it can't be cured must be endured. I write with eyes full of tears. *Adjeu*. I will write you a longer and more legible letter from Prague when I shall not be in such haste. *Adjeu*. I kiss you a million times most tenderly, and am ever thine, true till death,

stu—stu—Mozart.

Kiss Karl for me, and all kind remembrances to Herr and Frau von Puchberg. More very soon.

116. *To his Wife*

DRESDEN, 13th April, 1789.
7 o'clock in the morning.

Dearest, best little Wife!

We expected to reach Dresden after dinner on Saturday,

---

[1] This and subsequent letters were written on his travels with Prince Karl Lichnowsky through Dresden to Berlin. He refused the post of headkapellmeister (which would have ended his financial worries) offered him in Berlin by Frederick William II. "I am fond of Vienna," he said to a friend. "The Emperor treats me kindly, and I care little about money." Shortly afterwards the Emperor Joseph died.

but did not arrive till six o'clock on Sunday evening, as the roads are so bad. Yesterday I went to the Neumanns, where Madame Duschek is staying, to deliver her husband's letter. They live on the third story overlooking the road so that they can see from their room who is coming. When I reached the door Herr Neumann was there before me, and asked me with whom he had the honour to be speaking. "I will tell you at once who I am," I replied, "only pray be so good as to have Madame Duschek summoned so that my joke may not be spoiled." But at the same moment Madame Duschek stood before me, for she had recognised me from the window, and had said at once: "There comes someone who looks like Mozart!" They were all delighted. The company was large and consisted entirely of ugly women, but they make up for lack of beauty here by virtue. To-day the Prince and I go out to breakfast, then to see Neumann, then to the chapel. To-morrow or the day after we shall leave here for Leipzig. After receiving this letter you must write to Berlin, *poste restante*. I hope you got my letter from Prague safely. The Neumanns and Duscheks send their kind regards to you and also to Herr and Frau Lang.

Dearest little wife, if only I had a letter from you! If I were to tell you all the things I do with your dear portrait you would often laugh, I think! For instance, when I take it out of its case, I say, "Good morrow, Stanzerl! Good day, little rogue!—pussy-wussy! saucy one!—good-for-nothing!—dainty morsel!" And when I put it back I slip it in little by little saying all the time, "*Nu—nu—nu—nu!*" with just the peculiar emphasis this very meaning-ful word demands, and then, just at the last, quickly, "Good night, little pet—sleep sound!" Well, I suppose that what I have written is folly (to the world, at least) but to us, loving each other as devotedly as we do, it is *not* folly. To-day is the sixth since I left you, and, by God, it seems a year! I expect you will often find it hard to read my letters, as I write in haste, and therefore rather badly. *Adieu*, my dear, my only love. The carriage is here—that does not mean "Bravo, the carriage is there" but *male*.[1]—Farewell, and love me for ever as I love thee. A million tenderest kisses to thee. I am ever

Thy tenderly loving

Husband, W. A. Mozart.

P.S.—Is our Karl being a good boy? I hope so. Kiss him for me. All kind messages to Herr and Frau Puchberg. N.B.—You must not regulate the length of *your* letters by that of *mine*. Mine are short only because I am pressed with business, otherwise I would write whole sheets, but you have more leisure.—*adieu*,

117 *To his Wife*

PRAGUE, 31*st May*, 1789.

Dearest, best little Wife!

I am this instant arrived. I hope you got my last of the 23rd. It is as I told you in that letter. On Thursday, June 4th, between eleven and twelve o'clock, I shall arrive at the last (or first) stage of the diligence where I hope to meet you. Do not forget to bring someone with you who can deal with the Customs instead of me. *Adieu*. God, how I rejoice in the thought of seeing you again! In haste,

Mozart.

118. *To Michael Puchberg*

12*th July*, 1789.

Dearest, best of Friends!

and Honourable O.B.

My God, I could not wish my worst enemy in my present case! And if you, my best friend and brother, forsake me, I, unfortunate and blameless, and my poor sick wife and child, are all lost together! That last time I was with you I longed to pour out my heart—but I had not the courage to do so! And I would not venture now—it is only with trembling I dare do it in writing—I would not even dare do it in writing if I did not know that you know me and my circumstances—that you

---

[1] *Maledetto?*

are persuaded that I am guiltless of my most unfortunate, most tragic situation! O God! here am I with fresh entreaties instead of with thanks!—with new demands instead of with payments! If you really know me thoroughly, you must feel how all this torments me! I think I need not tell you over again how I have been prevented from earning anything by this unfortunate illness; but I must mention that despite my miserable condition, I determined to give a subscription concert at home, so that I could at least meet the great and frequent day by day expenses (for I was sure you would be kind and have patience with me), but—even this failed me! Fate is unhappily so against me (though only in Vienna) that I *cannot* make any money whatever I do. I sent round the list a fortnight ago, and the only name upon it is that of Swieten! Now (the 15th) that my dear little wife seems to be improving from day to day, I should be able to work again if this blow, this hard blow, had not fallen upon me.—At least they tell us she is improving—although yesterday (the 14th) I was quite cast down and in despair, she was in such pain again and I—with her! Last night, however, she slept so well and has seemed so cheerful all the morning that I am full of hope. I am now beginning to be disposed to work again—but I am now faced with misfortunes of another kind—though only for the moment! Dearest, best friend and brother, you know my present circumstances, but you also know my prospects. As to this, our agreement holds good. Thus, or thus—you understand me. Meanwhile, I am writing six easy pianoforte sonatas for Princess Friederika and six quartets for the King, all of which I am having printed by Kozeluch at my own charges. At the same time the two dedications are bringing me in something. In a few months my fate must be settled in every detail, and so, my best friend, you risk nothing by me. The point is now, my only friend, whether you will or can lend me another 500 florins? I would suggest that until my affairs are settled I should pay you back ten florins a month. Thus, within a few months at longest, I can pay back the whole sum, with whatever interest you ask, and at the same time acknowledge myself your life-long debtor. *That*, alas, I must ever remain, for I can never thank you sufficiently for your friendship and love. Thank God, *that* is over! You now know all. Only do not be offended by my trust in you, and remember that without your support the honour, the peace of mind, the very life, perhaps, of your friend and brother are forfeit.

Ever your most indebted servant, true friend and brother,

At home, 14th *July*, 1789.   W. A. Mozart.

O God! I can scarcely make up my mind to send this letter! And yet I must! Had this illness not befallen us, I should not have been forced to beg so shamelessly from my only friend. And yet I hope for your forgiveness, for you know both the good and evil of my position. The evil is only momentary, the good will certainly persist when the evil of the moment has been alleviated. *Adjeu!* Forgive me, for God's sake, only forgive me!—and—*Adieu!* — — —

119. *To Michael Puchberg*

July 1789.

Dearest Friend and Brother!

Since you did me that great and friendly service I have lived in such misery that, not only have I not been able to go out, but I could not write for very grief! —

At the moment she is quieter, and if she had not become so excited, which is fatal in her condition, she would be able to sleep. The only fear is that the bone may become affected.— She is amazingly resigned to her fate, and awaits recovery or death with true philosophic resignation. The tears flow as I write.—If you can, dearest friend, come to see us. And if you can, give me your advice and help in the matter you know of.

Mozart.

120. *To his Wife*

August 1789.

Most beloved little Wife!

I was overjoyed to get your dear letter. I hope you got my second yesterday with the decoction, the electuary and ants' eggs. I set off to-morrow morning at five o'clock. Were it not for the joy of seeing you once more and holding you in my arms I would not leave just yet, for *Figaro* is to be given soon, and as I have some alterations to make, I shall be needed at the rehearsals. I expect I shall have to return here on the 19th. But to stay here till the 19th without you would be impossible! Dear little wife! I will be quite frank with you. You have no need to be unhappy. You have a husband who loves you and does all he can for you. As to your foot, you only need have patience. It will certainly get quite well. I am glad it you are in spirits—of course I am—only I could wish you would not sometimes make yourself so cheap! You are too free, I think, with —— . . ., just as with —— when he was still in Baden. Consider that —— and —— are less free with other women, whom they know, perhaps, less well than they do you, than they are in your company! Even ——, who is otherwise a well-conducted man and particularly respectful towards women, must somehow have been misled into writing the most disgusting and coarsest *sottises* in his letter. A woman must always make herself respected or else she gets talked about. My dear! forgive me for being so frank, but my peace of mind demands it as well as our common happiness. Only remember that you once admitted to me yourself that you are inclined to be too compliant! You know the consequences of that. And remember, too, the promise you gave me. O God! only try my love—be merry and happy and kind with me—do not torment yourself and me with needless jealousy! Have confidence in my love—you have proofs of it, surely! —and you shall see how happy we will be. Do not doubt that it is only by her prudent behaviour that a woman can enchain her husband. *Adjeu*—to-morrow I shall kiss you devotedly!

Mozart.

121. *To Michael Puchberg*

Dearest friend!—   *20th February*, 1790.

If I had known that your beer was almost finished I would certainly never have ventured to rob you of it. I therefore

take the liberty of sending you back the other measure herewith, being provided with wine to-day. I thank you heartily
for the first, and when you have another supply of beer, pray
send me a little of it. You know how much I like it! I beg you,
dear friend, lend me a few ducats for a few days only, if you
can do so, as I have to settle a matter on the spot which
cannot be postponed. Forgive my importunity—it springs
from my complete confidence in your friendship and brotherly
love.   Ever your
                                                        Mozart.

122. *To Michael Puchberg*

March April 1790.

Herewith, dearest friend, I send you Handel's *Life*. When
recently I returned home after my visit to you, I found the
enclosed note from B. Swieten. You will perceive, as I did,
on reading it that my prospects are now better than ever. I
stand now on the threshold of my fortune—but the opportunity will be lost forever if I cannot this time make use of it.
My present circumstances, however, are such that, promising
as my prospects are, I must abandon all hope of furthering my
fortunes unless I can count on the help of a staunch friend.
You must have remarked that I have been labouring under
some constant oppression—and only the many good offices
you have already done me have held me back from speaking
out. Now, however, once more and for the last time, in this
most critical moment which will shape my whole future, I
call upon you, full of trust by reason of the all too frequent
instances of friendship and brotherly love you have accorded
me, to stand by me to the very utmost of your power! You
know how my present circumstances would damage the chances
of my application to the Court if they became known, and how
necessary it is that they should remain a secret, for at Court
they judge not by circumstances, but, unfortunately, merely
by appearances. You know—I am sure you are convinced—
that if, as I may now confidently hope, my application is

successful, you will certainly lose nothing. How joyfully I shall then discharge my debts to you! How glad I shall be to thank you and, in addition, confess myself eternally your debtor! What a pleasant sensation it is to reach one's goal at last—and what a blessed sensation to have helped thereto! Tears prevent me from completing the picture. In a word—my future happiness is in your hands. Act according to the dictates of your noble heart! Do what you can, and believe that you have to do with a right-minded and eternally grateful man, whose situation distresses him even more on your account than on his own!

Mozart.

123. To Michael Puchberg

May 1790.

Dearest, best Friend and Brother!—

    I am very sorry I am unable to go abroad and so get speech with you myself, but my toothache and headache are still too bad and I still feel very much indisposed. I share your ideas about a few good pupils, only I had thought of waiting till I was in my new quarters as I intended to give lessons at home. In the meantime, I beg you to spread this idea of mine abroad a little among people. I also propose to give subscription concerts at home in the three months June, July and August, so that it is only my present condition which presses upon me. When I move I shall have to pay 275 florins towards the new house—and I have to live, too, till I have arranged my concerts, and till the quartets upon which I am working are dispatched to the printers. I should be able to write with a fairly easy mind if I had actually to my hand 600 florins as a minimum now.—And ah! how I need peace of mind for work! But what torments me most at the moment is a debt to a certain jeweller who, although he at first saw my difficulty and said he was content to wait, now presses urgently and impatiently for payment. The sum is 100 florins. I wish with all my heart I were rid of this annoyance.—Now I have made frank confession to you, and I entreat you to do all that your means and true friendship permit.

Ever your
Mozart.

124. *To the Archduke Franz, Vienna* [1]

May 1790.

Your Royal Highness

I make so bold as very respectfully to beg your Royal Highness to be so gracious as to speak to his Majesty the King touching my most humble petition to his Majesty. Prompted by a desire for fame, by a love of my work and by a conviction of my own talents, I venture to apply for the post of second kapellmeister, the more particularly that Salieri, the very able kapellmeister, has never devoted himself to the ecclesiastical style in music, whereas I have made myself completely familiar with this style from my youth up. Some small renown accorded me by the world for my performances on the *piano-forte* encourages me also to beg for the favour of being entrusted with the musical instruction of the Royal Family.

In the sure conviction that I have applied to the best possible intermediary, and to one who is particularly gracious to me, I feel the utmost confidence and shall . . .

125. *To Michael Puchberg*

17th May, 1790.

Dearest Friend and O.B.!

You will have heard, no doubt, from your household that I called at your house yesterday intending to dine there uninvited (as you gave me permission to do). You know how things are with me—in short, being unable to find a friend to help me, I have been obliged to resort to the moneylenders; but as it takes some time to seek out the most Christian among this un-Christian class of people, I am at the moment so utterly penniless that I have to beg you, dearest friend, by all that is sacred, to help me with whatever you can spare! If I get the money, as I hope to do, in a week or a fortnight, I will at once

[1] Rough draft of a letter.

repay what you lend me now, though I must, alas! still ask you to have patience touching the sums for which I have been already long indebted to you. If you only knew how all this worries and troubles me! It has kept me all this time from finishing my quartets. I now have great hopes at Court, for I have reliable information that the E—— [1] has not sent back my petition, granted or rejected, like the rest, but has retained it.—That is a good sign. Next Saturday I intend to perform my quartets here at home, and request the pleasure of your company and that of your wife. Dearest, best friend and brother! Do not withdraw your friendship because of my importunity, but stand by me! I rely wholly on you, and am ever

Your most grateful

Mozart.

P.S.—I now have two pupils and would like to make up the number to eight. Pray spread it abroad that I give lessons.

126. To Michael Puchberg

12th June, 1790.

Dearest Friend and O.B.!

I am here to conduct my opera.[2] My wife is getting a little better. She already feels some slight relief, but she will have to take the baths sixty times—and go away again in the autumn. God grant it may do her good!—Dearest friend, if you can help with the present pressing expenses, oh, do so! I am staying in Baden for the sake of economy, and only go into town when absolutely necessary. I have just been obliged to part with my quartets (that difficult work!) for a mere song, so as to get ready money.—I am now working at some clavier sonatas for the same reason. *Adjeu.* Send me what you can most easily spare. An Office of mine is to be sung to-morrow in Baden. *Adjeu.*—(About 10 o'clock).

Ever your

Mozart.

P.S.—Once more I beg you to be so kind as to send the viola.

[1] Emperor.
[2] *Così fan tutte.* Mozart wrote the opera by commission of the Enperor.

127. *To Michael Puchberg*

14th August, 1790.

Dearest friend and brother!

Things to-day are going as ill with me as they went well yesterday! I could not sleep all night for pain. I must have over-heated myself with much walking yesterday and then inadvertently taken a chill. Picture my situation—ill and full of grief and care! Such a state of things sensibly delays recovery. In a week or a fortnight I shall be better off—for certain—but at present I am in want. Could you not assist me with a trifle? [1] It would make all the difference at the moment. You would, at least for the moment, bring peace of mind to

> Your
> > true friend, servant and brother,
> > > W. A. Mozart.

128. *To his Wife*

FRANKFORT-ON-MAIN,[2] *28th September*, 1790.

Dearest, best little wife of my heart!

We are this moment arrived—that is, at one o'clock in the afternoon, so we have taken only six days. We could have done the journey still more quickly if we had not rested a little at night on three occasions. We have just alighted at an inn in the suburb of Sachsenhausen and are excessively glad to have secured a room. We do not yet know our destination—whether we shall be together or be separated. If I cannot get a room anywhere for nothing, and find the inn not too dear, I shall certainly stay on here. I hope you have got my letter from Efferding safely. I could not write you more on the journey, as we stopped seldom and then only to rest. The journey was very pleasant. We had fine weather except for one day, and even this one day caused us no discomfort as my carriage (I should like to give it a kiss!) is magnificent. At Ratisbon we dined royally at midday, to the accompani-

---

[1] Mozart died in debt to this friend for 1000 florins. His widow ultimately discharged it.

[2] Mozart went to Frankfort-on-Main to attend the Imperial Coronation, with a view to financial advantage.

ment of divine music, with angelic cooking and most excellent Moselle wine. We breakfasted at Nuremberg,[1] a hideous town. At Wurzburg we warmed our precious stomachs with coffee.—It is a fine, splendid city. The living was passable everywhere— except that at Aschaffenburg, two and a half hours by diligence from here, mine host was pleased to cheat us abominably. I long for news of you, of your health, our affairs, etc. I am firmly resolved to make all the money I can here and then return to you rejoicing. What a fine life we shall live then! I will work—work *so* hard—so that no unforeseen accident shall ever reduce us to such desperate straits again.—As regards all this business I should like you to get Stadler to bring the . . . to you. His last suggestion was that the money should be advanced on Hofmeister's[2] endorsement alone— 1000 florins in cash and the rest on credit—that would more than cover everything, and I should then have nothing to do on my return but work. The whole business could be settled by a friend with *carte blanche* from me. *Adieu*. I kiss you a thousand times.

Ever thine, Mzt.

129. *To his Wife*

Dearest, best little Wife!

I now have three letters from you, my love—that of the 28th came this moment. I have not yet got the one you sent by Herr von Alt, but I will at once inquire about it at Le Noble's. You too must now have had four letters. This is the

---

[1] This estimate of the fine old mediaeval town which inspired Wagner's *Mastersingers* is characteristically eighteenth-century. Mozart, however, was not insensible to natural beauty. "In travelling with his wife through a beautiful country, he would first gaze attentively and in silence on the view before him; by degrees as the ordinary serious and even melancholy expression of his countenance became enlivened and cheerful, he would begin to sing, or rather hum, and at last exclaim, 'Oh, if I had but the theme on paper!' On her answering that that might easily be, he would continue, 'Yes, my treatment of it, no doubt. But how vexatious to be obliged to hatch all one's conceptions within doors.' Mozart always composed in the open air when he could. Thus *Don Giovanni* was composed on a bowling-green, and the principal part of the *Requiem* in a garden—two of his greatest works" (Edward Holmes).

[2] Hofmeister was a Leipzig music-publisher.

fifth. You will not be able to write to me any more for the present, for when you receive this I shall probably be no longer here, as I intend to give my concert on Wednesday or Thursday, and then on Friday—*tschiri tschitschi*—seek safety in flight! Dearest little wife! I hope that you have dealt with the business I wrote to you about—and are still dealing with it. I certainly shall not make enough here to be able to pay 800 or 1000 florins immediately on my return. But if the business with Hofmeister is at least so far advanced that only my presence is lacking, I shall at once have (the interest reckoned at twenty *per cento*) 2000–1600 florins in hand. I can then pay 1000 florins and shall be left with 600 florins. In Advent I shall begin to give small subscription concerts, and shall also take pupils. I need never pay the whole, as I write for H., so all should go right. Only do please conclude the arrangement with H.—that is if you at all wish to see me back! If you could only look into my heart! There the wish, the yearning to see you, to embrace you once more, struggles with the desire to bring home a large sum of money. I have often thought of travelling farther, but whenever I tried to force myself to decide to do so, the thought always came to me how bitterly I should regret it if I were to separate myself so long from my beloved wife without certain prospect of success, and perhaps quite fruitlessly! I feel as if I had already been away from you for years. Believe me, my dear, if you were with me I should perhaps find the decision easier, but— I am too used to having you—I love you too dearly to be able to exist long apart from you! And then all this talk of the free cities is mere boasting. True, I am celebrated here, admired and beloved, but, for the rest, the people here are still more penny-wise than the Viennese. If the concert has any sort of success it will be thanks to my name and to the Countess Hatzfeldt and the Schweitzer family, who are working hard on my behalf. But I shall be glad when it is over. If I set to work hard in Vienna, and take pupils, we can live pleasantly enough, and nothing shall persuade me to alter this plan except a good engagement at one or other of the Courts. Only do your best to bring off the affair with Hofmeister (through the help of some good fairy, if not otherwise!), and to advertise my intention to take pupils, and then we shall certainly not do badly. *Adieu,* my dear. You will get more letters from me, but I, alas, can get no more from you.

Ever love thy

Mozart.

FRANKFORT-ON-MAIN,
8th October, 1790.

The Coronation is to-morrow. Take care of your health—and be careful how you walk. *Adieu.*

130. *To his Wife*

Postscript. MAYENCE, *17th October,* 1790.

P.S.—Tears rained upon the paper as I wrote the foregoing page, but now let us cheer up! Catch!—an astonishing number of kisses are flying about.—The deuce!—I see a whole crowd of them, too! Ha! ha! I have just grabbed three—they are delicious! You can answer this letter, but must make the the address *poste restante,* Lintz. That is the safest. As I do not yet know whether I shall go to Ratisbon, I cannot tell you anything definite, but write on the envelope that it must be kept till it is called for. *Adieu,* dearest, best little wife. Take care of your health and don't go on foot in the town. Write and tell me how you like the new rooms. *Adieu.* A million kisses to you.

131. *To the Municipal Council of Vienna*

May 1791.

Most honourable, most learned Councillors of Vienna!

Sirs!

During the period of Herr Kapellmeister Hofmann's illness I contemplated taking the liberty of applying for his post, hoping, since my musical talents and achievements are known abroad, my name held in considerable estimation everywhere, and I myself have for several years enjoyed the honour of the appointment of Court composer here in the capital, that I might not be considered unworthy of this post, and might deserve the consideration of your highly learned corporation.

Kapellmeister Hofmann, however, regained his health, and under these circumstances, since from my heart I wish him long life, it occurred to me that it might perhaps be of service to the Cathedral and to you, Sirs, if I were to be appointed as deputy to the now ageing Herr Kapellmeister—for the present without salary—and thereby have opportunity of assisting this estimable man in his office, and of earning the regard of your most learned corporation by the actual performance of services for which I think I may justly deem myself peculiarly fitted by my acquirements in both ecclesiastical and secular styles of music.

Your most humble Servant,

Wolfgang Amadé Mozart,

Royal and Imperial Court Composer.

132. *To Choirmaster Stoll, Baden, near Vienna*

June 1791.

Leibster Stoll! (*seyens kein Schroll!*) [1]

Imprimo, I should like to know if Stadler [2] was with you yesterday and whether he asked you from me to send the Mass:

He was? Well, then, I hope to get it to-day; but if not, pray be so good as to send it off at once. N.B.—all parts. I will soon send it back.—

[1] "Dearest Stoll, do not be moody!"—put in for the sake of the jingle.
[2] *Not* the Abbé Stadler. This Stadler was an unworthy hanger-on of Mozart's, towards whose repeated dishonesty and betrayal of trust Mozart showed singular forbearance. See Letter No. 140.

Secundo. Will you please find some small lodging for my wife? She needs only two rooms, or a room and a closet, but it is most necessary that they should be on the ground-floor. The quarters I should greatly prefer would be those Goldhahn used to occupy on the ground-floor at the butcher's. Please go and inquire there first—they may still be to let. My wife will arrive on Saturday—or at latest on Monday. If we cannot get this we must at least look for something fairly near the baths—but the ground-floor it must be. The ground-floor at the notary's where D͞r Alt stayed would also do well, but the rooms at the butcher's would be best of all.

Tertio. I should also like to know whether the theatre is open in Baden yet? And please answer my three points as quickly as possible.

Mozart.

P.S.—My address is:

     In the Raubensteinergasse,

         Kayserhaus, No. 970. First-floor.

P.S.—This is the stupidest letter I have ever written in my life; but it is just suited to you!

133. *To his Wife*

Ma trés cher Epouse !

J'écris cette lettre dans la petite Chambre au Jardin chez Leitgeb[1] ou j'ai Couché cette nuit excellement—et j'espére que ma chere Epouse aura passée cette Nuit aussi bien que moi, j'y passerai cette Nuit aussi, puisque j'ai congedié Leonore, et je serais tout seul à la maison, ce qui n'est pas agreable.—

J'attends avec beaucoup d'impatience une lettre qui m'apprendra comme vous avés passée le jour d'hier ;—je tremble quand je pense au baigne du st. Antoin ; car je crains toujours le risque de tomber sur l'escalier en sortant—et je me trouve entre l'esperance et la Crainte—une Situation bien desagreable ! si vous n'etiés pas grosse Je craignerais moins — mais abbandonons cette Idèe

---

[1] A musician in the chapel at Salzburg.

triste !— — le Ciel aura eù certainement soin de ma Chere stanzi-Marini,—

Madame le Schwingenschu mà prieé de leur procurer une loge pour ce soir au theatre de Wieden ou l'on donnera, la cinquiemè partie d'Antoin, et j'etais si heureux de pouvoir les servir; j'aurai donc le plaisir de voir cet Opera dans leur Compagnie.

I have this moment received your dear letter and am delighted to see that you are sound and well.—Madame Leitgeb has made me a nightcap and cravat, but *how* has she made them! Heaven above! I always *said* her work would be like that—but that is no use now! I am glad your appetite is good, but he who eats a lot must also —— a lot?—No, *walk* a lot, I mean! But I should not like you to take long walks without me. Only do follow my advice exactly—it is meant for the best, I assure you. *Adieu*, my dear, my only love! Hold your hands up in the air—2999½ little kisses are flying from me to you and waiting to be snapped up. Now let me whisper in your ear — — — — now you is mine — — — now we open and shut our mouths — more — and more — at last we say, "It is all about *Plumpi—strumpi*——" Well, you can think what you like. That is the joke!—*adieu*—1000 tender kisses from thine ever,

Mozart.

6th June, 1791.

134. *To his Wife*

11th June, 1791.

Ma très chère Epouse !

*Criés avec moi contre mon mauvais sort !—Mad*selle *Kirchgessner ne donne pas son Academie Lundi !—par consequent j'aurais pu vous posseder, ma chère, tout ce jour de Dimanche— mercredi je viendrai sûrement.—*

I must make haste, as it is already a quarter past six, and the carriage goes at seven.—Take care you do not slip in the bath, and never go about alone. If I were in your place I would miss a day to avoid taking the treatment too violently. I hope someone slept with you to-night. I cannot tell you what I would not give to be with you in Baden instead of being planted here.—I was so bored that I composed an aria for the opera [1] to-day. I got up at five o'clock. I have let my watch run down, you will be amazed to hear, but as I had no key I could not, alas, wind it! Is that not sad? *Schlumbla!* There is a word to think over! I wound the big clock instead. *Adjeu*, dear one! I am dining with Puchberg to-day. I send you a thousand kisses, and say with you in thought, "Death and despair were his reward!"

Your ever-loving Husband,

W. A. Mozart.

Carl must be a good boy. Kiss him from me.

(Take an electuary if the bowels do not move—not otherwise.)

(Take care of yourself in the morning and evening when it is chilly.)

135. *To his Wife*

Dearest, best little Wife!

I can only write you a few lines now in haste, as I am going to surprise Leitgeb by going out to breakfast. It is now half-past five o'clock. After dinner I will write more. And I hope, by then to have had a letter from you. *Adjeu*—I only wanted to say Good morning. Take care of yourself—particularly in the baths. If you feel the least weakness stop at once. *Adjeu*. Two thousand kisses.—

Mozart.

Compliments to —— and tell him he must make himself a nuisance to So-and-So.

Ma très chere épouse!

I have this moment received your letter, which has given me extraordinary pleasure. I am already longing for a second

---

[1] *The Magic Flute.* The following letters refer to this opera.

to tell me how the baths are affecting you. I am sorry, too, that I was not at your lovely music yesterday, not on account of the music, but because I should have been so happy to be at your side. I gave —— a surprise to-day. I went first to the Rehbergs and got Frau Rehberg to send up one of her daughters to tell him that an old and dear friend was come from Rome and had been from house to house all over the town seeking him in vain! He sent word that I would please to wait a little, and meantime the poor man dressed up in all his Sunday best—his very finest coat and his hair resplendently dressed! You can imagine how we all laughed at him! I cannot resist making a fool of a man—if it is not —— then it must be —— or ——! Where do I sleep? At home, of course. I have been sleeping very well, only the mice bearing me honest company. I have had regular discussions with them. I was up before five o'clock. *Apropos* I advise you not to go to church to-morrow—these peasant fellows are too rough. True, you have a rough companion, but the peasants have no respect for him —*perdent respectum*, because they can see at a glance that he is a silly sheep. *Snai!*—

I shall answer Süssmayer by word of mouth—I would rather not waste paper on him.

Send this Krügel or Klügel word that you want better food —or perhaps you could speak to him yourself in passing. That would be still better. He is a good fellow in other ways, and has great respect for me.—

To-morrow I shall join the procession to Josephstadt, candle in hand! *Snai!*—

Do not forget my warnings about the morning and evening air, and about too long bathing. My regards to Count and Countess Wagensperg. *Adjeu.* I kiss you two thousand times in spirit, and am ever

Your

Mozart.

Vienna, 25th June, 1791.

P.S.—It might after all be a good thing if you gave Carl a little rhubarb. Why did you not send me that long letter?

Here is a letter for him. Ask him to send me an answer. — — Catch—catch—x x x x x kisses flying through the air for you; x there goes another one!——

I have just received your second. Be careful of the baths! Take more sleep, too — not so irregular! — or I shall grow anxious. I am a little anxious as it is!

Adieu — —

136. *To his Wife*

Ma très chère Epouse !

I hope you are feeling very well. I remember that you have not often been upset during pregnancy. Perhaps the baths are too relaxing? I should not wait for certain proofs—they are too unpleasant. My advice is that you should stop now! Then my mind would be quite at rest. To-day is the day to miss, and yet I wager the little wife went to the bath, did she not? Seriously—rather prolong it till late autumn! I hope you will by now have received my first little note.

Please tell that naughty boy Süssmayer [1] he must send me my score of the first act from the introduction to the finale so that I can orchestrate it. It would be a good thing if he could put it together to-day and dispatch it by the first coach to-morrow, as then I should get it by midday. A couple of Englishmen have just called, not wishing to leave Vienna without making my acquaintance. But, of course, the *real* truth is that they wished to know Süssmayer, and came to see me to ask where he lived, having heard that I have the good fortune to be intimate with him!—I told them to go to the Ungarische Krone and wait till he returns from the baths. *Snai !* They wish to engage him as lamp-polisher. I greatly long for news of you. It is half-past twelve already and I have got none as yet. I shall wait just a little longer and then seal my letter.— Nothing has come! I must close it. Farewell, dearest, best little wife! Take care of your health, for I care not whatever

---

[1] Franz Xaver Süssmayer, Mozart's pupil and assistant, who completed the *Requiem* after his death.

else goes awry as long as you are well and are kind to me. Follow the advice I gave you at the beginning of this letter and fare thee well. *Adieu.* A thousand kisses to you, and a thousand boxes on the ear to Lacci-Bacci.[1]

Ever thy
Mozart.

VIENNA, *Saturday, 2nd July,* 1791.

137. *To his Wife*

4th July, 1791.

Dearest little Wife!

I must be brief. It is half-past one and I have not yet dined. I wish I could send you more. Meanwhile, here are three gulden. To-morrow at midday you shall get more. Cheer up—keep up your spirits! All will yet be well. A thousand kisses to you. I am weak for want of food—*adjeu* — —

Ever thine,
Mozart.

I have waited till now, hoping to be able to send you more money!—

138. *To his Wife*

Dearest, best little Wife!

Do not be melancholy, I beg you! I hope you received the money. It is better for your foot that you should stay on in Baden, as you can walk out better there. I hope to hold you in my arms on Saturday, perhaps sooner! But as soon as my business here is over I shall be with you. For I mean to take a long rest in your arms. I shall need it, too; for the mental worry and distress and all the running about that accompanies it does, after all, exhaust one a little! I received the last parcel safely and thank you for it!—I am more glad than I can tell you that you have discontinued the baths. In a word, all I lack is—your presence. I do not feel I can wait for it. Really, when my business is over I could have you back for good, but

<hr>

[1] His son?

—I should so much like just a few more sweet days with you in Baden. —— is with me at the moment, and tells me I must do so. He has a *gusto* for you, and thinks you must feel that it is so!

And what is my second fool doing? I find it hard to choose between the two fools! When I reached the "Crown" yesterday evening, I found the English lord lying there quite exhausted still waiting for ——!—As I was on my way to Wetzlar's to-day I saw a couple of oxen yoked to a wagon, and as they began to pull, the oxen wagged their heads *exactly* like our foolish ——. —*Snai!*

If you need anything, my little sweetheart, write to me frankly and I shall indeed be delighted to try to satisfy my Stanzi-Marini.—

Ever thy
Mozart.

VIENNA, 5*th July*, 1791.

Carl must be a good boy, and perhaps I will answer his letter. *Adieu.*

139. *To his Wife*

Dearest, best little Wife!

You will forgive me, I know, for not having written till now. The reason is that I must keep hold of ——. I dare not let him escape. I am at his house every day at seven o'clock in the morning.

I hope you got yesterday's letter safely. I did not go to see the balloon. I can imagine all that, and, besides, I did not think anything would come of it even this time. But how the Viennese are rejoicing! They are as full of praise now as they have been of abuse hitherto!

There is something I cannot read in your letter and something I cannot understand. You write, "To-day, of course, my —— little husband will be in a numerous com. and in the Prater, too," etc. I cannot read the adjective to "little husband." As for com., I suppose it is *company*, but what company you refer to I cannot think!

Please tell Sauermayer [1] from me that I had no time to be forever running to his quarters, and whenever I did go I always found him from home. Only give him the three florins to dry his tears!

My one wish is that my affairs were settled, so that I could be with you again. You would never believe how long the time seems to me since I left you! I cannot describe my feelings to you—there is a kind of emptiness which hurts me sharply— a kind of longing, never ceasing, because never satisfied, but persisting, nay, increasing, from day to day. When I think how merry we were together in Baden—like children! And what sad, weary hours I live through here! Even my work gives me no joy, because I am accustomed to break off from time to time and exchange a few words with you, and—that pleasure is now, alas, impossible. If I go to the clavier and sing something from the opera, I have to stop at once—my emotions are too strong.—*Basta!* the very hour I finish my business I shall be away from here. I have no news to tell you. The illuminations in Baden were a little previous—as the true news is just the contrary! I will inquire at the Court apothecary's, where perhaps they can procure me the electuary after all. If so, I shall send it you at once. Meanwhile, if it should be necessary, I would advise you to take tartar rather than a cordial. *Adjeu*, dearest little wife,

Ever thy

Mozart.

140. *To his Wife*

7–8th October, 1791.
Friday, half-past ten at night.

Dearest, best little Wife!

I am but just returned from the opera.[2] It was quite as full as ever. The *duetto*, "Man and Wife," etc., and the glockenspiel in Act I. were encored as usual — the boy terzett in

---

[1] Süssmayer?   [2] *The Magic Flute.*

Act II. in addition. But it is the evident *quiet* approbation which best pleases me! It is apparent that this opera is rising rapidly and steadily in estimation. And now for my doings. Just after your departure I played two games of billiards with Herr von Mozart (the man who wrote the opera being played at Schickaneder's [1] theatre). I then sold my old nag for fourteen ducats. Next I got Joseph to get Primus to fetch me a cup of black coffee, smoking a splendid pipe of tobacco the while. I then orchestrated almost the whole of Stadtler's rondo. I have since received a letter from Stadler from Prague. All the Duscheks are well. It seems they have had no letter from you, though I can scarcely believe that possible! Enough—you already know that my German opera has met with a magnificent reception. But it is the strangest thing that, on the very evening on which my opera was given for the first time with so much success, *Tito* was given in Prague for the last time, and was also tremendously applauded. Bedini sang better than ever. The little duet in A between the two girls was encored, and, but for the fear of overstraining Mme. Marchetti, the rondo would have been welcomed a second time. Stadler himself ("Oh, wonder of Bohemia," he writes) got "*bravos!*" from the parterre and even from the orchestra. "But indeed I did my very best," he says. He also wrote (Stadler) that —— and now I see that he is an ass—, —— of course, not Stadler—*he* is only a bit of an ass, not much of one, but —— , well, *he* is an ass indeed! At half-past five I went out through the Stuben-thor and took my favourite stroll by way of the *Glacis* to the theatre. What do I see? What do I smell? Why, here is Don Primus with the cutlets! *Che gusto!* Now I am eating to your health! It is just striking eleven o'clock. Perhaps you are asleep already! Sh, sh! I won't wake you!

Saturday, 8th. You should have seen me at supper yester-day! I could not find the old tablecloth so I got out one as white as driven snow—and the double candlesticks with wax

---

[1] A theatre-manager. A "wag" and "good fellow" who defrauded Mozart grossly in the matter of the sale of the score of *The Magic Flute*. He took the part of Papageno in its production at his theatre.

candles! According to (Stadler's) letter the Italians are done with here already. Moreover, I see, now that Madame Duschek must have had a letter from you, as he writes: "The lady was very pleased with Mathie's postscript. She said that she liked the DONKEY just as he is." I am urging (Süssmayer) to write on (Stadler's) behalf, for he has begged me very earnestly to do so. No doubt you are very well pleased that I write this! The hairdresser came punctually at six o'clock, Primus having lighted the fire at half-past five and waked me at a quarter to six. Why must it rain this day of all days! I hoped you would have good weather. Only keep well wrapped up lest you should take cold. I hope the bathing will keep you well through the winter—for it was only the hope of improved health for you which made me drive you to Baden. The time drags for me without you—I foresaw that it would. If I had nothing to do I would have spent the week with you out there, but I have no suitable place there in which to work, and I am anxious, as far as possible, to avoid all chance of money difficulties. There is nothing more desirable than to be able to live in some peace of mind, which means that one must work diligently, and glad I am to do so. Give (Süssmayer) a few sound boxes on the ear on my behalf and pray ask (Sophie) A. (a thousand kisses to her) to give him a few, too. Do not let him want for them, for Heaven's sake! I would not for the world have, sooner or later, to bear his reproaches for not having treated him aright, so beat him too much rather than too little!—It might be as well for you to pull his nose, knock out an eye, or inflict some other visible injury on him, so that the fellow cannot deny having received something from you.—*Adieu*, dear little wife! The diligence is just going. I hope and expect to get a line from you to-day, and in this sweet hope I kiss you a thousand times, and am

Ever thy
Loving Husband,
W. A. Mozart.

141. *To his Wife*

8–9th October, 1791.
Saturday night, at half-past ten o'clock.

Dearest, best little Wife!

How great were my joy and delight to find your letter awaiting me on my return from the opera! The theatre was full—although Saturday, being post-day, is always a bad day —and the opera was received with the usual applause and encores. It will be given again to-morrow, but not on Monday, so Stoll must be persuaded to come on Tuesday, when it will begin again. I say "begin" because it will probably run again then for a few days in succession. I have just devoured a delicious dish of hare which Don Primus (my faithful servant) brought me, and as my appetite is rather large to-day I have sent him out again to bring me something more, if possible. In the meantime, therefore, I continue my letter to you. I was writing so hard this morning that I let the time pass till it was half-past one, when I had to run with all speed to Hofer's (to avoid dining alone), where I met Mama.[1] Immediately after dinner, I went home again and wrote till it was time to go to the opera. Leitgeb asked me to take him again, and I did so. I shall take Mama to-morrow.—Hofer has already given her the libretto to read. In Mama's case it may be said that she will *see*, not that she will *hear*, the opera! We had a box to-day, and all were delighted, but He, the Arch-Enemy, was so much the Bavarian that I could not stay, or I should have been forced to tell him he was an ass! Unfortunately I was with them when the second act began, that is, at the solemn scene, and he laughed at everything. At first I had patience, and tried to draw his attention to this speech and that, but he mocked at everything. It became too much for me. I called him *Papageno*, and went away, but I do not suppose the rascal understood me! I then went to another box occupied by Flamm and his wife. There it was very pleasant, and I remained till the end. Well, to-day I went behind the scenes for Papageno's aria with the glockenspiel, for I felt a great desire to play it

---

[1] Mozart's relations with his wife's mother were cordial at this time, and till his death.

myself. For a joke, I played an arpeggio when Schickaneder has to speak a few words. He started, looked into the wings and saw me. He stopped then, and would go no farther. I guessed his thoughts and played a chord again. He then struck the glockenspiel, muttering, "Stop it!" Everyone laughed. I think my joke disclosed to many for the first time that he does not really play the instrument himself!

You cannot imagine how enchanting the music sounds from a box close to the orchestra—far better than from the gallery. As soon as you come back you must try it.

Sunday morning. 7 o'clock. I have slept very well and hope you have, too. I have greatly relished a half-capon friend Primus brought me. At 10 o'clock I am going to divine service at the Piarists' chapel, as Leitgeb tells me I can then get word with the director. I shall stay there to dinner.

Primus told me yesterday evening that illness was rife in Baden. Is it true? Take care of yourself and do not trust the weather. — Primus has just come back by the slow diligence and tells me that the mail-coach left before seven this morning, and no other goes till midday, so that all my writing at night and early this morning were in vain, which vexes me greatly. Next Sunday I shall certainly come out to you. Then we can all go to the Casino together and travel home together on Monday.—

Lechleitner has been again to the opera already. Even if he is no *connoisseur* he is at least a true *amateur*—which —— is not. He is really an absurdity! He prefers a good dinner! Farewell, dear! I kiss thee a million times, and am ever thy

Mozart.

P.S.—Kiss Sophie for me. A few good nose-pulls to Siesmay,[1] and a thousand compliments to Stoll. *Adieu*—the hour strikes!—farewell!—we shall meet again!

N.B.—I think you must have sent the two pair of yellow

---

[1] Süssmayer?

winter riding-breeches to the laundry, as Joseph and I have hunted for them in vain. *Adieu!*

Mozart died on 5 December, 1791. There was not money enough for fitting obsequies. He was buried in the "common grave." Few friends followed the coffin, and even these turned back half-way on account of the bad weather. It is now impossible to identify with any certainty the spot where rest his mortal remains.

Constance Mozart to the Emperor Leopold II.

Your Majesty!

The undersigned has had the misfortune to suffer the terrible loss of her husband and to be left by him with two infant sons in circumstances closely bordering on penury and want.

To add to her distress she is aware that, according to existing regulations as to pensions, she has not the slightest claim on any kind of subsidy or grant, her deceased husband not having completed ten years' service, and consequently nothing remains for her but to throw herself wholly upon your Majesty's pity and well-known loving care for all who are in need.

But in order not to appear perhaps unworthy of the royal clemency, she ventures most submissively to give some slight account of her very precarious position and its origin.

1stly, her deceased husband was never, during his residence in Vienna, so fortunate as to secure an opportunity of exhibiting his talent to the world in a manner sufficiently striking to establish his prospects, and consequently was unable to leave any fortune for his family, while

2ndly, he might with the greatest ease have sought his fortune abroad and placed his family in brilliant circumstances had he given ear to the offers frequently made him, and not sought his greatest renown in the honour of serving the Imperial Court in this city.

3rdly, his comparative youth and the high probability that he yet had time enough to build up the fortunes of his dependants on the foundation of his own very rare talent, excluded from his mind all thought of the present situation. It was for this reason that it did not so much as occur to him to secure to his heirs a safe, albeit small, provision by incorporation in the Society for the Widows and Orphans of Musicians.

4thly, the picture becomes all the more pathetic in that he was taken from the world at the very moment when his prospects for the future were brightening upon all sides. For, besides the recent appointment to the reversion of the post of kapellmeister at St. Stephen's Cathedral, there arrived but a few days before his death the promise of a yearly subscription of 1000 francs from certain members of the Hungarian nobility, together with the advice of a yet higher annual amount from Amsterdam, in return for which he was to compose but a very few pieces each year for the exclusive use of the subscribers.

Once again the petitioner ventures to throw herself all the more completely upon the royal benevolence and well-known fatherly care for those in want, particularly in such cases as hers, in that her confidence that your Majesty will not exclude her and her two infant sons from the royal clemency is the *only* hope still capable in some slight measure of sustaining her in her affliction.

VIENNA, 11*th December*, 1791.

Constantia Mozart, *née* Weber,

Relict of Wolfgang Amadeus Mozart, deceased, Royal and Imperial Chamber-music composer.

SUMMARY OF EVENTS

(Adapted from E. J. Breakspeare's "Conspectus" in his "Mozart."
J. M. Dent and Sons Ltd. 1922.)

1756. Mozart born 27 January and baptised next day in Salzburg Cathedral.

1759–60. Received lessons on the clavier from his father and began to invent musical themes.

1761. First attempts at composition written down by his father, and, later, in his own handwriting. *"Op. 1, Menuett und Trio"* and three *Minuets* and an *Allegro.*

First public appearance in September as a chorister in college theatricals.

1762. *Sonata pour claveçin,* Mozart's first published work (published in Paris as *Opus 1,* 21 November, 1763).

First musical tour of Mozart family to Munich for three weeks in January.

Second musical tour to Vienna in October. Wolfgang played before the Empress Maria Theresa.

1763. Clavier sonata composed in October and published in Paris as *Opus 2.*

Third tour begun in June through France, England, Holland and Switzerland. (Not completed till 1766.)

Clavier sonata, *Opus 3,* composed in November.

1764. Ten clavier sonatas composed in London, dedicated to Queen Charlotte and published in 1765.

1765. Concerts in London. Mozarts left London in July for Holland.

1766. In Amsterdam and The Hague; pieces composed for the Prince of Orange. A *Kyrie* composed in Paris.

1767. Production of cantata *The First Commandment* at Salzburg. Second visit to Vienna. Mozart fell ill of smallpox.

1768. *La Finta Semplice*—Mozart's first operatic work—composed but prevented a hearing in Vienna. *Bastien and Bastienne* produced.

1769. Appointed Court Violinist and Konzertmeister at the Archiepiscopal Court of Salzburg, unsalaried.

1770. First Italian journey with his father, First string quartet composed. Went to Rome and Naples. Mozart decorated by Pope Clement XIV. with the Order of the Golden Spur, and admitted to the Fellowship of the Philharmonic Academy of Bologna. *Mitridate, Re di Ponto* produced at Milan in December, with great success. (Beethoven born in Bonn.)

1771. Return to Salzburg. Second Italian tour. *Ascanio in Alba* produced at Milan in October. Return to Salzburg.

1772. Installation of the new Archbishop of Salzburg, Hieronymus von Colloredo. Mozart's *Sogno di Scipione* produced on the occasion. A third journey to Italy and fourth visit to Milan in preparation for the production of *Lucio Silla*.

Mozart granted a small salary of 450 florins per annum.

1773. Left Italy for Vienna in the summer to join the Archbishop of Salzburg. Home in September. Financial results of journey disappointing.

1774. Much composition in Salzburg, concertos, etc. Visit to Munich for production of opera.

1775. *La Finta Giardiniera* produced in Munich in January. Return home in March. Violin concertos, etc., composed.

1776. A year of composition, Court duties, etc., in Salzburg. Difficulties with the Archbishop.

1777. Mozart dismissed by the Archbishop in August. Wolfgang and his mother set out for Augsburg, where he met his cousin, then to Mannheim, where he lingered in hope of a Court appointment and met the Weber family.

1778. Left Mannheim in March for Paris. A symphony, some ballet music, sonatas, etc., composed. Death of Mozart's mother. Mozart's father had in the meantime come to agreement with the Archbishop of Salzburg.

1779. Mozart returned home and received appointment of Court and Cathedral Organist with salary of 450 florins per annum. Music for *King Thamos* and *Zaïde* (an unfinished operetta in German) composed during the year.

1780. *Idomeneo, Re di Crete* composed. Munich visited.

1781. First performance of *Idomeneo* in January. Mozart summoned to Vienna by the Archbishop. He quarrelled with the Archbishop and resigned his appointment. Went to lodge with the Webers. Became engaged to Constance Weber.

1782. Mozart settled in Vienna. A German opera commissioned by the Emperor—*The Abduction from the Seraglio*—and produced in

July with extraordinary success. Mozart married Constance Weber on 4 August. Piano concertos composed, concerts given, etc.

1783. Mozart gave a concert attended by the Emperor and made 1600 florins (about £150). In August and September he went with his wife to visit his father in Salzburg. Composed a *Mass* for the occasion which was performed in the church of St. Peter, Constance Mozart taking part in the singing. Carl Leopold, the elder of Mozart's two surviving children, born in June.

1784. The string quartets composed (afterwards dedicated to Joseph Haydn), also quintet for piano and wind-instruments.

1785. Mozart became a Free-mason. Composed *Davidde penitente*. Leopold Mozart came to visit his son, returned to Salzburg, and died in May.

1786. *The Marriage of Figaro* produced in Vienna.

1787. Visited Prague with his wife. *Don Giovanni* produced there in October. In December he was appointed Chamber-music Composer to the Imperial Court at a salary of 800 florins.

1788. The three great orchestral symphonies composed, in C, in G minor and in E-flat major.

1789. Mozart visited Berlin and was warmly received by King Frederick William. He composed a set of string quartets for the king, who offered him an appointment at about £450 a year, but Mozart decided to remain with the Emperor in Vienna. Mozart's wife seriously ill.

1790. *Così fan tutte* produced at the commission of the Emperor. The Emperor died. Mozart's financial condition became very critical. Journeyed to Frankfort for the Imperial coronation.

1791. *La Clemenza di Tito* produced early in September in Prague. *The Magic Flute* produced at the end of September in Vienna. The *Requiem* composed but not completed.

Mozart died on 5 December and was buried next day in the churchyard of St. Mark's, Vienna.

INDEX